To Paul,

With Best Wis...

Geoff Horne

To Take a Sword

G. R. Horne

PublishBritannica

London   Baltimore

ISBN: 1-1437-0792-0
PUBLISHED BY PUBLISHBRITANNICA
www.publishbritannica.com
London   Baltimore

Dedicated to my grandchildren

Table of Contents

first encounter between Horn and Princess Cleona, daughter of King Aeden, and the talk of marriage.

The marriage of Cleona and Horn, and the mutual exchange of ambassadors and trade delegations between Westerland and Collona following the Treaty with King Aeden.

Prince Attaga of the Island of Laswindel appeals to Horn for help in repelling an Irish invasion led by their common enemy, Brinian. The Battle of the North-West and the success at the Battle of the Hills with the flight of Brinian from the field.

The capture of Dog in the woodlands by Terroc, the Knight of King Aelcane of Ireland, and his escape back to the hills. The news of a new force arrived to join Brinian at the woodlands and their subsequent defeat at the Battle of the Hills, finally with the rout and pursuit of the Irish to the coast.

Brinian on the run to the north-west coast with Dog blocking the escape route at the Quayside against the surviving Irish invaders in full flight. The release of the village hostages by the Knight Briscal followed by the fight to the death between Brinian and his Commander Ribatt. A chance word from a scout leads to the discovery of the dying Brinian in the Gorselands by Fenner. The return to the castle at Laswindel and celebrations of the victory. Horn and Lord Grenden muster the army to return by ship to a great welcome at Westerland, and the threat of invasion is replaced with peace and prosperity and the birth of a son to Cleona and Horn.

Characters in *To take a Sword*

Westerland

- Colver, alias Horn
- King Alymer of Westerland
- Queen Aethena of Westerland
- Lord Grenden, Commander-in-Chief of the Westerland Army
- Alric, cousin of Horn
- Ancour, the Chancellor
- Winloch, the Secretary
- Lords Wagnor, Sintel, and Sancto
- Richel, Commander for Lord Grenden
- Stelid, the Bishop
- Grindel, the Physician
- Briscal, a young Knight of King Alymer
- Backley, Kaldon, Cordo, Foxley, Alban, Horton—Knights of the Unicorn.
- Elvil, Knight to Lord Grenden
- Dog, the urchin
- Torvic, the Engineer
- Althon, Master of the Hunt
- Althreda, wife of Dog
- Redwald, son of Dog
- Greg, the Giant
- Malvin, Fenner, Boarset, Latten—the Scouts.
- Fretwin, the archer
- Blandon, the swordmaker
- Ruckle, the wound dresser
- Alfud, Knight Ambassador to Collona

Irish Invaders

•Ealcane, Mestig, Trelane—Irish Kings
•Brinian, the Irish Commander-in-Chief

The Alliance against Westerland

•King Aeden of Collona
•Queen Helda of Collona
•Princess Cleona of Collona
•Prince Aelman of Collona
•Eapden, son of Prince Aelman.
•Rogden, the rogue Knight and Commander-in-Chief
•Bosden, the brother of Rogden
•Ansell, Commander for Rogden
•Olten, Chancellor of Collona.
•King Stadd of Preyden
•Lackden, Preyden, Commander-in-Chief
•Halden, Lackden's Commander
•Yalden, 1st ram commander
•Hagan, Preyden Commander
•Werden of the battering ram
•Redel of the ram attack
•Yerden of the ram attack
•Astle, the veteran
•Marbeld, village leader
•Marbeld's sons, Juttom and Jacktor
•Terroc, Knight to King Ealcane
•Ligard, Knight to Rogden
•Maxam, the torturer

Laswindel Expedition

- King Plachan of Laswindel
- Prince Attaga of Laswindel

Irish Invaders of Laswindel

- Brinian, Commander of the Irish army.
- Terrroc, Knight to King Ealcane
- Ribbatt, Commander for Brinian

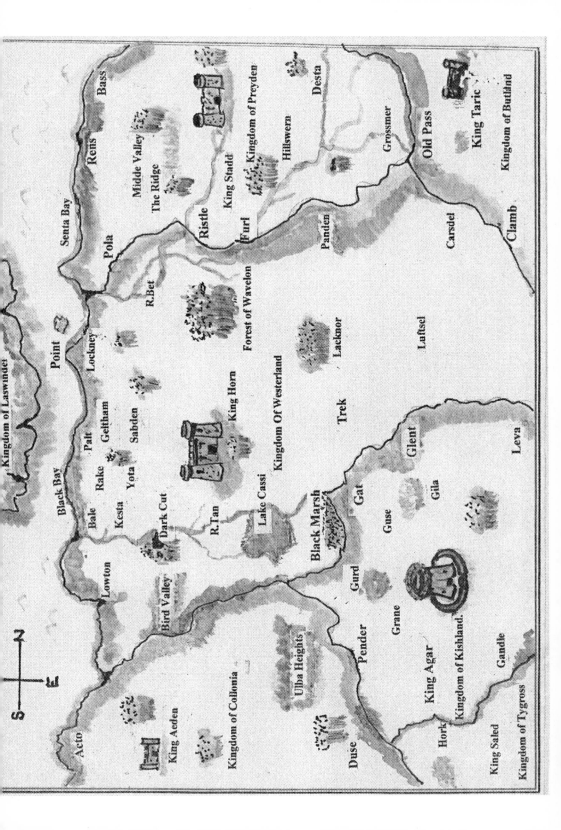

PREFACE

This story was influenced by the *Saga of King Horn* and the *Horn Childe,* the oldest recorded tale written in England in the 1200's. This tale of chivalry, romance, and treachery was written in 1,500 verses and was based in Westernesse (Cheshire). It was stolen by the French at the end of the 13th century. It was called *Horn et Rymenhild* and set in Normandy. This was followed by the Scots, who put it in Edinburgh in the style of nine ballads, calling it *Hind Horn*. The story was more or less identical to the original King Horn in each case.

Professors W.G. Colloingwood and W.P. Kerr, learned Professors in the early part of this century, prepared a paper which was read at Penrith on the 7th of July, 1936. They also read the paper of the Rev Thomas Lee from 1888 where he attempts to show the characters in the story were taken from actual historical figures of the time, namely in the 10th century. A key figure, "The Horn Childe," at the age of fifteen was a King's Champion and was credited with the slaying of the Viking King of York, Eric the Bloodaxe, at the Battle of Stainmoor. The story of "King Horn" is thought by many to be where the idea for King Arthur and the Knights of the Round Table was taken. There was no such title as Knight in the time that Arthur was supposed to exist. In the story of "King Horn," there was a sword "Blavian," a magician at court, and bondsmen in service to Horn instead of Knights. Some became traitors, and there was the beautiful Princess Rymenhild who fell in love with Horn.

The idea came to me to write a story of the emergence of a royal son as a warrior. In his youth, he was already a veteran of battles and a master in the art of war, who, with his companions, become legendary figures throughout all known kingdoms in a few short years.

The first book, *To take a Sword*, deals with his inborn desire to be a warrior. This is an introduction to the main characters which form his elite company in the castle, court and army. It includes his succession to the crown, treachery, and his romance with a Princess from a neighbouring kingdom.

G.R.Horne

Chapter 1

The Invaders

Horn studied the expression on the face of his father, King Alymer of Westerland, as the messenger, muddied and breathless, steadied himself and, bending low, addressed the King.

"Sire, I bring news of an Irish force landing on our shores near Lockney, led by three Kings. The people of Lockney cannot hold them!" The messenger, visibly shaken and supported by the Chancellor Ancour and Secretary Winloch, said, "My liege, the garrison had been overwhelmed; the men, women and children have been put to the sword, and I fear the village will be destroyed."

The King rose from his seat and approached the exhausted man,

"What is the strength of the invader?" The King waited for the man to reply.

When he had recovered a little, he spoke. "Sire, it seems that there are three Kings of Ireland with at least five thousand men, well armed and determined."

King Alymer gave orders for the man to be fed and rested, and at the same time, he dismissed the court with a sweep of his hand, with the exception of his Chancellor, to whom he spoke urgently.

Ancour was sent scuttling as the King called loudly for Lord Grenden, his Commander-in Chief of the army, to attend to him at once. The hall and castle rang with the call taken up by many throats. Lord Grenden was soon located, not unexpectedly in a ladies chamber, by the now quite flustered Ancour.

"My Lord, make haste to the King. He has need of your presence; the kingdom is under attack from an Irish horde at Lockney."

Lord Grenden, who was taller than most men, with strong features scarred from past wounds, was considered handsome. He was also the most experienced soldier in the land. He was the victor of many battles against the marauding Vikings over the years, and was still not much over the age of thirty.

"Ancour, go ahead, tell the King I attend at once. Call for the Lords Wagnore and Sintel to join me."

These Lords were able commanders and well versed in the art of war, and as such, had been trusted to lead the divisions of the King's army. Lord Grenden, buckling on his sword over his surcoat, took a hurried leave of his lady and left the chamber, calling for his squire as he hastened to the King's presence.

The Irish had made many invasions of Westerland, which was on a direct course east by sea, with a sailing time of less than four hours in good weather. Their usual lightning raids lasted for less than a day, in which time they could plunder the coastal village, then take to their ships before any major force could arrive. This time, however, it was different. With the intention of conquest, a large fleet had been prepared with three of the most powerful Kings on board.

There had been a long standing hatred between Ireland and Westerland, which had not lessened over the years. It stemmed from the capture of King Alymer's young cousin Alric during one of their raids near the village of Lockney. The unfortunate youth was taken back to Ireland and held in chains until they tired of sporting with him. Knowing that a ransom would be paid, contact was made through a messenger. It was agreed to land him on the shore near Lockney in exchange for five thousand gold coins; he was to be accompanied by no more men than was needed to carry the ransom. The exchange, it was said, failed miserably, owing to so much distrust between the two parties. The luckless captive was hacked to pieces and thrown overboard; his mutilated corpse was finally recovered from the sea later the same day. His body was taken to the castle amid much grief and renewed hatred of the Irish.

Horn, having understood the situation that now fell upon his father's kingdom, could hardly contain his excitement. Could this be his chance?! Now at the age of fifteen, and having been taught since the age of seven by Lord Grenden, this could be the time for his first encounter with a real enemy. After all, it was usual for boys to accompany their fathers and brothers to war. Horn was well built; his years of swordmanship had developed his shoulders and chest for someone beyond his years. No other sons of the Lords or Knights could stand against him in mock combat. Lord Grenden strode purposefully into the hall and addressed the King.

"Sire, I have called my captains, and they will attend me shortly to marshal the men. We could have two thousand men under arms and ready to move in two hours."

King Alymer knew that his Commander would act without losing any precious time, and they together formed their plan of action to attack and destroy the enemy, before they could penetrate too deeply into the kingdom.

"My Lord Grenden, you will take half the force to engage the raiders, while I and the Lords Wagnor and Sintel round the enemy, making straight for the coast and cutting off any possible retreat should he change his mind. We can meet up at a given point to destroy the remnants of these Irish before they can take to their ships."

Lord Grenden bowed out of the King's presence and made haste to the courtyard. Already men were assembling under their commanders, who were shouting orders for a weapon check as to their condition and readiness. The women, as was their custom, bustled round their men, helping them into their brown protective jackets adorned with metal studs. The women, with a last kiss and words of encouragement, bid them farewell as they moved into the sections directed by the commanders.

Horn, his excitement increasing with the din of action within the castle, made his way into the yard unnoticed by the King or his courtiers. He passed through the mass of men to a group of boys, all who seemed eager to join the men in the coming battle. Suddenly, he realised his clothing would mark him out from those about him. Looking round, he spotted an old beggar sitting on a pile of sacks wrapped in what could be only be described as a long cape. It looked as if it had been worn by a hundred others. He approached and looked at the beggar, who returned his stare, hostility clearly mirrored in his watery eyes, and spoke.

"I have a gold coin here; I want your cape for it."

The beggar snatched the coin. He bit hard on it, and tearing off the cape, threw it at Horn. He then sat down, his pathetic body now exposing his few rags. Dazed with disbelief, he clutched the coin tightly in his claw-like hand in awe at his good fortune.

Hiding the cape, he went in search of Lord Grenden and, finding him in conversation with Lord Sancto, made his presence known. Seeing Horn, he broke away and turned to face him.

"My Prince, I would advise you to return to the hall at once; this is no place for you. His Majesty would wish to know of your whereabouts before he moves out of the castle with his force."

Horn realised that the Lord was really dismissing him by suggesting he returned to the hall and replied, "My Lord, is it not time for me to take my place with the men, and have you not said that I would tax and have the better of most who dare stand against me? You are my only master at close quarter combat." His eyes spoke with energy as he made his plea. "I see many boys here in the yard with their fathers and brothers, why not me?"

Lord Grenden had still to give his final orders to his commanders before moving out and spoke sharply to Horn. "Go swiftly, young Prince, to your father for his blessing on this, as we must be gone within the hour."

Horn knew in his heart that his father would not agree to him taking part, so moving away, he uncovered the cape from its hiding place, Drawing it around his body, he made sure it covered his clothes. At first, the smell of stale bodies and putrid vegetable matter assailed his nostrils. His attention was now drawn to his fine shoes, which must be disguised. He found the answer in a dung heap, which not only covered them with unpleasant dark stains, but gave off a smell that would not be found in any chamber in the castle. His next move was to somehow alter his obviously clean face and well kept hair. He achieved this by scooping up the damp earth and applying it lightly to his face and head. Feeling that his disguise would pass a cursory inspection, he made for the group of boys that were still huddled together close to a group of men.

Their obvious intention was to go with the army, possibly hoping to be asked to work as arrow boys or messengers for the commanders. Particularly, they wanted to collect weapons and strip the bodies of anything worth taking after a skirmish or battle. This would give them the opportunity to secret away small trinkets to sell at the market or to barter for food. Most of these boys would not fight unless they were caught unawares by the enemy and had to defend themselves or die.

As Horn approached them, he could see that their ages were between fourteen and sixteen, and it seemed as though they were also aware of the smell he was now giving off from his cape and shoes. They stared at him. The boys turned to talk loudly among themselves; after all, they gave off the same offensive smells of stale sweat and unwashed bodies. He listened to their boasting of previous encounters and found it was not too difficult to imitate their swaggering postures. He was careful not to be too obvious in making any claims that would be questioned. One youth, very much the older in years and the loudest of them all, caught him roughly by the arm.

"Who might you be then? I don't know your face. Come to that, what are you fighting with? You don't expect the Irish to give you a sword, do you?"

Horn looked at the speaker and was shocked at what he saw; the face was horribly twisted into a sneer, which made him look even more threatening because of a facial deformity. This was caused by a very ugly harelip, which seemed to dominate his entire face. He had never seen such ugliness. Occasionally clowns entertaining at the castle could make the most frightening faces, but this was for real. He felt, here was a youth who would not hesitate to take advantage of any sign of weakness among his peers. He made a mental note not to upset him! This contorted face attempted a smile, the effect of which was difficult to watch. Horn was tempted to avoid direct eye contact with him, as to do so might be taken as an affront, and that he could not risk.

"I could get you a sword or spear, if you have a coin or something, before we leave the gate," he said with an attempt at a wink, which was somehow lost in that twisted face. "Have you any money?" His voice sounded threatening as he stuck his face too close for Horn's liking.

Horn, not intending the youth to see his purse, fumbled under his cape, and feigning reluctance, handed him a small coin, which was snatched from his hand and quickly pocketed. The youth raced off to the nearest group of men standing close together, deep in animated talk and awaiting their orders. The men had placed their weapons of swords, shields and spears in neat order against the wall. As he approached, the youth, with one movement, without pausing, using skills learnt since childhood, scooped up a sword, and in seconds was back among the boys. With a look of triumph and accomplishment he produced the weapon for Horn.

"Quick, get this under you cape. Keep it there until we have left the castle gates with the army."

Horn took the hilt of the sword and it felt good under the cover of his cape. The quality was a lot to be desired, but the weight was good enough.

The youth asked, "Who are you? Does your father work at the castle for a Lord?"

Horn had to think quickly. "He works at the castle," he said, hoping to sound convincing.

Asking the youth his name, he tried to avoid direct eye contact with him. His reply was almost spat out defiantly. "I have no father I know of. Some say he was probably hanged for stealing at the castle. My mother died before I was three, so I had no name. Everybody called me what they wanted to. They mostly called me Dog because someone once said it. They just saw my scars.

I got used to it."

A commotion was heard in the courtyard from the group of men whose member had lost his sword. With the mass of men now beginning to move out and the size of the watching crowd, he had no chance of finding the culprit now. Orders were given for both forces to move out through the gates. Lord Grenden's force, being the smaller of the two, wheeled off to the west, while the King and his Commanders, Wagnor and Sintel, took the shorter route, northwest to the coast. Both forces expected to pick up men from the villages as they passed through. This proved to be the case; the scouts sent on ahead had done their job well. One party had been sent out as soon as the messenger reported the presence of enemy at Lockney. He had located one or two small groups of Irishmen infiltrating into the northeast region.

The King was particularly pleased with those that joined his force from the villages. Old faces he recognised meant that his subjects had answered the call. One veteran Astle, the lord of his village, called out, "My Liege! My sword is sharp! My eyes are clear; my arm is strong; and my kinsmen are eager for the fight."

The King saluted the old warrior with his sword as he and his men joined the force. The chosen route was to close the main paths to the sea; he did not want the enemy to feel they could withdraw should they lose the battle. A wide sweep was needed so as not to encounter any small breakaway groups of the enemy looking for spoils. Lord Grenden steeped up the pace of his march, as the men were making good progress. His scouts reported that they were in contact with the enemy. Their strength had not yet been confirmed, but they did say Lockney had suffered looting and burning. This could mean that the Irish army were now on their way to the next village, which would be Geltham, some five miles to the south-east, and much larger than Lockney. It had many old veterans who could put up a spirited defence to hold up the enemy, but only for a limited time.

Lord Grenden's men neared Lockney and were soon aware of a great deal of noise in the area of the woods south of the village. Orders were given for silence as they approached. They could see several men in pursuit of some luckless villagers, who, having escaped the initial massacre, had attempted to hide. To the enemy, seemingly, it was a good sport, with little or no danger. Women and children would prove no match for their pursuers and would soon give up trying to run from them and their inevitable fate. Their screams as they tried unsuccessfully to protect their children from the sword only hastened their end. By the time Lord Grenden had sent out a party to deal with the enemy, all was quiet. As they entered the woods, the sickening sight of the bodies of the villagers drew gasps and oaths from even the hardest veteran. He recalled his men to continue their march to seek out the main Irish army. With the evidence gathered at the scene, it pointed to there being no more than a dozen men involved. Affected by the slaughter in the woods, he detailed Fenner, the scout, and a small party to track down and destroy them, then to return to the force as soon as possible.

It proved correct. The easy chase of the villagers and the pitiful collections of loot they were carrying gave them a sense of well being; there was no need to hurry. Perhaps they would find more people to chase and rob, to satisfy their appetites and add to their spoils. Catching up with the enemy, Fenner, who was small in stature, would pretend to be a villager in hiding who escaped them. Then, farther down in the woods, his men would lay a trap. He would, on their approach, hide his sword, pretend to foolishly to step out into their full view, and turn and run into the bush where they would certainly follow him. It worked! As soon as he was seen by the Irish, they whooped with delight at this further sport. He cunningly froze for a moment, feigning surprise and terror. He then turned and seemingly ran into the bushes as though to escape. He raised his hand, the signal to his waiting men. On they came, entering the trap, intent on killing this little man. They were engaged with lightning speed before they could recover from their shock and surprise. They died one by one, except for one who threw down his sword in a hopeless gesture. He was cut down by a mighty blow without mercy. No survivors meant no warning to any other stray groups, who had broken away from the main force to rob, kill, and create terror among the villagers. Sadly, the easy targets were mainly women, children, and old men.

Fenner, with his small group travelling fast, caught up with the main force of Lord Grenden and reported the successful outcome of their mission in the woods. After a brief rest, the party were sent out to scout in the area of Geltham.

They arrived at the outskirts and adopted a silent approach in case any stray villagers should unwittingly give them away. Their attention was suddenly drawn to a noise caused by a raider dragging a protesting women from a barn. Fenner loosed an arrow from his bow and dropped the man without a sound.

The woman, realising she was free, ran away, never to know her rescuer. The scouts approached the scene and carried the body to the thick scrub nearby. Making sure that they had been unobserved, they carried on into the village itself. As they neared the lanes of the village, they could hear the enemy and see that the defences in and around Geltham were completely destroyed. All would have been easily overrun by the overwhelming numbers of the Irish. Unlike Lockney, the men here had undergone some form of training, so they would have some resistance. Taking stock of the enemy, they could estimate that although there had been many Irish in the attack on the village, all the signs led to the fact that it was not the whole Irish army involved. Sporadic fighting was still going on around the slopes, with the enemy outnumbering the defenders.

In spite of the heroic stand of the village men and their meagre defences, the Irish force had made quick inroads into the village. The sheer number of the enemy took its eventual toll. Many brave fathers and sons fell exhausted, their swords and spears becoming too heavy to wield by their leaden arms to hold off the Irish, who soon made sure of victory. The village Lord, Marbeld, and his two sons, Jutton and Jacktor, were among the last to die on the crumbling slopes in fierce hand to hand fighting. Although they killed many of the enemy, even they had to succumb to the inevitable. The scouts had witnessed this last stand brave stand and were tempted to charge down and join the one-sided struggle, but their job was to observe and report. Also, there was still the threat of the rest of their army arriving.

"Hold fast, Boarset! You will get your chance to face them before long. Save your head and strength for the battle to come. Your courage will be tested for sure," whispered Malvin to his young scout. He spoke quietly to the others.

"Lord Grenden will be here within the next hour. There is nothing we can effectively do without betraying our presence and the fact that our army is approaching. This would put us all in danger; we do not want them to have the advantage of an attack on our force, as we would be outnumbered. Surprise will be vital!"

A scout arrived from Lord Grenden to say the force would be with them very shortly and would make their attack on the right side of the village. The enemy was reported mainly at the northern end and was seen moving into the centre, clearing out huts as they went. When the force arrived, orders were given for strict silence in approach. Weapons were to be muffled, so no undue noise would carry to the ears of the enemy. For their attack to succeed, it would have to be one of surprise and speed, compensating for the difference in the number of men.

With looting becoming a priority, the Irish swarmed into the first row of huts. Daggers were drawn over a small chest which might or might not contain valuables. This was to cause an early breakdown in order. Soon they were stumbling out into the lanes, arms heavy with goods. Their two leaders, conspicuous by their finery, shouted and cursed at the men to stop, wait and rest, as other parts of the village could wait for their attention.

The women who had survived were not given the opportunity to run for cover into the countryside. They were roughly handled by the enemy, who with loud guffaws, made them perform and dance to the tune of a whistle. The unfortunate ones among them were carried off, struggling and screaming, by the grinning men. The noise of the resting and celebrating Irish soon became louder and more boisterous as the local brewhouse was discovered. This new found thirst of the men began to take its toll. With the supply of ale being send round by their comrades, even the few sentries that had been posted relaxed. The enemy were now in a happy mood, only interrupted by the occasional squabble over looted goods. Any remaining women had now become the prize objects of their celebrations. They were going to enjoy themselves before the main army arrived, when there would be more competition for the women.

The Westerlanders could not have wished for a better situation, and the celebrating enemy had not expected any further opposition. They were now obviously out of control. Their leaders seemed to have let the men have their heads. Perhaps they had already decided that all defence had been wiped out or was of little consequence. Geltham, being a well stocked and prosperous village, was a good place to pause before a general advance was ordered by the Irish Commander-in Chief.

Lord Grenden now called in his commanders in order to discuss final plans for the attack on Geltham. It was now intended to surprise the Irish at first light when they would be at their weakest. They would fall upon them with great speed and purpose before they could muster their full strength to retaliate in anything approaching an organised force. First, and later in the evening, they would send in Fenner with two other scouts to mark out the positions of the sentries. Most would, by now, be suffering from the boredom of their watch and would be very easy to approach closely.

Gradually, the noisiest of the enemy dozed off were they where or staggered to a hut not yet burned. A strange quiet crept through the village. The stars began to show in their thousands in the night sky. Only the chirping of the courting crickets and the hoot of a lone owl could be heard. Fenner knew that he would have to wait until the sentries had been relieved, and their replacements posted, to give the assurance that no other movement by the enemy would be likely. He was to expect a signal just before the main attack. It was enough time to deal with the sentries quickly, before any alarm could be raised and before the element of surprise was lost.

As the dawn was about to break, and the half light still provided cover, Fenner and his scouts moved with stealth towards their targets. They could be seen and heard yawning, scratching themselves, completely relaxed, and not at all interested in their surroundings. It was easy to take them out of this world. Fenner took the first man, a bearded giant who dwarfed him, but as his knife slid into the victim's throat with speed, he gave only a soft surprised gurgle, abruptly halted by the sudden gush of his life's blood. Fenner held him as he crumpled and lay still. His second target, twenty feet away, turned unexpectedly as if to greet a friend, but found someone with a drawn knife already in motion. It was delivered with great force into the chest. He dropped, clutching at Fenner's jacket. His eyes were already rapidly glazing as he lost his grip and, with it, his life. Within minutes, all the sentries had been dealt with successfully by the scouts. The job was well done, with no chance of an alarm being raised of the intending attack.

The scouts signalled their mission completed. Lord Grenden moved his men into the outskirts of the village, splitting them into four sections with the object of fanning out to the huts that were occupied by the Irish. Orders to destroy the occupants as quickly and quietly as possible was given, and the attack would have to be as one assault to be totally successful.

The attack went as planned, taking the enemy by surprise. The first signs they had were, in most cases, their last. Totally unprepared, many had no time to arm themselves to mount a defence. Shouts and cries of the dying men alerted a small group of the Irish who had strayed to the far end of the village in quest of loot. These few came rushing up the lanes, joining others who had emerged from the few huts that had been overlooked. The Irish engaged the King's men, who were now leaving the huts in the centre after their devastating assault. As the opposition grew by the minute, there now seemed to be more of the enemy. Lord Grenden now had to face this new threat.

Horn had been involved in the first attack and found himself in close company with the youth called Dog. They had skirted around Lord Grenden to avoid being sent back to join the other boys and, in the case of Horn, being recognized by the Lord. Although, by now, his disguise had taken on a natural hue. His clothes were stained and spoiled by crawling through woodland and contact with the wet earth and mud. He felt confident with the sword in his hand, and at the signal, he rushed into the nearest hut with Dog close on his heels. The occupants startled to find themselves attacked. One grabbed at a spear, but before he could use it, Horn ran him through. The expression on the man's face was of complete bewilderment. Horn, spinning round to his left, sidestepped another who had got to his feet and delivered a lightning blow which all but decapitated the unfortunate man. Dog, in action himself, had glanced across at his companion. He noticed the speed and grace of the swordsmanship of his new friend. It was clear that this was no ordinary lad from the castle; he would find out more later. They slashed and cut at anyone who managed to get on their feet, until there was none left to challenge. Dog made his way out into the lanes to join in the general fighting, which was now raging freely in small groups. He had a charmed life, escaping blows that would have split his head in two or smashed open his chest. His style of combat had the hallmark of a certain talent that could be developed. Coupled with a vision of sheer ugliness, his contorted face struck fear into their hearts. It was complete savagery, combined with an unusual strength in his young body, rather than his weapon skill, that enabled him to overcome men in their prime. His ferocity driving them back enabled him to deliver a mortal blow as they struggled to defend themselves.

Lord Grenden, himself now in the lanes, could be seen in the thick of the fighting, a great warrior of stature who not only led his troops well but fought with them. His enemies fell before him as he wielded his great sword, and occasionally death came to those unlucky enough to try to round him.

Horn, nearby in the lanes, caught the sudden flurry of movement towards his back to see an axe raised to strike, but with a deft stroke parried the intended blow. The axe flew from the man's hand with the force it met, and Horn drove his sword through the body before he could recover his balance and weapon. It was becoming clear that the Irish were beginning to fall back, assuming wrongly that they were facing a large army. Aware of losing many men in the first attack on the huts, including both their commanders, they began to look for ways of escape. Some that managed to break away made for the northern area of Lockney, where the main Irish army was reported. Lord Grenden gave the order to ease off when possible, but also ordered the scouts to follow at a distance.

He estimated that his force had accounted for something in the region of fifteen hundred of the enemy, which meant some three or four thousand were still left of the original estimate of five thousand. If so, where were they? And more importantly, where are the three Irish kings known to be among them? There was a chance that the fleeing remnants from Geltham would run into the King's force, heading towards the coast. Horn joined the boys who were rapidly stripping the bodies, including Dog, who as Horn approached, could be heard addressing his audience, giving them an account of his new friend's part in the attack. Dog mentioned Horn's amazing talent with the sword and, of course, his own tally of the enemy at his companion's side. Dog sidled up to Horn

"Who are you? You are not one of us. Where did you learn to use a sword like that?" Although his voice sounded threatening, it also carried a hint of respect for the action he had witnessed first hand. He and Horn were the only boys to take part in that attack, the rest had hung back and waited, out of range of the fighting. Horn thought quickly, *what name would be acceptable to them?* The last thing he wanted at this moment was to be exposed. This would reveal his presence to Lord Grenden and worse still, possibly his father, the King.

"My father was a servant at the court called Colver." He hoped it sounded convincing. "He was well known for his skill in weapons. He taught me from an early age the bow and the sword, and I was able to engage in mock combat with the young men of the court." He prayed that would satisfy them for the time being.

Dog, still studying him, grunted, "Some people have all the luck."

Horn thought that might shut him up for a while, and changed the subject to food, which was always a priority for the young. Scraps had been taken from the huts left by the Irish, and these were now divided among them and eaten in minutes by the ravenous boys.

Lord Grenden had anticipated correctly the result of his assault on Geltham, which cost him only a handful of men. He decided to follow on towards

Lockney, behind his scouts at a discreet distance, not wanting any Irishmen to escape to their ships before the King's force in the north could deal with them. Fenner, with Boarset extremely close, was suddenly brought to a halt at the sight of several horsemen who seemed to spur on the fleeing men. The scouts came to the conclusion that this group of horsemen were no ordinary men, but of high stature and bearing. These could be the three Irish Kings and their bodyguard. Boarset was sent back to report these findings to Lord Grenden while Fenner kept in touch with the enemy.

As he watched, the horsemen left and galloped off at speed to the north-west. Ahead of their men, the Irish horsemen had unknowingly bypassed the King's army as they made for a point overlooking a small inlet. They had also made plans should a retreat be necessary. A rearguard was to be formed to allow as many men as possible to board the ships with little loss. The road out of Geltham was strewn with discarded loot, particularly the heavier items which tended to slow down the fleeing men. Staying alive was a priority when escape was a possibility after a defeat. There was always another day to fight on better terms.

The commanders of the Westerland force gave instructions for the booty to be collected and put in a place of safety until it could be claimed by any surviving villagers. Horn noticed that Dog and one or two of the boys took a keen interest in the collection. Their remarks led him to believe that, given the opportunity, they would lose no time carrying off some these goods—not to the villagers, but to the market. Lord Sancto, also aware of their interest, reminded all that swift punishment would be given to anyone looting or stealing goods; he would spare no one. Horn thanked the Lord under his breath for his awareness of the possible intent of the boys. After all, he would hate to lose Dog's company at this moment because they had a respectful understanding. To steal for the sake of stealing, well, he understood it was a way of life for these boys at the castle.

A messenger arrived, putting paid to that subject, as he informed all that the King's force had the enemy in its sight. The strength of the Irish was still not confirmed, but they would attack them when they reached the area of the village of Lockney. This, being near to the coast, was the first place the invaders overran and ransacked on landing. Lord Grenden was ordered to close on the fleeing Irish from Geltham and attack them, keeping their attention from the approach to the village from the north by King's men. The scouts had reported that the main Irish army was now approaching Lockney and would be in the village within the next half an hour. Closing on the remnants of the Irish from Geltham, Lord Grenden ordered his force to head straight for the village of Lockney, hopefully to engage the enemy and trap them between his force arriving from the south-east, and the King's men now bearing down on them from the north.

Lord Grenden, nearing the village, could see a great deal of activity and was surprised that, to all intents and purposes, his force had not yet been seen by the Irish. He entered the lanes into the village and gave the order for his men to bang their weapons on their shields as they charged forward. The enemy, now fully aware of the attack, began to marshal their men into a defensive formation as they turned to face the onslaught by the Westerlanders. Fierce fighting erupted on a large scale as the Irish Commanders called on their entire force to rush to the area of conflict. The first wave of Grenden's men in the charge came to an abrupt halt as they clashed with a determined enemy. Many fell on both sides, but with the advantage of superior numbers of men, the enemy gaps were soon filled. In a matter of seconds in swept the second wave, which was more successful. It began to create havoc among the Irish. The fury of the attacking men tested their courage to the limit. Some broke away, in spite of the threatening curses of their commanders as to their fate should they flee. Soon the dense lines of the Irish broke away into small groups, the fighting still intense and savage. Many men lay dead on the ground, and the wounded were trampled on as the fighting spilled over them. The men cursed as they tripped and fell among the bodies, their faces twisted in the agony of their violent end. Some struggled to their feet, lucky to join the fray once more. Horn had swept in with the second wave, shouting as loud as anyone. With Dog at his side, he parried, cut, and stabbed, swinging his sword with devastating effect. Suddenly Dog slipped! Horn, fearing for his safety, leapt over his body, killing an Irishman who was in the act of bringing his sword down on the youth's head. Now on his feet, Dog pressed forward into the attack, quickly despatching two of the enemy. He called out to Horn, who was carving out quite a gap among the enemy ranks. "To me! To me!" he said as he was forced to take on too many at a time.

The inevitable now took place as the King's army entered the northern end of the village and attacked the rear of the invaders with little warning. The enemy now realised they had been ushered into a trap, and were in great difficulties, although still with superior odds. This was mainly because of a rumour that had been spreading quickly through their ranks. It was said their kings were making for the coast instead of supporting the army, leaving them to their fate should the Saxons defeat them. Many more in the village tried to find a way of escape. Some made it into the countryside; others never reached safety before being cut down by their pursuers.

Lord Wagnor, aware of the scouts report of the horsemen, came to the conclusion that they were men of high rank, perhaps the kings among them. He made for the coast. He was close on their heels and, riding hard, was almost on them when they split into two parties. One opted for combat, while the other group sped on. They gave a good account of themselves until the last of them fell, but this hold up had given the others the chance to put some distance from Lord Wagnor's men, who had lost two of their number in that encounter. Taking up the chase again at breakneck speed, he arrived at the coast to find the kings had dismounted and already boarded the nearest ship from a small boat. It was now too late to pursue by boat. Fretwin, the archer, decided to try his hand with a shot at the figures on the ship. He was acclaimed for his accuracy. He drew back hard and loosed his arrow. The flight was true, the distance right. It was seen to hit one of the kings, who fell to the deck. No further shots were possible as the ship now turned and pulled away, the sails already filling as it headed out to sea. Lord Wagnor cursed his bad luck. He had been so close to taking them prisoner. He now prepared to return to the main army at Lockney, disappointed, as the capture of these kings would have been the subject of a great ransom, which would have pleased King Alymer.

The casualties had been much lower than expected in spite of the fierce fighting, and now the main battle was taking place in the open. The enemy, having been driven out of the village lanes and into the open, gave the Westerlanders the advantage; their bowmen created havoc and panic among the desperate Irish.

Horn, full of confidence, was in pursuit of a group that had broken away, making for the nearby woods. Again he was accompanied by Dog, who seemed to sense his companion Colver had the luck of the devil or had a greater calling. He decided to stick close to him, whatever happened. Closing on three of the enemy, the tail end of a group turned to face their pursuers and fight, although they were still short of the woods and safety. Horn took the first Irishman, a huge man, and sidestepped his raised axe. With an immense roar, the Irishman swung his axe higher as Horn feinted with his dagger. At the same time, Horn drove his sword through the man's unprotected body. The roar died in his throat as he crashed to the ground. Dog had the better of one, killing him after a short exchange. The third man had now leapt onto Dog's back, his dagger poised to strike home, but Horn, turning as his man hit the ground, saw Dog's peril. With a speed too fast to follow, he threw his dagger with unerring accuracy and struck the man's back. Falling, the man clawed desperately to reach the dagger without success, allowing Dog to deal him a crushing blow, which laid open his skull.

Dog called out to Horn, who bent down to retrieve his dagger from the body and wipe it on the inert body, "Again, I owe you, Colver."

Horn was already moving towards the woods, as the hunt was still on; Dog had to run to catch him up. There were still many groups of the enemy in the woods and the nearby shrubland, which afforded good cover. Sections of Lord Grenden's men joined in the hunt of the fleeing Irish. Their task, now the main battle, was reaching a conclusion. The enemy's huge losses meant that they would soon be unable to fight as an organised army. Lord Grenden rode over to the fringe of the woods with four of his section leaders. They dismounted to outline a plan of the final roundup of the scattered invaders within the woods.

Without warning, a group of the enemy came at Lord Grenden's party with a rush, surrounding them; fierce fighting began against heavy odds. The sound of clashing steel, coupled with the shouts and cries of the action, reached the ears of Horn and Dog, who turned and ran towards the sound. Both covered the distance in seconds. They took on the first that turned to face them, and with ease, laid them low. In the thick of fighting, Horn could see the tall figure of Lord Grenden in the centre, wielding his sword. He almost stopped; he might be recognised! But he was now committed. If he survived, worse still, he would have to explain his actions to his father, the King. His thoughts were interrupted by a man who came at him. Using his favourite ploy, he parried the axe blow aimed at his head. As the axe dropped from the man's hand by his powerful counter, he closed on his enemy. Using his dagger, he plunged it deep into the chest. Again and again they pressed forward until the last of the Irish was despatched by Lord Grenden. With a massive downward stroke with his great sword, he almost cleaved his enemy in two. Dog, of course, had made his presence known by his shouting. Horn, making the initial attack to aid the Lord's party, had been seen to take on the enemy with unusual skill. In spite of the situation, this had not gone unnoticed by Lord Grenden. One of the officers asked him his name.

"I am Colver." Horn avoided his eyes.

Dog butted in rudely, "That's right, and I'm called Dog."

The officer, taken aback by their youth, asked where they had come from, at which Dog assured them that they had been with the army since it left the castle. Lord Grenden had not missed this conversation, and he knew he had witnessed in that skirmish a style of swordsmanship second to none, and by the hand of such a young boy. As for the youth with him, well, he was a warrior in the making, who relied on his brute strength, savagery, and a lot of luck. He was impressed.

"I know you, boy. I commend you to my Lords and Knights. You will join my staff now; come along with my Lords."

Horn looked across at Dog, knowing he heard the Lord's command to join him, but not that he had recognised him in spite of his disguise, but by his weapon skill.

"My Lord, if I am to join your staff, may I have the boy standing there to act as my servant?" he asked, pointing at Dog.

Lord Grenden looked at Dog, really for the first time, and was visibly shocked. He had never seen such an ugly boy; he had to partially avert his eye. However, he had seen the crude power of the youth. Obviously there was already a successful association between them that seemed to work well in combat, even under great pressure.

"You will have to quarter him with the other servants when we make camp. Ye Gods! My Prince, where did you find this one? Oh yes, you did say you left the castle together."

Horn called out to Dog to join him.

"Dog, you must come with me. You must remember to call me Colver at all times, and do not steal anything from the Lords or Knights. Do you understand?"

Dog sensed that his fortunes were about to change for the better, and that his friend was, after all, the son of some important person, maybe a Knight! Or even a Lord! He had suspected this all along, but in any case, he had found favour with the Commander-in-Chief of the whole army! Dog replied, "Colver, I am your man. I will follow you and fight with you!"

With that, the small party moved out from the wooded area to rejoin the main army. There were enough men hunting down the enemy deep in the woods. So far the skirmish had cost them only one officer. Thanks to Horn and Dog, the enemy group had been wiped out.

In the north of the village of Lockney, the main army was still engaging the last of the invaders, now no longer in thousands, but in hundreds. The possibility remained of more than a thousand scattered towards the coastal areas of the north-east. In the north-west, some were still trying to make for the borders of Preyden and to the south-east towards Collona. They would be hunted down and would have to run the gauntlet of the King's men, who were now busy setting up points of ambush along the main routes to both neighbouring kingdoms. A great toll had been taken of the enemy in the area of Geltham and on the road to Lockney, but at a cost. Sadly, the King had lost many old warriors and friends. These included the old veteran Astle, who went down in fierce fighting. Pushing too far forward, he had been cut off and surrounded. Although he took the lives of more than a dozen, he finally succumbed to heavy odds. He and his kin would not be forgotten.

Lord Grenden spoke quietly to Horn. "Is the King aware of your absence from the castle, my Prince? Or did you disregard my advice to ask for the King's blessing to join the army?"

Horn admitted he had left the castle on impulse, as he knew the King would deny him the chance to go, even with a special escort, which had always accompanied him outside the castle.

Horn took a moment to reply. "My Lord, I pray you, let the King know I was in your party during the attack to explain my presence in your company, but that I was in no danger to my life."

The Lord nodded in agreement,

"As much as the King would be impressed with any knight in the kingdom who had done as well in your recent action, he would readily dismiss your great talent with the sword. His Majesty would think only of the risks you had incurred by taking on an enemy such as the Irish."

Horn thanked him, but he knew that eventually there would come a time to face his father and account for his actions. Not only that, he could imagine his mother, the Queen, would now have realised he was missing. She would raise a hue and cry throughout the castle when she found out he had not been seen.

He could see the King's army ahead. Their task in the area of Lockney was almost done, with the exception of rounding up stragglers in the immediate countryside. The invasion had failed; it was at an end; the Irish Kings had deserted their army, and most of their ships were now in the King's hand. It would be some time before any of them would ever set foot on Westerland's shore. Then again, the Irish were not the only enemies that cast their eyes on this fertile land and its treasures. It would always remain the envy of kings, princes, and pretenders.

King Alymer, standing on a small hillock, could see not only the final demise of the main army of his enemy, but also a small group approaching. Lord Grenden led with the banner unfurled; it was decorated with falcons in salute to the King. He dismounted and knelt before him.

"Sire, I am pleased to report the hated Irish were destroyed by an army of your men of Westerland. Some sections are now hunting down the remainder, wherever they may run to. The Gods were kind to us, our losses are small, and your loyal subjects are in high spirits, as you see."

The men around the hillock raised high their weapons and voices in one accord, shouting his name. "Alymer! Aylmer! Aylmer the Great!"

Saluting with a raised arm, the King acknowledged the praise of his men, and after further compliments, rested and ate. Horn had deliberately kept his distance from the King by standing back behind the knights. It would not have been a good time for the King to have recognised his own son in the army. He and Dog filled their stomachs from the ration cart and treated their parched throats to the strong ale. Within a short time, both had succumbed from the rigours of the day's battle, falling into a deep sleep as the sun began to fade and night fell.

Horn woke with a start. He heard the sound of men moving and the loud shouting of orders. He shook Dog, who could have slept forever. Speaking quickly, he said, "Dog! Something is up! Get on your feet!"

Looking, they could see men running to form up under the commanders, and heard the voice of Lord Grenden calling to make haste to join him. He then wheeled round to spur the men into action. A force of roughly a thousand Irish, seen by the scouts, had not yet been accounted for under a leader called Brinian. His force, after reaching the coast and then being unable to take to the ships, made the decision to attack the King's force. He believed it to have been seriously weakened by losses and the many search parties that had been sent out to hunt down his countrymen.

The King's force had set camp in a position by a small group of hillocks, while Lord Grenden's men were camped about a third of a mile away. Brinian had not seen the commanders's force, believing the King's men to be the entire Westerland army in camp. At the onset of his attack, which took place with little or no warning, his men were able to penetrate deep into the King's force, as they were still scrambling into some form of order. The fighting began to spread into groups over a wide area. Confused and shaken by the surprise attack, they fought hard. One large group of the enemy broke away to close on the King and his bodyguard. The King, already in action, wielded his great two-handed sword, whirling it above his head. It took a toll of those that faced him. His Lord's Wagnor and Sintel held their own against heavier odds, but the arrival of this new determined group was to put the King in mortal danger. Wagnor, taking on two of the Irish, stumbled over a tree root, lost his balance, and took a spear through the chest as he struggled to his feet. Lord Sintel took a heavy blow on his sword arm, causing a deep wound and rendering it completely useless. He switched his sword to the other hand, feinted, then ran his opponent through as he came to finish him. Another Irishman took his place, landing a mighty blow to Sintel's shoulder. This opened up a massive gaping wound, which now meant he was defenceless. His opponent then delivered a powerful thrust to Sintel's body, which took his life. King Aylmer had now lost two of his most able Knights.

Lord Grenden and his men arrived at the scene and at once engaged the enemy with vigour. Lord Grenden noticed the King's knight Briscal fighting hard to reach his side.

"My Lord, the Lord's Wagnor and Sintel are lost! And the King over the ridge is in a dangerous situation. He is hard pressed by great odds. Assistance is required at once, before it is too late!"

Lord Grenden called to Richel to break off and take six Knights with the two youths, Colver and Dog, saying he would join them as soon as he could. They covered the distance quickly to the hillock, joining in the action. Horn and Dog, shoulder to shoulder, pressed forward into the thick of the enemy, gaining ground towards the King, who had noticed Richel and the Knights fighting their way through to him. This gave him new strength to his sword arm as they joined him. The King became aware of a small figure whose dexterity with the sword caused devastation to the enemy. At his side, another youth, his face contorted in a hideous scowl, slashed and stabbed at the Irish with little regard for his own safety. Many fell before these two. They seemed, to the King, to be fighting perfectly in tandem. Gradually the number of the enemy pressing forward began to lessen, and it was clear that they were on the point of defeat. Some sensing defeat, including Brinian himself, managed to avoid the King's pursuers, and made for the cover of the nearby woods. Others, too exhausted by the fight, became easy victims; their chance of escape were dominated by the men of Lord Grenden's force. The Lord, flushed with his part in the success of this latest skirmish, arrived at the King's side.

"Sire, I am pleased to see you in good order and your men in high spirit. My force is carrying on in the hunt for those who escaped our swords. The scout Malvin informs me it could be in the hundreds. We will account for them either in the woods or hills, and there is, Sire, very little threat of a new attack in anything like serious numbers."

The King thanked his Lord for his command of the situation, which, with lesser warriors, would have meant a heavy defeat with dire consequences for the kingdom. After further discussions between them, the King now had time to think over the action he had survived, and recalled the two young men he had seen in the relief party that came to his aid when sorely pressed. The smaller had extraordinary swordplay, and the other had tenacity. They were a good pair that worked well together; they had fought outstandingly.

"My Lord Grenden, I must enquire of you, who are the two young knights with Richel? It is good to see such talent and bravery in such young men. I must talk with them before we leave the field; go bring them forth at once!"

Horn was resting with Dog, who, as usual, was recounting his exploits to anyone who would listen.

"Oh! How easy the fight—" He was stopped in mid-flow by Horn.

"Stop spouting your own part in this Dog; we all did well today."

Dog did not like to be halted, but took the hint from his friend Colver. After all, attachment to him could bring better things to his life without stealing. If it meant taking the part of a servant at times, so be it! The Knight Richel rode over to them and commended them for their part in the last action."

"I now understand why Lord Grenden included you both in my party to go to the King's aid. Your name, I believe, is Colver, and your companion carries the name of Dog."

Richel took the nods as confirmation, but he thought of the King's reaction when he faced the one called Dog. Even in happy moments, his attempts to smile only succeeded in producing a scowl. He would be taken aback! Horn wished the ground would swallow him up, rather than face his father and account for his presence in the army. Lord Grenden would also be at risk by not revealing his presence to the King earlier. Although, in fairness, he had done his best to assume a disguise to fool the Lord.

Richel entered the King's shelter with Horn and Dog close behind him; their presence was recognised at once by the Knights. Cheers greeted their entry as they approached within a few feet of the King and halted. The Knights formed a gangway as the two were announced and brought forward. Horn kept his head lowered and remained a step behind Dog as they bowed before the King. Richel, bowing low, announced the two youths.

"Sire, the two men known as Colver and Dog at your command."

The King looked at Dog. He could not believe what he was seeing. He had to look away briefly, and then asked his age, for it was difficult to judge such a face. The scar dominated his countenance, which also betrayed his way of life since birth. Trying hard not to stare, the King thought only of the boy's prowess on the field.

"Knight you are not! Base born you may be! Courage is not given to all men, whatever their birth, but reward you shall have to mark this day, and your King's gratitude."

The King motioned to Ancour, who produced a purse containing gold coins, and presented it to Dog, who was then dismissed and led out of the shelter. Horn found himself standing alone before his father. He was convinced he had been recognised, and hoped for a softer rebuke for his disobedience.

"Step forward and let me look upon this young warrior."

As he spoke he recognised the features of his own son, in spite of the torn and muddied clothing, which had suffered much on the marches and sweat in combat.

"Come closer! Come closer!" commanded the King. "Let me look upon the face of a Knight, and so ye shall be from this day, Colver."

Horn felt a tremendous feeling of relief as his father had not publicly reprimanded him in front of the Lords and Knights. Bending low in homage, he replied, "Sire, you honour me more than I deserve. I am hardly worthy of the accolade of Knight."

The King cut him short and addressed his Commander-in-Chief. "My Lord Grenden, you have done your work well. This kingdom is now richer by one warrior Knight. He will take the place of our fallen Knights on merit earned.

You will take him into your company in close attendance to continue his service. He will serve us well. His skills displayed on the field please me and, I am sure, his noble tutor."

Lord Grenden caught Horn's eye and smiled the smile of a man who had passed on gifts to an eager worthy student, and now, after some years, had the privilege of seeing this talent displayed on the battlefield. He was happy.

With that, the King ordered the huntsmen to seek out game to provide a feast that night in Lockney, because there no longer was any threat from the Irish. Most of the survivors were still on the run from the groups of King's men eager to catch them and send them to their Gods without delay. That night at the feast, the King bade Lord Grenden to sit a much washed and cleansed Horn at his table, a place among the Lords and Knights. All had, by now, seen through the name Colver. They recognised him as the King's son and witnessed the pleasure it gave to both the father, King Alymer, and the Prince's tutor, Lord Grenden. Health was drunk many times for the fallen Knights, Wagnor and Sintel, whose exploits and service over the years were commemorated. Some notable action of the two were personally told by Richel. Lastly, they spoke of Horn, the new Knight. He could now mingle freely with them, for he was no longer just a member of the royal family, a Prince of the Blood, but now a Knight and a warrior. For him, a dream had become a reality.

Dog was sitting with the men, but his mind was in another world. His head spun with a thousand thoughts. *He was now the possessor of a purse of gold coins and it felt good!* He felt for it. *Yes! It was there!* Never could he have imagined he would be the recipient of such wealth by honest means. He smiled at the thought of himself, once a common thief, snatching purses which usually contained nothing of value. Men who once kicked him as a beggar, or worse, would envy him his new found wealth. What was even better, as a warrior, he was noticed and commended by the King himself.

He snapped out of this dream world as the ale flowed, and the tales of the number of the enemy he had despatched grew. His aggressive talent had been seen by many, but who cared; he was in good company. All were anxious to be drinking with him. His unfortunate countenance was now quite accepted and seldom referred to, not like the bitter days of defending the stinging and, at one time, hurtful jibes. He had become used to them. He either reconciled himself, shrugged them off, or responded with a flow of curses. *Yes!* he thought. *Life is going to be better, and now my curiosity about Colver is, more or less, resolved.* Colver was now a Knight and, indeed, the son of a very important person. He would accompany him when he asked for his service and anywhere he directed. He wandered over towards the King's table, careful not to be seen. He noticed his companion was the centre of attention. Having been cleaned up for the King's presence, he sat with grace and bearing in that noble company. He mused, *this young fellow, his companion, will go far.* He could picture him as a great lord, but then, would he still be needed? Perhaps only in battle, where he could serve and fight with him, but not with the same closeness as before. They had enjoyed the thrusting forward through the enemy ranks and sharing the taste of victory. *What would tomorrow bring? Would Colver ignore him?* Maybe the other young Knights would constantly demand his company. Perhaps his new found status would go to his head, and he would seek new companions when he returned to the castle. Dog did not know that Colver was, in fact, the Prince. Knights and the Lords felt honoured in his company. He belonging to the royal house of Westerland and was now a proven warrior.

Morning broke with the men thinking of returning to their homes and the castle. It was always good to be welcomed back as victors over an old enemy. There would be tales to be told to wide-eyed sons of great deeds in battle, and sadly, the news of those who would not be coming back, most buried where they fell. Lord Grenden, aware of his position as supreme commander, began to marshal his men into a semblance of order. He did not want any of the men to break away to villages or make an untidy entry into the castle. Also, there was a small risk from groups of the enemy laying low in the woodland or countryside. An ambush could be laid by any small number of men along the route, if they had the advantage of numbers.

Horn had woken to a new dawn, fresh and happy in his mind. No further deception was necessary. Life could be good now. He had the recognition of his father, the King, and not the punishment he had feared would be his for joining the army. Now, on the way back to the castle, he decided to walk, rather than take the horse offered to him by the Commander. He wished to be with Richel and the young Knights, who had preferred to walk themselves. It was a chance to know them better. The castle would be reached in three hours, marching at a comfortable pace. Horn, looking back, fancied he could see a figure keeping a regular distance behind them. Falling back from his group, he could see it was Dog. *Of course! How could he have forgotten Dog so quickly?* He called out, "Hey Dog! Follow on to the castle. I will send for you this day. I have something important to tell you." Dog waved in response.

A small group of the enemy broke from their cover, startled by the approaching force. Richel detailed three knights to deal with them. When the knights caught up with the fleeing men, the men threw down their weapons. It was all to no avail; no mercy was allowed to an invader. There were a few more isolated incidents that ended with the same result, but soon the castle came into sight. The watching sentries of the garrison gave the signal for the war horn to be sounded. It gave out its triumphant blast, which echoed through every nook and cranny and carried to the ears of the approaching force. This brought the entire population to life. The courtyard rapidly filled with eager wives and mothers, all making for the best position to see their loved ones as they entered the gates. Gaily coloured banners were quickly hoisted on vantage points, and there was an air of expectancy. Excited children ran, ignoring their mother's scolding to stay close, less they were crushed by the crowds of inhabitants at the gate area.

At last, the moment arrived. The army reached the gates, led by the King and Lord Grenden. An immense roar sounded from hundreds of throats. Wives, mothers, sweethearts and parents embraced their men as they were allowed to break ranks. Smiles were everywhere. Small boys grabbed eagerly at their father's weapons, impatient and pleading to hear stories of the battles. Who were the heroes? How many Irishmen were killed? A thousand, two, three, four, or all of them? Questions would be asked time and time again until they had been answered. Mothers would have to wait for the opportunity to have their husbands to themselves. Sadly, some of the women turned away when the face so desperately sought failed to appear among the ranks of the army; then they knew that he was among the fallen. Names had not yet been listed, but their hearts sank, and those with children hugged them close in a tearful embrace. The childless woman ran to her shelter, flung herself down in grief, and would lay there for many hours through the coming days.

Horn, with the King, greeted the Queen, his sister, and members of the royal family. Both had noticed the absence of Horn from the castle soon after the army had left and had feared the worst. They had been deeply afraid for his safety, so the relief of seeing him enter the castle swept away their fears. No scolding would be forthcoming as the Queen embraced her son and then her husband, the King.

A change of clothing and a bath worked miracles. The only item left of Horn's old apparel from the action in the field was his dagger, a present from his father on his twelfth birthday. It had been well and truly tried and found not wanting in quality, as a few Irishmen, no doubt, would testify, if they could. He suddenly remembered his words with Dog! He begged to leave his mother's presence and almost ran into his father as he entered the chamber.

"Horn, I would have you attend me later. I have to discuss your position at court in the light of your escapade. You are now a Knight, as well as a Prince of the kingdom."

Horn replied he would and dashed off into the courtyard, which was now bustling with activity, to seek Dog. It was not difficult to find him. A gathering of boys and urchins revealed him in full flow as he made public his part in the battles. Horn noticed that Dog had found time to buy new clothes of quality and was carrying himself with confidence, rather than his usual aggressive swagger.

"Dog, you look better than you did a few hours ago. Come to the entrance of the hall, as I have something I wish to say to you."

Dog turned, bade his audience farewell, and followed Horn to the hall, wondering what his elevated friend Colver had in mind for him. Arriving there, Horn looked at his companion and gave a friendly smile.

"I have acquired a healthy respect for you, Dog, as a warrior. We fought well together, my friend. I hope when next an enemy attacks us, you will be beside me. I can think of no one better."

Dog grinned; his face assumed the awful grimace which Horn was now accustomed to.

"Same for me, my Lord," he said, using a title he now thought was more appropriate for his friend. He would, in the future, always address him so.

"Dog, tomorrow I will go hunting. I wish you to join my party and assist me personally. Should you agree, I will provide you with a horse. We leave at ten o'clock from the main courtyard."

The courtyard was alive with men and horses. Everywhere was a scene of purpose and expectation for the day's hunting. Horn found himself the centre of attention, with many wishing to ride with him. Brushing aside their offers, he called to Dog, who was standing a respectful distance from the Lords. He had wondered if Colver would call him or if he would be expected to run with the servants of the hunt.

"Take this big grey, Dog. He is a good horse. Ride with me and stay close till we spot a quarry worthy of our chase."

The hunt moved off quickly through the gates. They were a party of some thirty Lords, Knights, and courtiers. Their retainers ran to keep up, carrying bows and staves. As they passed the villages, many turned out to see and wave at the sight of the riders in high spirits. There had been recent reports from the foresters in the area of Wavelon of an abundance of red deer and wild boar of good size, which was confirmed later from the same forest.

The hunt arrived at the forest and sent in their retainers to start to beat the undergrowth and to make enough noise to put any wildlife to flight.

The first to break cover was a large boar, which Horn shouted was his, and laid claim to the chase. He set off at great speed after the squealing animal as it made straight for the thickest party of the forest. Pursuit on horseback would be highly dangerous. They decided to dismount and chase on foot. The boar had the advantage of cover, but they could see him now and again, crashing through one thicket after another. The thrill of the chase, and the excitement, gave the two young warriors that extra boost to their legs, but who would tire first? At last, the sound of the boar crashing his way through the forest ahead of them lessened in intensity. Suddenly, they were on it. At close quarters it lay in front of them, a huge animal, larger than first thought. It seemed to be studying them. Its cruel red eyes were filled with hate, its mouth covered in foam. Now at bay, the ferocious beast decided to charge its pursuers. It was no timid animal, but born with the heart of a lion and equipped with the means to cause serious life threatening injuries to a man on foot. Horn steadied himself as it charged. Taking aim with his bow, he loosed an arrow which hit the boar full in the chest, dropping him. But with a sound resembling a scream of hatred, it got to its feet and charged again. This time Dog waited until the huge, pain-crazed animal was almost on him. He thrust his spear straight through the neck. The impact knocked him backwards off his feet. The boar tried desperately to struggle to its feet once again, but collapsed with a grunt; its flank heaved as it sought for breath. It was left to Horn to step in quickly and finish the animal with a dagger thrust as men came running to join them to take charge of the beast.

Admiring its great size and evil tusks, they slung the carcase between poles and made their way out of the forest. Even with four men it proved to be a heavy burden. The dead animal would become even heavier as they carried it to the castle. The hunt had been a great success; they had two boars, three red deer and many fowl to grace the table. That night there would be celebrations in the hall. Horn extended an invitation to Dog to attend and to sit with the young Knights and those who were proven warriors

The great feast began as the royal party took their seats. The enormous platters were carried in by the servants, red faced, puffing and blowing with the weight. Musicians played quietly until they heralded the entrance of the great boar. It received tremendous cheers, and the hall filled with the distinctive smell of the roast, which caused many lips to be smacked in anticipation of this most favourite of dishes. The barrels were set up at each table to supply the vast quantity of ale that would be consumed. Serving men and women would be kept busy with the constant chain of drinking vessels in use on each table. The consumption of ale would keep mounting as people kept eating. King Alymer and his Queen sat with Horn, his younger brother and sister, Lord Grenden, the important courtiers, and the close household officers at the royal table. Again, Horn was the bombarded with compliments from members of the court who had heard of his exploits in the field, and the skill displayed during the rescue of the King's person against great odds. To them, this was unexpected from the young Prince.

The night went well and Horn glanced across the hall to where Dog was seemingly holding the attention of the young Knights. No doubt once again recounting his action in the last engagement, with an added something in excess of the actual happening. Well, he was entitled to embellish his story. He was a proven warrior, and he had fought alongside Colver, the great swordsman. Horn smiled to himself. He remembered his father's expression as Dog was presented to him.

Leaving the castle, he thought he must really find a position for Dog within the household. He resolved to talk with Ancour about it the next day. Now that he had respectable clothing, he would be acceptable to most in the castle, and even his ugliness could be overlooked in such a warrior. Meanwhile, at the feast, Dog wondered why whenever he spoke of Colver in the company of the young Knights, they tended to be amused. After repeating his question, they finally told him that he had, in fact, been in the company of the King's son, the Prince, Horn.

So the boy he had met in the courtyard, stole a sword for, shared so much danger with, and had come to admire really was the Prince! No wonder he possessed the talented swordplay he had witnessed. No doubt this Prince had been schooled from an early age in the martial arts. This would explain everything, even the boy's confidence. And, he had noticed that Colver sat at the King's table. Perhaps he had pinned too much hope on his companion who could have steered him to fame and fortune through his patronage, but a Prince! That was a bit too high above his lowly station. Well, what did it matter? Now, with his new status as a recognised warrior, and welcome in the company of Knights, he felt he had advanced himself to the point of being invited to sit and eat with them. A week or so ago he would have been stealing to eat. Now he could afford a roof instead of a pile of vermin-infested sacks. Even the girls were showing an interest. Before, the looks he got were of shock; that is, if they dared to give him a second look. Now, one girl had given him more than one glance beneath her lowered eyelids, and actually smiled. Her name was Althreda. Her father was a servant in the household and a huntsman with two sons. Dog dreamed on. One day, perhaps, if he distinguished himself further, this lovely creature could be approached. Dreaming still, he stole a look across at this vision who sat at the next table with her family. He resolved to do all he could the further his station and be worthy enough to win her hand. It would be necessary to be on equal terms with any rival suitor, as surely there must be for this beautiful maiden. Her brothers would obviously be protective, so there would be a need to foster good relations with them in the future, if he ever hoped to ask for her hand. Dog watched her retire from the feast with her father. *She possessed grace as well as beauty,* he thought for a moment. She turned her head in his direction. His heart leapt! He would sleep on that.

Most of the people and guests slept heavily after the long night of feasting and drinking. Not many heard the cockcrow, and the castle took its time coming to life. Some were woken by the sounds of servants running along the passages shouting at the boys who performed the menial tasks. The chattering women fetched the water from the springs, but most of all, the shouting and noise of activity made the servants feel important in the household of the King. Even the dogs scuttled out of the way of the flying feet. The slow ones yelped as a shoe lifted them in the air. Those that dodged this fate barked furiously to show their disapproval at being disturbed. As life slowly returned to the castle, the ladies were attended by their servants in their chambers, leisurely bathing and dressing, accompanied by much chatter and gossip on events of the night before. The Lords called for their servants to attend them, in readiness for their appearance at court.

King Alymer was anxious to hear of men who had been lost at Lockney and Geltham against the Irish. Their dependants would be given a purse from the King's hanaper. Many deeds of valour that had been seen or reported by the commanders, but not yet officially rewarded or recognised, would now have the King's attention. Chancellor Ancour hurried here and there to summon those mentioned to be presented to the King during the day. These included Lords Grenden, Sancto, Richel, the scouts, Malvin and Fenner, and many others.

The assembled court stirred when the first name called was Colver. It even surprised Horn that his father was reverting to his assumed name. The King received his son, now a Knight, with obvious pleasure.

"Horn, known as Colver, I commend your prowess on the field of battle against great odds, and your courage. I now invest you with the title of King's Champion, a true son, and worthy Knight of this kingdom. I charge you with the defence of the King's person at all times."

Horn received the congratulations of Lord Grenden and all who got within touching or talking distance. He took a great interest in the awards to others, and particularly the scouts, Malvin and Fenner. Their missions were nearly always fraught with extreme danger; so much depended on these men. The majority of their travels and good reports, combined with their accuracy, saved many lives. Their skill as assassins when needed was acknowledged by all except the luckless enemy. Malvin had trained others in the role of scout, one called Boarset, who was proving to be an asset on his first mission at Geltham. No doubt he would, in a very short time, prove to be worthy of the status of a lone scout, to be sent by a commander for the all important watch on the borders of the kingdom.

Chapter 2

The Challenge

As the summer faded into autumn, less tournaments were held, but the Knights were kept at practice to sharpen their skills. At Horn's request, Dog was invited to attend these training sessions to hone his swordsmanship. Albeit, his style was born naturally and crude to the eye, but it was effective against most opposition by virtue of his strength and sheer aggression. The smith and his men were busy forging new weapons. The cattle out in the fields around the castle were fat and well, yielding good quantities of milk from the rich pastures. The women gathered to gossip about their men, or their neighbours, while children ran and played. Men spent long hours in the fields, hay making and gathering the harvest. The great barn would be full, a good and all important necessity for the winter feeding of the animals. There was much corn for the millers and the domestic fowls. The condition of the deer, game and pigs looked promising for the next few months and into the main hunting season.

The winter passed without a great deal of activity. Keeping warm was one of the main occupations, and new household appointments were made. One, at the direct request of Horn, was that his companion, Dog, be given the title of Master of the Hunt, to take the place of old Althon. This post also carried a favoured apartment within the castle; it also meant that Dog would be on hand should Horn require his service in a hurry. What Horn did not know was that this appointment would bring Althreda's father and brothers under his charge as servants of the hunt. It could be, if the Gods were kind and Dog kept his head, the opportunity to gain the respect of the family. Life had certainly improved for Dog: regular food, fine clothes and footwear, his standing with the Knights. He was assured and at ease. His continued success in this field was applauded by most, as his reputation for the quick kill brought many compliments from the King. Horn felt justified in appointing Dog to the household.

The approaching summer was viewed with anticipation of long warm days, which is kind to newly born animals, particularly the foals. The horse was now becoming increasingly in demand by the army, in their request for speedy response to an emergency. No further sightings of the few Irish that had fled into the countryside had been confirmed, in spite of rumours of small bands that had been seen in the north by villagers and travellers. Scouts sent to look and report found most to be false. A number of the enemy were known to have escaped their pursuers, and crossed the borders of the neighbouring kingdoms. To this end, a force had been kept in readiness, which, from time to time, visited the areas prone to raids. These areas were hard to get to, this owing to the rough terrain of the north, which was covered with a variety of tall gorse. It could tear through a man's clothing, inflicting deep lacerations, which could often lead to fatal results if not attended to at once. A secretion from the long spines of this shrub contained a toxic substance, harmful to man and beasts

This force often wished they could encounter a real attack from the men of Snowdonna, or those from the far north who were oddly dressed, with wild eyes and flaming red hair, who came at you with a rush in mass, uttering the most ear splitting screams, and who died hard with curses on their lips. The King had told Horn of their persistent raids, stealing sheep and game some years back. They spoke in a tongue which was not to their understanding. When captured alive, these men caused continuing problems which often led to their deaths within days.

Over the years, only one of these men had survived in Westerland: a bearded giant with hair cascading down over massive shoulders. Around his powerful neck hung a Celtic motif of yellow gold. This he kissed every day as he awoke from his sleep; it was much admired and noticed by many because of its size. How to possess it was not a challenge to take, if you valued your life! Also, this man had the protection of Lord Grenden. It was the Lord who had captured him, and curious of his size, spared his life. The giant was normally a placid man, until provoked or committed to action. Lord Grenden nurtured this man and moulded him into a formidable member of his army, particularly being a master with the spear. This giant had also taught Horn his methods with this weapon in combat, and how to withstand a charge on foot against the spear in the hands of an enemy.

Horn had accompanied this last mission with the force, and after two days of marching with nothing to report, with no incident to cause excitement or interest, returned to the castle and made for his quarters. Casting off his equipment and weapons, he bathed and changed into court attire to attend the King.

"Nothing to wet your blade on, my young Prince?" the King asked. "Since becoming a Knight, it seems you are not being challenged, but tarry awhile, your time will surely come. Our kingdom is a high prize to many who only wait for the opportunity to see a weakness in our capacity to defend ourselves." The King then added. "Take note of good men, and those of stout heart that will look kindly on you and will be at your side, for surely a Prince needs an escort to be of the highest calibre, one willing to die for you without question."

Horn looked at his father and asked, "Sire, what makes a King tell his son to be so ready? Is there something I should know? Have you an illness?"

The King replied in a slow voice, leaning towards his son. "I am not well. I have been warned by our physician, Grindel, that I have but a short while. I have a malady that nothing known to men can cure. Therefore, before I take to my bed to await my death, when that time comes, I need Lord Grenden and the Chancellor to come to me. I shall name you as my successor, but beware! There are, in the kingdom, others who aspire to take the crown. Some are known to Lord Grenden and myself, and they will be taken care of after my death."

Horn was shaken by this unexpected news. He had always considered his father immortal. He assured the King he would carry out his orders when the time was at hand. He also realised that no word should come of this conversation, in case those capable of treachery should decide to act before he was crowned before all the people. The activity of the court betrayed nothing of the King's condition. Day to day events took place as usual. They sat to hear complaints often brought by villagers against others of the same or neighbouring village. They also dealt with, and made known, the trespassers in the King's forest who took game. So the days passed with the King looking no better and no worse. Horn was beginning to think that old Grindel was wrong, and the disease he had prophesied would not take the King to his ancestors.

Horn now concentrated on the young Knights and involved them in most of his activities, and through this close contact, he was able to select the most talented to enter his personal service. Those selected were to form a new found bodyguard to be installed in the "Order of the Unicorn." This decision was openly encouraged by Lord Grenden, who knew nothing of the King's illness, but thought it fitting that Horn should have his own bodyguards for the future. The chosen Knights were Alban, who was tall and fair-headed, and who excelled with the javelin; Backly, a short, powerful horseman who was ruthless with the axe; Kalden, who was fresh faced and looked younger than his years, but who was a swordsman of note with an amazing strength of arm. He also chose Cordo, an expert with the lance and highly skilled with the bow, and Foxley, who had made his name at tournaments, who was skilled in all weaponry. The last was Horton. Although he was the youngest of these Knights, he was the possessor of great talent at close quarters and was capable of moving at great speed. These six would then form the escort for Horn. Each was chosen for their skill as a combatant Knight, and after taking an oath of allegiance to the Prince, each began their role at once.

The King, informed of this development, was delighted. He gave his blessing individually to each Knight, feeling his son had chosen wisely in his selection of the most talented. One last appointment was made. Dog was promoted to the rank of captain. He would be in charge of people chosen later as personal foot escorts to strengthen the bodyguards. New quarters were found for these Knights that were paces away from the royal chambers. Servants were appointed as messengers to be on watch, day and night. Also attending the daily training sessions, they would be in attendance on the Knights. Although younger by some years, Horn felt comfortable in their presence. His respect for their skills, and their respect for his authority, plus his reputation as a warrior, worked well, and soon they had formed an ever strengthening bond. And so the King's wish became a reality. Although, of course, these Knights, like all in the kingdom, knew nothing of his illness, save Grindel and Horn, nor that it had given rise to the founding of the Order, whose sole purpose was protecting the Prince's succession, for the life of the King could be threatened should his condition become known.

Dog played his part in selecting men to form this escort of foot. He had already mixed with many that had taken part in the previous battles against the Irish invaders. He was able to single out those men who had been seen in the thick of fighting and had shown their mettle. Gradually, he was able to marshal the men into their own quarters, which were situated in the main courtyard and near to the grand hall. His priority was improving their weapons. He attired them in the dark brown, studded clothing that was now favoured by the army. Soon, they to began to form into a close company, aware of their part in the newly formed bodyguard for the Prince.

Horn had noticed the effect all this had on Dog and was pleased. He had used his talents to ferret out a company of trustful warriors. He was confident that he could rely on Dog to ensure constant training with their new issue of weapons and, the most crucial factor of all, to lead his men by example. Dog had absorbed and learnt much from his immediate betters, gleaning new mannerisms and habits from the young Knights, whose company he often sought. For many weeks Horn and his Knights worked at their skills. Dog's men trained hard until they became a highly proficient fighting group, one that could strike at any threat mounted by a claimant, or defend the crown at a minutes notice. Their creation would not be made public until it was deemed necessary. This bodyguard, then, could also play a major role in the combined force under Lord Grenden in case of a serious invasion by an enemy. Lord Grenden was kept abreast of this development. He was not worried that the formation of this elite body of Knights, responsible only to Horn, would, in any way, weaken his overall authority as commander of the whole army. They would be available to him if required, and his recent unexpected appointment to Commander of the "Order of the Unicorn" by the Prince sealed the alliance between the army and the new group.

On a hot and still August day, while the King was discussing matters of the State with Secretary Winloch and Chancellor Ancour, he suddenly had to find a support to steady himself, as a sharp pain racked his body. This caused him to double up in agony and cry out. Both the Ministers called out in alarm.

"Sire, what is it! Shall we summon for help?"

The King, in increasing pain, gasped out, "Take me to my chamber! Call Grindel to attend me at once."

His face was now contorted with consuming agony, which seemed now to run through the whole of his body. He commanded them to say nothing about this but to call Horn, Lord Grenden, and the Queen immediately. Grindel received the news he had long feared from Secretary Winloch. He hurried through the passages to the King's chamber and entered to find him with his Chancellor and, by now, almost incapable of speech.

"Grindel, tell me, have I now arrived at the point you predicted?"

Grindel made an inspection of the King's eyes and noticed that they had lost their usual brightness; he could see apprehension mirrored there. "Sire, we are fast approaching the time for you to make arrangements with your family and ministers."

The Chancellor, aware for the first time just how serious this was, asked

Grindel to give them his opinion: was the King dying? Grindel nodded his head slowly. "Ancour, the King is losing his battle with an illness and will not last until the morrow. I would advise you to arrange the King's matters at once, while he can still communicate by mouth, albeit with great difficulty."

The King, in intense pain, his face ashen, interrupted them as the Queen and Horn arrived in the chamber, followed closely by Lord Grenden. Raising himself slightly with great effort, he spoke. His voice was barely audible. "I fear my time has come. I wish to name my successor to the kingdom before I leave this earth. It will be my natural and rightful born son, Horn. I require each of you to accept my wishes. Swear allegiance to him on this my deathbed, and swear that you will support him faithfully, as you have done during my long and happy reign."

All in the royal chamber chorused their approval, as the King's voice was now reduced to a series of hoarse gasps. As he fought for breath, he ordered all to leave the chamber, except Horn and the Queen. He commanded Lord Grenden to ensure that he, and the ministers, would not make the news public until he had departed this life. He said his goodbyes to them. With no relief from the life consuming agony, he could only weakly move a hand to hold the Queen's, and then his son's. The King fought hard the losing battle of attempting to speak, but the Queen, with a finger on her lips, eventually quieted him. As they sat with him till the first onset of dawn, he began to slip quietly away.

The bantam cock strutted in the courtyard, then preened his brilliant, glossy coat of feathers, shook himself, and mounted his point of advantage. With an arched neck, he threw back his head to herald his existence and to challenge the world. With that, King Alymer of Westerland, the king for thirty triumphant years, with a long and soft sigh, now mercifully relieved of pain, left his kingdom to join his ancestors in the great hall of warriors.

A long blast of the war horn from the castle walls stopped the everyday hubbub of the court, who was meeting, as usual, to await the King's pleasure in the great hall. The castle inmates and villagers in their daily pursuits wondered what had happened. Could this be another invasion? It was always a sign of bad news to hear the solitary long blast. Again, the horn shattered the morning air. The Chancellor and Lord Grenden descended into the main courtyard, which was now crowded with alarmed people. In the adjacent courtyard, others were quickly assembling in great numbers. Lord Grenden raised his hands for silence to speak.

"Good people of Westerland, this day your great King Alymer has been called to his ancestors; the King is dead!"

As Horn stepped to his side, the Lord lifted his arm to the crowd. "The King is dead! Long live the King!" All the assembled people repeated this with great voice and true feeling. Horn and the Lords retired to the grand hall for the coronation ceremony, which Lord Grenden and the ministers thought it advisable to hold at once. Stelid, the Bishop, called on all of the assembled Lords and Knights to witness the coronation of the young Prince. He led the Prince to the throne. Lord Grenden stood there, waiting for him to sit. The Bishop raised the crown high to be seen by the Lords, before gently lowering it to adorn the Prince's head. The great shout again rang out in the hall.

"God save the King! God save the King!" This was repeated by hundreds of throats, time and time again with immense feeling.

The Queen and the royal family were the first to approach the throne and kneel in homage. They were followed by Lord Grenden and the whole assembly of ministers, Lords, and Knights. The day passed quietly, with no further celebrations allowed, as the family mourned the King's passing. The funeral of King Alymer was carried out in the simple manner he had directed, and was only attended by the family and a few close friends, such as Lord Grenden and the Chancellor Ancour. The body, being interred in the castle keep, was encased in lead, then covered with a massive stone with the simple adornment of a single "A" carved deeply into the fabric. The Queen kept to her chambers with her ladies and did not attempt to advise her son on any matter of State. He had the wisdom of Ancour and Winloch to introduce him to the affairs of government and the strength of Lord Grenden in military matters. Horn had always regarded the Commander as a second father since childhood.

Gradually, the news of the death of King Alymer spread far and wide to even the most remote parts of the kingdom, and eventually fell on the ears of some who were not sorry to hear it. One such person had been banished from the kingdom some years ago. He had been accused of treason and consorting with an enemy for profit. He had caused the death of a company of men while in pursuit of a vast treasure caravan over the Preyden border. Ambushed, he had left his men to their fate against heavy odds while he made his escape; a solitary survivor returned to condemn him. Rogden, the Knight, once highly thought of by the King as talented and courteous, was exposed. He had harboured ambitions to replace Lord Grenden. Now, he was on the King's list as being dangerous to his son's succession. He was a cousin, by marriage, to a sister of the King.

Hearing that the young Horn had succeeded his father as King, Rogden could see an opportunity. Horn, at his young age, would not have the experience in dealing with an invasion, let alone an attack on the realm, or even an assault on the castle itself. Being at one time in the service of the Lord, he knew the tactics and method of their approach to battle. He decided that he could take the kingdom with the right men behind him, and set about recruiting them from the borders. He gave the promise of rich rewards, easily earned, with vast amounts of booty for the taking. He attracted men mostly wanted for crimes, branded as outcasts, to whom the chance of easy pickings would appeal. As the news became general knowledge along the borders of the kingdom, almost five hundred men were quickly mustered. With this strength, he began to raid the villages in the west for provisions and weapons, giving dire threats to the inhabitants should they betray him.

However, one brave villager escaped the attentions of Rogden's men. Slipping out unnoticed, he travelled fast through the night, stopping only to regain his breath and to drink from a stream. Arriving at the castle, he was taken straight to Lord Grenden.

"My Lord, I bring news of the knight called Rogden near the village of Bale. He is terrorising the nearby villages and taking all he needs in food and weapons. His army of wild men is growing daily, and it is believed he intends to attack the castle when his force is doubled."

Lord Grenden asked him if he could estimate the strength of Rogden's army.

"Some say it is nearly a thousand, my Lord!"

Lord Grenden thanked him and gave orders for the man to be given food and new clothing, then asked for an audience with Horn. There would much to discuss, and quickly. They needed to mobilise men for this possible attack. The news of Rogden's intentions did not altogether surprise Horn. His father had warned him that these men existed; this was why he had formed his bodyguard. He was quite capable of entering into combat with anyone on fair terms, but treachery was another aspect to be aware of constantly.

One other Knight who was thought to challenge the succession was Barda, who claimed to be an illegitimate son of King Alymer from before his marriage to Queen Athena. Four years older than Horn, he claimed succession by right of his royal blood, which made him the first son and heir of the crown. Lord Grenden had always been aware of this claim, and the close association of the beautiful Acta from Sabden, renowned for her dancing and singing, with the then young King Alymer. Whether it was true or not, the association could not lead to marriage, as Alymer had been already promised to wed Athena at the age of sixteen. Barda had been allowed to remain in the kingdom when Acta claimed her son to be fathered by the King. It was on the condition she did not pursue it any further; the alternative would have been banishment for both her and her son. In time, he had even been allowed access to the castle, joining the army to earn a Knighthood for his bravery while serving under Lord Grenden. It was now time for a confrontation between the Lord and the Knight after King Alymer's death. It came to a head unexpectedly when Lord Grenden was on his way to Horn's chambers. He found himself facing a group of men in the narrow passage. He recognised Barda at once, and realised that this was possibly an attempt to gain unauthorised access to the King. Taking as few paces forward, he called out, "Barda, what is the reason for your presence here?"

Barda took a step forward towards him. "My Lord, I am here by right of birth, as you well know. It is unfortunate you have seen us."

Lord Grenden quickly summed up his position. This was a narrow passage, allowing no more than three abreast, which could be in his favour. The noise of any action would carry through the passages, bringing Knights and guards to the scene within minutes. He made a count of the men behind Barda. There were possibly ten or twelve at the most. Some he recognised as footmen, who would not be expert swordsmen. Again, he spoke. "Barda, give way! Do not go any further with this treachery. Nothing could come of this. Only your blood on this stone floor will mark your presence here."

"My lord, for many years have I waited to be recognised as the King's son. It is my destiny. The day had finally come; so stand in my way at your peril!"

Lord Grenden drew his sword and advanced. Even against these heavier odds, he was now committed to defend the King. Barda he knew his own capability as a Knight. He would fight hard. His men were an unknown quantity; it would depend on how determined they really were. In seconds they clashed chest to chest. The Lord took the weight of Barda and, with immense strength, forced him off balance to canon into his own men. Two of Barda's men surged forward. The first presented no problem, as he received a mighty cut to the chest too powerful to parry. The second was easily despatched. The returning swing of Lord Grenden's sword opened up a massive wound in his neck area. His cry of pain echoed along the passage, carrying to the guard of the royal chamber, who sounded the alarm. Now all were alerted in the immediate passages. Men came running, guided by the sound of clashing steel.

Lord Grenden accounted for three others before again confronting Barda. Pushing through his men, Barda came towards him with his sword and dagger raised to strike. The guards were now able to join the fighting, and Horn, who had been alerted by the noise of the guard, came running, shouting orders for the passage to be sealed off. Forcing his way through the guards, he recognised Barda and immediately knew what was happening. He called out to Lord Grenden and the treacherous Barda as the two were closing on each other. "Barda! Traitor! I have the right of challenge. It is me, Horn, that stands here, the only rightful son of Alymer. Lord Grenden, it is my duty to defend my crown. Stand back!"

Lord Grenden looked at Horn to see him coming, although he remained on guard as Barda turned to meet this challenge from the King. Barda said, with his voice splitting with hate, "Horn, gladly will I send you to join our cursed father. For many years have I waited to take what is mine!"

Horn, now at close quarters with the traitor, had time to reply before they came to blows. "Treacherous Barda, you have made a mistake this day. The only throne you will win is the four arms of the men who will take your body for crow's meat.'

Barda made the first attack. His sword rang against the steel blade of the King's as he parried. For a moment, both stood locked together, their eyes meeting with fierce determination. Breaking away, a flurry of sword play by Horn drove Barda back a few paces. Barda defended well, taking most blows by the middle of his blade. Horn was taken a little by surprise; most opponents would have made a mistake and exposed a weakness under such an attack.

Lord Grenden anxiously gripped his sword hilt, wanting to assist his King, but he realised to do so would be a personal affront to Horn. He consoled himself with the thought of a victorious Barda breathing for a minute before he stepped in and killed him. The traitor would not die quickly; he would slowly cut him to pieces as he stood, the blows lessening in strength to inflict small telling wounds. Lord Grenden realised his thoughts did not reflect Horn's talent as a swordsman and dismissed them as foolish ideas inspired by his concern for the young king. Back came Barda with a series of strokes which ended again in a clinch. Both bodies pressed chest to chest, looking for an advantage. Barda, his left hand suddenly free, managed to draw his dagger. Aiming to penetrate Horn's stomach, he struck the sword belt as he was again forced back by sheer strength of the King. Horn closed on him, delivering a bewildering display of swordplay. Barda could do little to retaliate under such a sustained attack except to fend off most of the blows and thrusts towards his body. He received many cuts in his attempt to get back on equal terms with Horn. Knowing this would, in time, weaken him by the serious loss of blood, he desperately lunged forward. Horn caught him squarely across right shoulder, laying it open to the bone. His sword arm dropped, sending his weapon clattering on the stone. Barda, with only his dagger for protection, was lost. He sank to his knees, with his eyes still focused up at Horn. The glittering hatred shown earlier was now replaced with the look of pain and apprehension. He knew what would be coming next. He was not disappointed. Horn stepped closer to the traitor and, with a clean thrust of his sword, pierced through the body, withdrawing immediately. For what seemed like minutes to Lord Grenden, Barda remained kneeling as if in prayer, until blood appeared to trickle from his open mouth. He then pitched forward, quite dead.

Lord Grenden could see that the men who had fallen in with Barda's weak and ill planned attempt to kill Horn were all but taken care of by the guards. Those that surrendered were put to death on the spot. His relief at the outcome of the attempt on the King's life showed plainly on his face.

"Sire! I thank the Gods for their kindness, and for guiding my footsteps to your chamber at this hour to come upon the traitor on his treacherous mission."

"My Lord, the Gods were, indeed, with us. It will increase our vigilance in forestalling any further attempts in the kingdom, as it is possible there are still others among us who cannot be trusted."

"Sire, I will remove the bodies from the castle for burial in an outside pit as they deserve. Then I'll let the lime work its purpose in a final act of justice."

Lord Grenden, as Commander-in-Chief of the army, was now under the authority of Horn in the same capacity as he held under King Alymer. The War Council was called to the hall. Lord Grenden, sitting beside, Horn spoke. "Sire, we have heard from the villager of this Knight Rogden's ambitions. I would beg you, Sire, to intercept this force now. I will readily lead such a force as we think necessary to go to Bale. It would be wise to send the scouts now to the area around the village, to assess their numbers and weapons."

Horn looked at Lord Grenden. "No, my Lord, it is not my wish that you lead such a force. Richel and Sancto will deploy the men. I have need of your presence here to take charge of the defences, if the need arises. Away with the scouts at once to make contact with Rogden."

A force of a thousand men was quickly assembled in the courtyard. Their weapons were checked and, where necessary, replaced with new swords and spears. The usual farewells, shouts and cheers were heard as they moved out of the courtyard and through the gates. The force was to face a march of almost two days to the village of Bale, where the villager had reported the presence of Rogden's men. Then again, it could be that they had already moved on to other villages, looting as they went. Bale could have been only a starting point. It would be up to the scouts to locate them as soon as possible and report their findings to Richel and Sancto.

Malvin, the chief scout, with Fenner and others, set off at speed towards Bale. Their method of travel had been developed into a fine art. They could cover distances over the roughest terrain like deer, with the acquired skill of the hunter, using the smallest amount of cover at an instance. While the force from the castle would take a full day to reach the area of Bale, Malvin and his scouts could be there in half the time. Their lighter weapons and clothing enabled them to jump ditches and ford rivers with fewer problems than the force would encounter. Towards the end of the morning, the scouts were now nearing the village. Fenner had been sent on, while Malvin and the other scouts followed at a short distance.

This was Fenner's skill. He could move almost unseen to within a few yards of anyone, provided there was a minimum of cover. Being a small man, he could literally melt into the ground. He was the quickest and surest of assassins. Suddenly, as Fenner turned a corner on the outskirts of the village, he could see a villager making his way towards him. He gave the man time to get really close, stepped into his path, and put a finger on his lips for silence. The startled mam almost turned and ran, but Fenner spoke to him quickly, but quietly. "Stay, friend! I am with the King's army. Where are the men who raided your village? Are they nearby?"

Recovering his fright, the man answered, "The men are but two miles away, settled near the village of Lowton, for the night approaches."

Fenner thanked him and asked him if he knew how many men had entered his village.

"Many hundreds, and they stripped us of everything they could carry. They also took some of the younger women with them, killing at least twenty of the men who tried to stop them."

He bade the man be careful not to betray the army's presence, and hurried back to report to Malvin. After hearing Fenner's encounter with the villager, Malvin decided that the scouts should move out at once towards the village of Lowton under the cover of approaching darkness.

They covered the distance in less than half an hour, and slipping into the bush nearby, could actually hear the voices of men at ease. Sadly, the occasional scream carried to them, as the rebels abused the women for their entertainment. Most of Rogden's men occupied the north end of the village in some twenty huts. The scouts, having made sure that the raiders had not posted sentries, waited for an hour until all was quiet. Using familiar skills, they were able to approach the huts, even listening to the small talk and the snores of those that slept. Malvin decided to move out quietly into the surrounding area of the village, satisfied that the numbers did not amount to more than five hundred, or slightly more. This could also mean the possibility of another group of similar strength somewhere nearby. One scout was sent back to meet up with Lord Sancto's force that was still moving towards Bale. His men only halted their march for a short rest, expecting to reach the village at first light. When the scout made contact, he found them taking a rest and checking their weapons in preparation of a hard fight that could only be hours away. Lord Santco gave orders to move out immediately. He cautioned all to be quiet. This would enable them to use the element of surprise. There was no unnecessary talking or noise from their weapons as they went forward towards Lowton.

Rogden had not been idle. His men might be resting in the village but once having served in the King's army, he realised that before long, a large force would be sent out to engage him. Although no sentries had been posted, he had sent out men to act as lookouts to strategic points along the routes, from the east and north, before he left the village.

It was one of these lookouts who first spotted the King's army approaching. He quickly sped off towards Rogden and his force to warn them. Catching up with the raiders who were not in a hurry, he reported his findings to the leader, who at once sent another man back to the village with orders to evacuate at once, and join him on the road to Collona. The man tore into the village, and at once, panic and confusion were rampant, as the Commander left in charge shouted curses at those who were slow to respond, kicking them into action as they scrambled out of the huts, grabbing their weapons, still half asleep. The men left hurriedly, in some disorder, to catch up with their comrades on their way to a place named Bird Valley, near the border of Collona. Rogden had decided on this place because of the nature of the valley; he could prepare an ambush. Sure that the King's army would pursue them, and would use the valley as the quicker route towards Collona, he instructed his men with the details of his plan.

The valley, which ran for about half a mile, featured slopes covered in woodland, and was an ideal setting; men could swiftly charge down on an enemy from the gentle slopes without losing their footing from almost perfect concealment. The neck of the valley was invitingly wide, but within a short distance narrowed considerably, where men in numbers would find it difficult to move quickly. Men would be restricted in the free use of their weapons. Rogden had guessed correctly.

Lord Richel, arriving at the now deserted village, met the scouts who reported that the raiders had moved out and were heading towards the border with Collana. He decided to take the short route through Bird Valley to cut off Rogden's force before he could reach the border and safety. Lord Sancto would be following close behind him to meet up at the valley. The Commanders hoped to catch Rogden on the open plains beyond. Out in open, his trained men would have the advantage against the hastily recruited misfits of Rigden's army.

Richel's scouts reached the entrance of the valley and could see none of the tell tale signs of an army having moved through, certainly nothing that would have alerted the King's force of a possible ambush. In the meantime, Lord Sancto had caught up with Richel and his men just prior to arriving at the valley and listened to the report of the scouts. The scouts included two who had ventured some distance into the centre, and who had been left unhindered by the raiders to return to their Commanders. Rogden had been wise enough to split his men into two parties before reaching the valley, skirting round each side to climb the slopes into the woodland, to position themselves on both sides from which to make their charge on the King's men below.

Having been given the all clear, Lord Sancto gave the order to enter the valley and move quickly through. Soon his men were shoulder to shoulder as the valley narrowed, which had the effect of slowing down their progress as they began to push and crowd each other. This was what Rogden had hoped for; his men waiting in the woodland cover grasped their weapons firmly, waiting for the signal to attack. His plan was for the King's men to have reached the middle section of the valley, then charge down before they could mount an organised defence. He had estimated their numbers were almost equal, but he had the element of surprise.

He gave the signal, and his men began their charge down the slopes, the initial effect of this unexpected onslaught throwing Richel into complete confusion. Many good men fell before they could defend themselves against this mass of charging men. The King's men had little time, or room, to draw their weapons until gaps caused by their fallen comrades provided them the opportunity to engage the enemy on equal terms. Many gallant actions were fought. Richel, himself a target, found he was soon surrounded by six of the enemy; he killed one with a thrust of his sword as he was pulled from his horse, unable to get to his feet. He was cruelly despatched by a dozen blows or more, his corpse mutilated and stripped in seconds.

Lord Santo, now on foot with his men, his horse having been killed, screaming under him by thrusting spears, took a great toll as he urged his men forward, their object to reach the end of the valley and the open ground. Sadly, the losses were beginning to tell as their escape route was now under serious threat of being cut off. Richel's men, now leaderless, and having taken most of the casualties from the initial charge, began to look for escape back to the entrance. Some made it, but most perished in the pursuit by the enemy eager for blood. Soon it was the ritual of stripping the bodies of anything worth taking; after all, the spoils of victory, the weapons, were highly sought after. If a trinket of great worth was discovered, it often led to a fierce argument with fatal consequences. Rogden, having seen the success of his plan, the near destruction of the King's army, was elated.

The handful of Richel's men who had fled from the fighting and attempted to escape back to the entrance were pursued; most never made it, being caught and killed by the eager raiders. The remnants of Lord Sancto's force no longer posed a threat to him, their fighting spirit evaporated by the shock of the ambush, and the subsequent hard fighting under difficult conditions. He had lost about a third of his men, and rather than risk losing more, called off the engagement. Gradually, the fighting slowed down until the valley suddenly became quiet. No furious clash of steel could be heard, only the whimpering of the unfortunate King's men lying seriously wounded, their fate certain; they would be finished off with a dagger or sword. They hoped that it would be with one quick strike, as the body strippers worked their way towards them, pleading would be to no avail to the men Rogden had recruited.

Lord Sancto, thankful to see the enemy break away from the fighting and leave them when they had the advantage of numbers, urged his men on to reach the end of the valley and on to the open plains. He sent a scout at once to the castle, to report to the King the sad loss of Richel and most of his men. There was a faint hope that there had been some survivors from the Richel force that would make for the castle by the south easterly route; he then gave orders for his men to prepare for the journey back to the waiting Lord Grenden.

Rogden's men counted over five hundred dead of the King's force in the valley, a great loss and an unexpected defeat. Heavily laden with good weapons, he ordered them to return the village of Lowton, safe in the knowledge that it would be some time before the King would send another force. He guessed correctly on his arrival, any of the King's men that had been in occupation had fled at the news of the defeat at Bird Valley. Rogden and his men feasted long into the night; tomorrow, he told himself, was the day of decision, having now demonstrated to his men he could take on a trained army of comparable size and beat them. Recruiting would now be easier, and when reinforced, he would mount a serious challenge to the boy who now wore the crown of Westerland. His confidence was high with expectation for the coming days.

Chapter 3

The Threat

Horn, disappointed to hear of the near destruction of his force, led by Lord Sancto and Richel against the rogue Knight Rogden, instructed Lord Grenden to examine and question every man returning to the castle from Bird Valley. What hurt most were the loss of Lord Richel and something in the region of five hundred trained men, whose replacement would take months.

"Lord Grenden, I now charge you with preparing as large an army as you can muster; send your commanders into the kingdom. I need every honest and fit man available to join the new force, particularly those who have in the past been trained. Their women must not hold or dissuade them, the call of their King cannot be challenged, be he Knight or peasant. Remember, our time is short, so set about at once, my Lord!"

Lord Grenden called in his Commanders and ordered them to leave at once, but to be aware of the enemy's presence in the area of Bale and Lowton, where they were reported to be occupying. The need was so great that men and boys must be taken from the fields, from their families, as had been done before in the reign of King Alyme, when the kingdom was under threat by a serious Viking invasion. The Commanders and their men pushed their way into huts and barns, ferreting out those men and youths who were not so ready to soldier, even for their King. There were others who were eager enough, and slowly but surely, each Commander's group grew larger by the hour; the feeling was now one of purpose. At last the recruiting had reached an impressive number in the space of two full days, and the order came for them to return to the castle to be counted and assessed by Lord Grenden's staff. The total was surprising, nearly two thousand, even after sending away those who were keen to serve, but not totally fit. This, with the standing army of four thousand, could be a basis with which to adequately defend the castle or take to the field to protect the kingdom against a major attack.

The scouts had now returned to the castle, with the exception of the two who had given the all clear at Bird Valley, and had led Lord Richel's men sadly into an ambush, with fatal consequences, both dying in the charge by the enemy. Death was their penalty for overlooking the men in the woodland slopes, where they might have been able to pick up a sound, however small, or the glint of a weapon in the sun.

The news of the destruction of the King's force at Bird Valley had not escaped the notice of others, like the neighbouring kingdom of Collona to the south-east. At one time they had been sorely beaten by King Alymer and had since not dared to cross the border. It was a refuge where dissenters such as Rogden had always been welcome, and in fact, some of the men in their border region had already joined the ranks of the rogue Knight to taste victory. On the north-east lay the kingdom of Preyden, whose King, on hearing the news, sent a messenger to Rogden, offering him support should he decide to attack the castle, promising to send a substantial number of trained men to assist him. He asked in return for a part of Westerland as a prize, should they be successful.

These two kingdoms, combined with Rogden, would be a major threat to Horn and his people; if they did unite as a common enemy, it could raise an army of ten thousand or more. Such odds could not be defeated on the field and would incur enormous casualties, even the bravest would succumb against such tremendous odds. Lord Grenden and Horn, deep in talks with their Commanders, were not yet aware of this new threat. Their immediate concern was to deal with Rogden and his force, bearing in mind that he would still be recruiting. This was made easier by his victory at Bird Valley, now common knowledge to friend and foe alike. They were still discussing their plans to seek out Rogden when a messenger arrived and was ushered in with great haste; he gave his report.

"Sire, it is reported that a group of Preydens have been seen crossing the border into the kingdom."

This could mean that they had heard the news of the defeat at the Valley at the hands of Rogden; this incursion had to be contained before it became an invasion of the kingdom. Horn gave the order to send out a small force of trained men to the border, to look for signs of a major build up of a Preyden army. Their task was to catch and kill any Preyden they found, to spread out in stealth parties, approaching silently, and slitting the throats of the intruders before melting into the night. Small groups on their way to join Rogden were encountered and dealt without allowing any alarm to be given. The force had been instructed not to challenge and fight, but to kill silently, which they accomplished with quiet efficiency.

Rogden again had been busy, his success had much enhanced his standing as a Commander, especially by the Collonians; crossing their border, he was accorded the reception of a conquering hero and invited to sit with King Aeden at a feast in his honour. The main talking point centred on marching in strength into Westerland with an army of great size and taking the castle from the young King, while he was still reeling and trying to come to terms with his army's defeat, with loss of so many good men. Both King Aeden and Rogden now realised that with the King of Preyden also prepared to send an army to join their alliance, it almost guaranteed success; with an army in the region of ten thousand, they would be unbeatable on open ground, too strong for Horn. It was enough to take the castle by storm or lay a siege effectively, in spite of the reputation of the Westerlanders as warriors.

Their confidence running high, they made appointments in the new alliance army. It was no surprise that Rogden was installed as Commander-in-Chief, who would take overall control of the army, his brother Bosden taking command of the Collonians at the request of King Aeden. The next few days in Collona were spent in hurried preparation. It was necessary for all weapons to be inspected by each of the new Commanders; those found in poor condition were replaced with the weapons taken from the King's men killed in the Valley. Tactics were discussed; plans were laid to meet most situations that would arise should they meet Horn's army in the field. As this might not become a reality, other plans would be put into operation when they met up with the Preydens in a few days.

Meanwhile, Lord Grenden's scouts had been observing Rogden's progress into Collona, with Malvin and Fenner actually crossing the border. Both had observed the preparations and build up of the enemy, who seemed to be attempting a form of training; this was an army in the making, and a large one at that! The chief scout, having seen enough, sent Fenner with all speed to report to Lord Grenden at the castle, sending his other scouts to the routes beyond Lockney towards Preyden. He stayed at the border himself to watch for the expected signs of Rogden's army on the move into Westerland. More importantly, he watched the direction they would take. Would they stay in the south or march northwards directly towards the castle?

The Castle was now under strict military control, the gates strongly guarded; sentries had been doubled on the battlements; everywhere fevered preparations could be seen, such as the precautions for siege. There were great barrels of water to quell flaming missiles, molten pitch in large cauldrons to pour down on the heads of invaders attempting to put up scaling ladders, and large boulders to crush the attackers milling below. An eventual attack on the castle itself was expected. Should Horn decide to attack the enemy in the field, he could then retreat. Plans had been made to divert or split the gathering enemy forces at their meeting place before they could reach maximum strength. The scouts would need to identify where that would be; at a guess it would be fairly close, possibly within two miles from the castle and towards the north-east.

Fenner arrived and reported on the training of the enemy in Collona; this confirmed Horn's worst fears that not only would Preyden join in an attack, but now also Collona. He would be outnumbered by his enemies possibly two to one. He had hoped Lord Sancto and the two hundred men who had gone towards the Preyden border region would have been able to thin out some of the men crossing their border. They were skilled assassins, but no word had been received from this group. Sadly, the messenger, sent from the group, had been snatched by the Preyden scouts only a mile from the castle. Although tortured, he refused to give details of the operation on their borders, so the brave scout died as a result of his ordeal.

The role played by Sancto's men was paying handsome dividends. They were skirting the border of the kingdom. This provided them with exactly the result that was intended, picking off small groups of men making their way from their villages to join up with Rogden, without any loss to themselves. They came upon a camp of fifty of these men and attacked them under cover of darkness, all were put to the knife or sword swiftly. A few offered resistance until they were overcome, but no one escaped to give warning. Within three days they had killed over four hundred men. Lord Sancto was convinced that the Preyden's main army was about to march over their border into Westerland in mass; a report from his scout had led him to believe that this army was massing in strength only a mile away, so it could be a matter of hours before they crossed into the kingdom. It was time to return to the castle, while they still could. His small force had done their job well; an added bonus was the capture of the Preyden scouts after a short chase, the very ones who had intercepted their messenger; their pleas were ignored.

In sight of the castle they could see that in even in a few days much had been done in laying defensive obstacles; an escort party took them through the gate, again heavily guarded. Once inside they were greeted to a warm welcome as their families rushed to greet them. Lord Sancto hurried to the King with his report. Horn was saddened to hear of the fate of the young messenger, but he was full of praise for their efforts on the Preyden border. After hearing the news, that at any time the Preyden army would be entering the kingdom in mass to meet up with Rogden's men, he suggested it would be of prime importance to find out which direction the Preydens would take. Would they go north to meet them? Or would they advance to within a few miles of the castle to wait for their allies to arrive? Time was now important for Horn; news from the scouts at both borders was vital to him. The chance to engage a smaller force of the enemy before they could meet would be a damaging blow to their alliance. The chance of the Preydens splitting their army could not be counted on; they, in their turn, would be aware of this possible move by Horn.

Rogden the Knight was pleased with himself; things were going well, better than he had ever dreamed. He was the Commander-in-Chief of an army of thousands. All looked up to him, he was their hero, a victor over the famed King's army. In a short time he had created an army that could take the highly prized kingdom of Westerland in one battle; no one before had succeeded. He had heard that Horn could only muster an army of some four or five thousand, and with the alliance, he could outnumber them by more than two to one. With the arrangement with King Aeden of Collona to unite with the Preydens, the total army would be assembled near the village of Sabden, lying on the south-east, some twelve miles from their main objective, the castle.

This would give Horn the option to meet them in the field, and if he was not to challenge them, they would march on to take the castle; he was confident of success. King Aeden and King Stadd had agreed to receive parts of Westerland near their own borders, but he, Rogden, would claim most of the kingdom and the castle! The other dissenters would claim their share of the spoils, as this was the price of service; as for the masses, well, they may expect some form of pickings, but the chances of that being realised could be nil.

The scout Malvin watched as the army of Rogden moved out of Collona and marched towards the north in the direction of Sabden. He then set off for the castle, first with this news, and to return at once to follow Rogden's progress. Working out the route they would take, where he could catch up with them the following morning, was a priority.

Rogden, at the head of his army astride a magnificent black horse, looked and felt the part of a great Commander, safe in the knowledge that at this moment there would be no attack, or resistance, before arriving at the village they had selected. Shortly, he would take the journey to his expected destiny. What next? In spite of the alliance, would not his ambitions stretch to Preyden and Collona one day?

Horn heard the news of the departure of the enemy out of Collona and decided that action must be taken at once to prevent these allies meeting at their appointed place, and thereby becoming an army of great size. Lord Grenden's task would be to take a force towards Sabden, beating Rogden to the village. They would then await the arrival of the Preydens, who had been marching now for two days, and had, in spite of the risk, split into three large sections. The object was to conceal the size of their force from any scouts of the King's army, but it carried the risk of a sudden attack. This was discounted by dismissing the possibility that the King's men would be too busy at the castle with strengthening defences against their intended attack.

Lord Grenden took a force of five hundred men and arrived quickly at the outskirts of the village. He sent in two men, who reported they could see some of the enemy already in occupation, the villagers subdued, and most had been herded into a series of huts at the extreme south end village. There was no sign of a lookout; clearly, they were not expecting any opposition as they were aware of the main body of their army already on the way, and the villagers had been easily overrun. The scouts, moving in closer, estimated that the number of the enemy did not exceed three of four hundred men and youths. Lord Grenden could not wait any longer to attack the enemy, as he wanted to leave the village before a larger force arrived, and certainly before Rogden's arrival. He decided to attack in three sections: one to attack from the east side, skirting round and using cover; another section to attack from the west, while he and the remainder charged straight into the village from the north, into the heart of the village. The attack by the section led by Lord Grenden would immediately draw most of the enemy towards them, leaving their flanks exposed to the attacks from the east and west simultaneously. The scouts from the north-west had reported no large groups of the Preydens, the nearest within a few miles, at least two hours march away. Rogden's progress was such there could be a chance of his arriving before dark, but he may yet call a halt for his tired men.

Lord Grenden gave the order for the attack to begin, his section rushing into the centre of the village, taking the enemy by surprise. He detailed groups of a dozen men entering each hut. The startled occupants, who had not been run through as they grabbed their weapons, were swiftly dealt with, joining their comrades in the long sleep. The fury and speed of the attack carried all before them, the pattern being repeated at the other ends of the village. The few that managed to break out of the huts took only a yard or two before ending on the point of a sword. The whole operation was over in half an hour, the slaughter final; no one was spared. At first the villagers were afraid to leave the huts where they had been herded by the enemy. They were warned of the approaching enemy, and strongly advised to take their possessions and what valuables they had and go to the countryside. Lord Grenden's losses amounted to fifteen men, while the piled bodies of the Preydens deliberately left at the northern approach of the village bore testimony to the success of the attack by the King's men. When more of the enemy arrived at the village, they would find a grim warning, and more importantly, this setback for the Preydens would worry and annoy Rogden when he arrived at Sabden, giving the clear message that the Westerland forces could, and would, attack at any time and at any place.

Arriving back at the castle, Lord Grenden learned that Horn had also left to attack a small group of Rogden's men. He was following a report by the scout Malvin that a small advance party was ahead of the their main force, heading northwards towards Sabden from the south-west, where they would have to pass by way of Bird Valley, the shortest route. This was the scene of the recent ambush of his Knights Richel and Sancto. Horn, with five Knights and accompanied by Dog in his role as Commander of his footmen, made rapid progress in that direction, hoping to meet this group of the enemy before they had a chance to enter the valley, with the intention of laying a similar ambush in revenge for the loss of Richel and his men. Moving in close to the valley entrance, the scouts reported that the enemy party had not yet arrived, but a strong company of Rogden's men had been left to guard the valley itself and could be seen in the distance. This now ruled out the ambush in the valley itself; another plan would have to be put into being quickly.

Half a mile from the valley lay a small tree covered ravine, aptly called Dark Cut, the direct route north by which any travellers would have to pass. The route wound round the right hand side of the ravine on approach, with the tall trees creating an umbrella, reducing the daylight. Five hundred yards before the Cut, the enemy's view would be momentarily lost as they approached a low ridge, which could take them a few minutes to surmount. As there would be a scout ahead of this party, it would be necessary to dispose of him before the enemy appeared over the ridge. Fenner was given this mission; it would be his responsibility to carry out this operation without arousing the suspicion of the following party. On the left of the ravine covered with dense undergrowth and shrubbery there was good cover, adequate enough to conceal Horn's small force from the enemy. Horn called out to Dog to join him.

"Dog, as we cannot employ our original plan to use the valley, we will take advantage of the cover at Dark Cut. It could be possible to take the party by surprise. The force will be split into two sections, of which you will take command of one, and I, the other. We will plan further when we arrive there."

"Sire, we will remove these people from our land; they can meet their Gods early, unannounced and unready."

Horn smiled, but he recognised the keenness of Dog and most of the men to face an enemy. Arriving at Deep Cut, Horn took his section to the left with Dog, with the intention of attacking the expected party from that position.

"Dog, I will remain here while you will take your section to the rear of ravine. When the enemy are already on the left path, we will break cover and attack their rear. Your men will then round the trees at the rear to meet them. It might, if the attacks were timed perfectly, result in many of the party being driven into the ravine itself."

There could be no escape once entered, as it gave only the opportunity to turn back after two hundred yards, or to plunge into a seemingly bottomless pit. Malvin, watching at the valley, could see the party half way through and joined by the men stationed there. He left at once, and not finding Horn near the scene, took the north route which passed the ravine, where he made contact with Horn.

"Sire, the party is making its way through the valley. I estimate the numbers to be about seventy; if the guards accompany them, it could total a hundred. They seem in good spirits, with much excited talking directed to a figure who appears to be in charge."

Horn realised that this party could be at the ravine in an hour. He sent off Fenner to make contact with the enemy, particularly their scout. It would be left to his unique experience as to how he would plan his moment to take him out. The surprise, and the advantage the King's men needed, rested entirely on his small shoulders, and if he failed, it could cost them dearly.

Fenner moved quickly over the ridge towards Bird Valley, using cover as he drew closer to the enemy, now emerging from the valley seemingly in good spirits. Their behaviour gave the impression of total confidence brought about by their feeling of belonging to a great army; they would be invincible, already victors about to share the spoils promised by the Commander. In reality, only Rogden, and his close confidants, the two Kings, would take the lion's share of everything. Their men would return to their villages too afraid to voice any serious complaint over broken promises; after all, they would have the chance of discovering a worthwhile trinket while stripping the dead and dying on the battlefield.

Fenner's keen eye caught sight of the scout who was well ahead of the party, noticing that at intervals he raised his arm towards them, his signal for all was well. With the scout now identified, he moved quickly back to the ridge to await his arrival where he would be dealt with, while the party was still out of sight. Finding sufficient cover at the top of the ridge, he could still see the approaching scout as he began his ascent, arriving no more than a few feet from the hidden Fenner. As he cleared the ridge, the scout looked about before giving his signal, dropping for a moment out of sight of his party. Fenner judged it correctly as he pounced. Taken by surprise, the scout had no opportunity to draw his weapon against the speed of the attack. A soft gurgle was all he would be allowed as the knife went home; he slid from Fenner's hold to the ground. He then dragged the body away to a clump of dense gorse where it would be hidden. Stripping off the man's jacket, he found it covered his small frame well before returning to the top. The party, now much closer as they neared the ridge, could see their scout had returned to give his signal that all was clear. Fenner then raced back to the ravine, sure that the party would feel nothing was wrong. He made sure that they would see him take the path on the left, before joining the force. On they came over the ridge, mostly keeping together. Fenner, ahead, gave them the signal as he disappeared down the path and out of sight. Horn could now see that the party numbered something in the region of eighty to a hundred and called quietly, "Wait until they have entered the path; there must be no noise! When I give the signal to attack, we must go as one section, while Dog and Greg attack from the rear."

Dog received the orders and awaited for the signal; he must not be too early or the enemy may turn back before the King's section could be in a position to surprise them. The approaching party seemed interested in their surroundings, in particular, the ravine. One man actually broke away to look at the entrance, passing within a few feet of the hidden men. Fortunately, he was called back to join the party, being told to keep with the main body as they kept to the path alongside the ravine. The last of the slow moving men passed the entrance until, out of the sight of the waiting Horn, men grasped their weapons in anticipation of the impending assault. The King's men emerged from their cover and quietly assembled into order, then as a body, surged past the entrance, taking the left hand path. The startled enemy turned at the sound of running feet to find they were being attacked. Hastily drawing their weapons, they had no option but to defend themselves. As the path itself was not wide, many men were forced to break away into groups off the path into the adjoining field. Fighting spread along the edges of the woodland, the advantage of surprise being with the King's men. Horn, in action, sailed into the enemy, his sword busy driving them before him, intent on reaching a figure who stood out from the others around him.

He, at the same time, became aware of this figure, slashing, hacking and cutting his way in an effort to reach him. Would this be Horn? In such a small army and so far from the castle? Why would he risk engaging an enemy when the vast army of Rogden would shortly be on its way north? His swordmanship elevated him above his men, this surely identified the King of Westerland. Within minutes they closed, the man almost spitting words through clenched teeth to Horn.

"I am Bosden, brother of Rogden; I take your crown!" Horn parried his blow, and they locked together, straining for advantage.

"So, as Horn, I will take your life!" he said pushing him away, feinted, and landed a stinging blow to the man's shoulder, which immediately opened up a deep wound. With curses steaming from his lips, Bosden charged forward, his strength aided by desperation and rage. Horn caught him again as he came on, this time a lightning cut to the chest stopped him in his advance. Spinning round, he presented an easy target to Horn's dagger hand. Bosden crashed to the ground, his curses dying with him.

A loud triumphant shout was heard above the din of battle, heralding the arrival of Dog and his men; they now blocked any chance of retreat. The Collonians realised they were in a desperate situation; they now had no option but to fight to the front and rear, towards their ultimate end. Dog, in the company of the giant Greg, took on two at a time. Slowly but surely, the numbers of the fallen enemy mounted as the minutes ticked away. The giant, sidestepping a sword thrust, caught the unfortunate man with a huge hand and hurled him against a large rock, his skull shattering with a sickening sound as his limp corpse slumped to the ground. He engaged another that came at him, spearing the man through the body; the impact lifted the man clean off his feet, wriggling like a fish newly caught. His screams were short lived as the giant stamped on his body and withdrew his spear, applying another merciful thrust to finish the man's agony. Dog was in full flow; he could see Horn ahead of him and waved his sword in salute, then set about creating havoc with wild oaths and scant regard. Luck was with him as he urged his men on to finish the job.

Suddenly, a quiet descended in the valley; the grunts and screams of the dying had ceased; the shouts of the victors tailed off as they began the task of collecting weapons from the dead. Many swords were recognised as being forged at the castle; the wounded men were attended to as they made preparations to leave to return to the castle as quickly as possible. This action would have a demoralising effect on the enemy passing through on their way to Sabden, again a warning that the Westerlanders were not going to be the walkover that had been promised; many of them would not be alive before any major battle took place. The piles of corpses of their comrades who had set out from Collona with high hopes were proof enough, and when they reached Sabden again, they would be witness to the slaughter there of the Preydens by the King's men.

The scouts reported to Horn, now on his way to the castle, that the main army led by Rogden was approaching. His army was entering the valley to march to join the main Preyden force, now nearing the village in large groups. Horn and Dog had split their force into two parties, Dog taking the south-east route, while Horn made due east straight for the castle. On arrival he waited for Dog, who reported that he had run into a small group of ten Preydens; they were easily disposed of with no loss to his men.

Horn reported his success at Dark Cut to Lord Grenden; he congratulated the Lord on his great assault on the Preydens at Sabden. Both felt they had seriously shaken the confidence of Rogden and his allies with these two actions, and the previous toll of the Preydens at the border by the hands of Lord

Sancto and his men. They assessed the tally on the enemy killed in the last few days at well over a thousand men, but the damage to Rogden's reputation was doubly important to Horn and Lord Grenden. Horn called a meeting to inform his Commanders that there were to be no further expeditions to take on groups of the enemy beyond the castle, as the main army of Rogden, and his allies would, by now, have assembled at or near Sabden. They could be awaiting orders to march on to a point from where they could consider the best way to attack the stronghold of the kingdom, and time was on their hands.

Rogden had indeed noticed with concern the massacre at the ravine as he approached it, cursing the scout who had failed to report the presence of the King's men. He had failed to give warning to the party before they entered the area over the ridge. It was, of course, the skilled Fenner who had taken him out of commission, making sure that the party suspected nothing until the attack. *I should not have sent off that advance party*, Rogden told himself. *I should have kept them in the army, safe from attack instead of suffering losses.* He soon heard the news of the Preydens slaughtered at Sabden; well, there was nothing he could have done about that. It was their own undoing due to their lack of vigilance; they paid for their over confidence. He realised that he lost nearly a thousand men, at little cost to the King's men, but the greatest blow was that his brother Bosden, who had been the Commander of the advance party, was lost; his decapitated body was shown to him. He raged and swore vengeance against the Westerlanders in his grief, swearing to kill a hundred of them for his brother; his sword would not be idle; he would spare no one, and called on the Gods to give him the strength of ten men for the battle to come.

Rogden arrived at Sabden. The report of the massacre turned out to be just that, the Preyden advance army had now materialised into a great mound of corpses. At this sight he screamed at the Preydens, demanding why they had not removed their own men; he ordered them to dig a pit away from the village. The two Kings, Aeden and Stadd, now having joined the main body of the army in the light of these two setbacks, asked Rogden for an assurance that he could, in fact, produce the promise of the expected, having committed their men to his command. To this, Rogden's reply was that there could be no doubt of our ultimate success in the campaign, and the two incidents mentioned were the result of swift attacks by the Westerlanders on two small groups when they were most vulnerable. This could not possibly happen again in view of the massive strength of the allies now acting together as a large army.

Instructions would be issued by him to Commanders to ensure whenever they rested, sentries would be posted, and that scouts worked well ahead of the army while on the march. With both armies now together, differences would have to be settled between the Commanders as to what role they would each agree to. One named Lackden, a noted Preyden Commander, demanded to be given equal rank to that of Rogden, which was made a condition by order of King Stadd. So after three hours of bickering, it was agreed upon that Lackden would have the opportunity of succeeding Rogden, should he be unable to take full command of the alliance. Rogden addressed the Kings and his commanders.

"Sires, Lords, Knights, men of this great army, this is a historic merger of two kingdoms into one army, for the purpose of defeating our common enemy, this kingdom of Westerland. It is the will of the Gods that we go forth in strength to destroy the forces of Horn and his cursed commander, Grenden. We will conquer them! We will exact justice for the years of domination and incursion into our lands, taking our treasures, the lives of our young men and women, and the destruction of our villages."

This short speech had the desired effect on the men as they raised their voices.

"Death to the Westerlanders! Death to their King! On to battle!"

The cry went up from thousands of throats together as one, all accompanied by the wild brandishing of their weapons, the demonstration reaching almost a state of frenzy.

"Rogden, we command you to take us now with our great army and lead us into battle against this kingdom, and to destroy them!"cried the two Kings.

Rogden called to his Commanders to move their men out, to take the easterly direction towards the castle, which would mean a circular route of four hours to the woodland, near Wavelon, on the north. This provided they did meet any determined opposition, which brought forth a few mutterings of dissent from the Preydens, who had already travelled this route to the village of Sabden, and now were being asked to return two thirds of the way back. Because of the Preyden Commander, Lackden's insistence, and his standing with his own Knights, he was to lead one wing of the main assault force of three thousand men to be held in reserve, while Rogden led his force of roughly five thousand in the first attack on the castle, assuming that they would not be challenged in the field.

Malvin and his scouts, observing the enemy moving out of the village of Sabden, sent the news at once to Lord Grenden. The castle was alerted and told to standby for a possible attack, either later that day or, more likely, the following morning. Estimates of between eight and nine thousand of the enemy were given by the scouts, so the odds were they would be outnumbered by more than two to one. The advantage, however, would be with the defenders at the onset of the attack, until the walls were breached, but first that had to become a reality. The defenders would make sure that the enemy paid dearly in the attempt.

Final preparations were made, and speeded up on the ramparts. Large rocks had been winched up onto the battlements, to drop on to tightly packed bodies below trying to erect their scaling ladders. Boiling pitch was now already bubbling in the large cauldrons. It was the most feared missile by an attacker, as it not only scalded its victim, but stuck to the skin and could not be wiped off. Long poles were carried up to engage the laddermen, hopefully pushing them away to crash below. The contents of the human waste pits stood ready in containers, along with anything that could be hurled or poured down to kill, injure, or at the least deter an invader trying to reach the battlements. Lord Grenden himself had taken charge of the battlements, the walls, and gate defence, and busied himself with his Commanders. All weapons were inspected. He visited the men on the walls to give encouragement, as they would be the first to receive the enemy's attack. The walls would be manned with men evenly spaced out, standing three deep, one archer, one swordsman, and one spearman, who also doubled up as polemen, to strengthen them in support. Added to these, there would be fast mobile groups to deal with any possible breach of the walls, able to reach any part in seconds. During his inspection one veteran took it upon himself to speak.

"We are ready, my Lord, to invite the enemy to meet the devil this day!" another cried out.

"My Lord, our arms are strong! Our weapons sharpened to cleave bone and flesh! My sword is hungry to take part against the enemy!"

The old campaigner Astle's only surviving son, returning to his village from the action at Sabden, bade farewell to his family, to take up his position on the walls. As the Lord approached his position with a smile of recognition, he called out, "All's well, my Lord. I am with my kin, our Gods are with us, victory will be ours, and the enemy dead will rot below our wall." With that he cut a figure of eight with his axe in anticipation of combat.

Lord Grenden was pleased with the reception he had received on the battlements; moral was high among the men, with the veterans such as young Astle among them; others would be driven by their example in battle. His Commanders had carried out his orders to the full, and with the men in good heart, he felt confident that they could hold the castle against double the enemy's army and, if necessary, withstand a long siege.

Horn received the report from Lord Grenden on the defences. "My Liege," he spoke with confidence. "The men have prepared well on the walls and gate; all are in good spirits; they will give the enemy a hard fight in any attempt to breach our walls. The gate has been strengthened to withstand the possible use of the heaviest rams, and a special group has been formed at the gate, led by Dog with the giant Greg, thirty men and a company of archers."

"Will they be strong enough to stem a charge should the gate go?" asked the King.

"As well as the ring of men, Sire. We have devised a huge rope net behind the gate, and should they crash through, they would have to attempt to cut the rope of immense thickness to gain a foothold in the courtyard. Meanwhile, the archers will wipe out those who reach the net; this will cause confusion and panic to those of the enemy still pressing forward from outside the gate. This will give us time to bring in reserves to deal with them, before it could become a major problem."

Horn thanked Lord Grenden for his efforts and organisation. "My Lord, my trust and faith in your command has always been repaid with honour and personal bravery. May the Gods look on you with great favour as my special Commander, and Knight, in this coming battle."

Lord Grenden knelt before his King. "Sire, it is my great calling and my bounden duty to carry the sword for one who is born worthy, and is a proven champion of kings and men. Once the boy Prince, who was my keen student in warfare, his destiny is to become a legend among kingdoms far and wide."

Horn decided that his role in the castle against the attack would be the control of the main courtyard, his choice of support being his own Knights of the Unicorn, plus a hundred knights and men chosen for their talent in hand to hand fighting with the axe, sword, and dagger. Also, in the event of the enemy gaining a foothold in the courtyard, then the women and children would be taken to the castle and kept on the high floors, which can be easily defended by a handful of good men. They could rely on the backing of the main force that would be marshalled at the entrance to the great hall. The possibility of a long siege was not ruled out; provisions had been laid in; the barns were full, and the water from the springs was plentiful, All cattle outside the castle had been brought in and housed in the great barn for safety. Also, this would deny the enemy the chance to take them for their own use. The castle and its defenders were now ready should the enemy decide to attack; all means of defence had received a thorough inspection; an air of purpose and determination could be felt and seen on the faces of the subjects of Westerland.

Chapter 4

The Attack

The scouts were now aware that all would depend on them to watch closely all routes to the castle area for the first signs of Rogden's army. The lookouts on the battlements now paid full attention to their part of the landscape, determined not to miss the smallest detail or indication of the arrival of the enemy. The stage was set for battle! It was expected that there might be an explorative attack in the first instance to test the defence and their weapons at close quarters, and to betray the position of the defenders, with the remainder of the enemy waiting well outside the range of the archers.

The enemy force arrived in the late afternoon at the woodland, near the forest of Wavelon, and set up camp, an hours march to the castle. Malvin sent his scouts to take up their positions half way between the enemy and the castle itself, while he remained as close as possible to observe their movements. He was surprised to see that they were dividing into two separate forces, making their camps a few hundred yards apart, a definite division, but Malvin was not aware of the friction between Rogden and the Preyden Commander, Lackden. He would not settle for less than equal command, which was eventually agreed upon as long as it did not have the effect of weakening their combined strength, which was imperative for a sustained battle and victory.

It was to be a force of fifteen hundred of Rogden's men to attack first, making straight for one section of the wall with ladders, with another thousand men five hundred yards from the castle, well out of arrow range. The remainder would be held in reserve at the woods. Lackden would take two thirds of his force to a point a few hundred yards from the opposite walls to await the signal to take part in the attack, hopefully through the gates into the courtyard, where their numbers would count against exhausted defenders. Confidence had grown between the two Kings as they watched Rogden's preparations in the woods. The construction of ladders and the eagerness of the men were all good omens; they could taste victory even now before the attack. These two Kings were not warriors and would not take to the field, preferring to watch developments from a safe distance, with their own appointed guards. The fact being, they were really puppets of their Lords, only ruling by their consent. It was a necessity to have a king, which pleased the people. He was a colourful figurehead surrounded by courtiers, a King who could be seen in splendour by his subjects, adored by the common people.

A party of Lackden's men were felling huge trees to be used as battering rams. It would take some hours to shape them and create a sharp nose. The carts that would be used had to be strengthened to take the great weight of the trunks when they made their charge at the castle gates. Strong rope hoops would be needed for the selected men to control the speed and direction of the ram, as they could not afford to miss their target while possibly under an arrow attack. Malvin stayed, watching these preparations until dusk. Fires lit by the enemy made his position impossible, so he moved back to join his scouts near the castle walls.

Morning broke to reveal a swirling ground mist, and the great war horn sounded throughout the castle, warning of an attack. Men braced themselves for the pending onslaught and the task ahead, defending, and looking to give no quarter. The positions on the battlements now fully manned; fires were stoked under the cauldrons filled with bubbling pitch, the large rocks were rolled nearer to the edges, ready to be rolled over the battlements. Archers checked their bowstrings and examined their arrows, awaiting the first targets to appear under three hundred yards, and these would be the first enemy to fall as they charged towards the walls with their ladders.

They did not have to wait long. Rogden's Commander of the first assault section gave the order to advance at a run. Leading his men, he was the first to meet a withering storm of arrows which laid low a third of them. Ladders were quickly picked up from the fallen men to continue the rush to the walls. Only two ladders were successful in being placed upright and mounted, but these, and the men clinging to them, were quickly destroyed by the huge boulders rolled off the battlements above. Broken bodies tumbled to the ground entwined in the wreckage of the ladders, the air filled with shrieks of the dying. Below, those pressed against the foot of the walls were the first to receive the baptism of scalding black pitch, blinding them. They screamed in agonizing pain, from which there would be no respite from a horrible end. Many stumbled back in an attempt to reach safety to become easy targets for the archers, only a few survivors from this first assault made the five hundred yards back.

It did not bode well for the next attack; new tactics were needed, or these losses could be expected each time they tried to reach the walls. This setback for Rogden was not entirely unexpected; he had been involved in attacking strongholds before, and keen observations had been made of the defenders response, their employment of missiles. Although the initial attackers would take the full force of weapons from above, there would come a time when, after repeated attacks, the missiles would be exhausted, or lessen as a dangerous threat, then it was men against men, and he had the superior number.

As the afternoon approached, he decided to try another attack, but this time the scaling party would be protected by shields from the archers, carried by extra men until they reached the walls and raised their ladders into position. This, in fact, worked on the open ground; few men were hit, and six ladders were put against the walls. His next ploy became apparent. A section of his archers conducted a duel at three hundred yards with those on the battlements, while others erected a barricade made of entwined willow at two hundred yards, at little cost to themselves. The shorter range gave them the chance to really challenge both archers and defenders on the wall, taking most of their volleys away from the laddermen.

This worked well; only two men were lost, and Rogden's archers were now able to loose volley after volley at the defenders on the battlements at this short range, occupying the attention of their archers while the ladders were rushed forward. One ladder in place was quickly mounted by the enemy. As they reached the top of the wall, a defender's pole made perfect contact, sending it spinning backwards, the men still clinging desperately as they crashed to the rocks below, only one man getting to his feet, blood pouring from a head injury. Another ladder successfully raised came to grief. As the first man reached the top, he took a spear thrust through his chest, causing the stricken man to fall backwards, taking the others with him to the ground. The sections of the ladder were still entwined with men, splintered into a mass of wood and broken limbs to scatter over the rocks. Only one ladder proved anything resembling a short lived success; the defenders had been struck with a volley of well aimed arrows by the enemy archers. Although the attackers managed to gain a foothold on the battlements, they were met with the determined mobile group who swiftly overcame them.

One wounded Collonian was picked up and hurled over the wall, his shrieking protest of fear abruptly cut off as he hit the ground with a sickening thud. This pattern continued until more than twenty ladders parties were proven unsuccessful. Under a sustained volley from his archers, Rogden called off the attack. He estimated he had lost something like three hundred men in the last attack, and called for a general withdrawal.

He must find a way to restore the spirits of the men who had witnessed the violent end of their comrades, who never had the chance to draw weapons. Most were sent to their deaths, either from the ladders, or the variety of deadly missiles that rained down to crush or scald them. He withdrew his men back to the small woodland area which lay fifteen hundreds away, and began to plan with Lackden a surprise raid on the south east wall. His scout had detected a weakness; it was to be carried out as soon as it was dark with a small company of men, at a point where the walls dipped, and using a large crack, which would provide footholds.

This plan had a chance to work when the sentries might be carrying out other duties; this section of the wall had not been attacked as yet. These guards would be keen to fetch food and water, reducing their numbers, and would obviously have to be relieved at some time from wall duty. They would not be expecting an attack at night, as the main assault had been on the heavily defended front walls of the castle and both sides of the gate area. The attackers had been seen to withdraw and presumably rest till the morning light. The leader chosen to lead this group was Halden, a Preyden, who was a veteran of many battles over the years, a proven assassin when needed, with catlike agility, a man to avoid in an argument, if you valued your life.

The men selected for this party moved silently from their cover, crossing the open ground to the wall, and pausing at the foot for a moment to listen. Hearing no sound or challenge, they began climbing. Edging their way upwards, their fingers and feet groping for holds offered by the crack. The first man nearing the battlements froze as he heard approaching footsteps. Waiting until they passed, he slid over the top; in the half light he could make out two sentries nearby who were leaning on their spears. It was not going to be possible to pass them or remove them without the chance of discovery. This was soon confirmed by a sudden call from the sentries to others, bringing the response he did not want to hear. Their Commander's voice was asking if they were on guard, or were they enjoying each other company? He would be with them in a couple minutes. The Preyden sliently slid back over the wall, descended to the ground, and spoke softly to Halden.

"There is too much activity on the wall; we will either have to wait, call it off, or proceed and attempt to overpower the sentries. This will prove costly, and it will alert the whole castle to our presence. Our timing seems to be wrong for this raid."

Halden agreed that it was not no longer a mission with a chance of success. He gave the order to return to Commander Lackden with their report. Lackden was not pleased; he had wanted to make an impression, a mission that would have reached the ears of Rogden. Now he would have to wait until tomorrow and lead his men to victory in what was to be the main attack on the gate. His assault parties had been picked for their strength, which would be needed to propel the battering ram and to set the cart moving at great speed. This, combined with the sheer weight of the ram, would hopefully damage the gates so severely, it would give the following men the chance to rush through in mass and engage the defenders in the courtyard, or at the least weaken it so much that the second charge with a new ram would bring success.

Morning broke again with a swirling white ground mist which gave the enemy a little cover. Peering through this mist, Rogden could see his archers taking up their position at two hundred yards; it could not be better; more men would be able to reach the walls and the gate area. He now knew the type of missiles used by the defenders.

Horn gave the order for the war horn to sound. Standing in the courtyard, he spoke to all within earshot. "We are again to be attacked by the whole army of our cursed enemy, who is determined to destroy us, but we will deny them that pleasure. They will find us, as all our enemies have found us, too strong in spirit and too strong in purpose. We will spare no one! The Gods are with us!"

A great shout greeted this speech, which must have carried to the enemy's ears hundreds of yards away.

"Commanders, to your men!" shouted Lord Grenden.

The sound of running feet echoed across the courtyard as they took up their positions, some racing to the battlements to be first in action. Horn strode to the gate area and called out to Dog, who was marshalling his men and checking weapons, "Dog, all depends on you and your men at the gate. Let this be a sorry day for our enemy; fight with strength and spare no one!"

Dog, with purpose, replied, "Sire, we are ready. Come ten thousand at this gate, they will never return to their miserable hovels. They will only fill the buzzard's stomachs or be picked over by the carrion. As we live, they shall perish!"

Lord Grenden, straining hard to see through the mist, could now see the enemy moving forward towards the walls, and noticed that they were using different tactics with some success. His archers on the walls no longer had the advantage because of the mist, but also they had to conduct a duel with the enemy archers, who had moved their barricades during the night even nearer. This meant they could easily pick off the men on the walls while they themselves had good cover, with the enemy reaching the walls in great numbers with little loss. Many ladders were being mounted against the walls, although most polemen managed to push away the attackers, cheers ringing out from the defenders every time a ladder with its cargo of wriggling men crashed to the rocks below. The boiling pitch in the cauldrons had been simmering all night, and those unlucky enough to be under it as it cascaded down rented the air with horrific screams, running blindly in terror in any direction until they collapsed or fell victim to an arrow. Some ladders were reduced to tangled heaps of wood among the crushed bodies, but those that survived were eagerly seized as more men took their place to join in the assault of the wall.

Lord Grenden's attention was drawn to beyond the gate area where he was could see a party assembled with a battering ram, and noted that they were to be protected from the archers by shield men as they trundled the cart, slowly at first, to stop within forty yards of the gate. He gave orders to the archers to try loosing their arrows at the cartmen's lower body, particularly the leg. As he did so, the cart began to move forward, and within seconds reached a surprising speed. Rogden, seeing the start on the ram's charge, gave the order for an all out attack of the walls, after noting gaps now appearing on the battlements. This was due to the sustained efforts of his archers. He urged on all his Commanders to attack, regardless of the cost, sure the day would be his. The ram hit the gates with a resounding crash, spilling men in all directions. The gate groaned but was still intact. The party turned the cart to begin the race back, but the cart itself had suffered much damage. After a few yards it had to abandoned; half of the men became targets for the archers; bruised from the impact, the survivors were lucky to reach the safety of the woods.

Lackden prepared the second cart and its crew of fresh men. The next charge would be from a greater distance, in the region of sixty yards, and again at speed. The plan being, as the cart began to outpace its pullers and pushers, for the men to throw themselves aside at twenty yards, with the object of them being able to regain their feet quickly for combat, followed by the footmen close behind. Lackden, having given the order for the second ram to begin its charge, and under the command of the Knight Yerden, left to begin the assault of the south wall with his entire force of over a thousand men. The ram started slowly and gathered speed quickly, the footmen behind finding it difficult to keep up as it gathered pace. Within yards of the gate, the men leapt clear as it crashed into the target, wood splinters flying in every direction, but the gate again held, although now seriously damaged. The men, risking the volleys of arrows aimed at them, pulled and pushed the cart back towards the sixty yard point with the aid of the footmen. Once again the archers took their toll on the heaving and sweating men, now without the protection of the shieldmen; some broke away to run and were cursed by their comrades.

The attack by Lackden was not going well. He had already suffered heavy losses. Only one ladder group actually gained access to the battlements, but were quickly dealt with. Those killed or wounded were thrown over the wall by the defenders to land on their comrades below. His group under Halden would have to wait for a better moment, probably when the gate was destroyed, and his other part of the force had gained entry. The defenders on the south wall would have to rally to defend the courtyard, giving him the opportunity to take the south wall.

The next ram party was made up to full strength, and in command was the Knight Yerden, as once again they trundled the cart with its weighty cargo to within forty yards, but this time with a hundred men at arms. This time, success was vital! But with so many men running along side the car, it would attract a storm of arrows. Yerden screamed out the order; the ram moved quickly into a fast trot, picking up speed within a few seconds. Soon it was flying as never before, the men determined that this was the final charge at the gate; their new found strength served them well. With a horrendous crash, the ram struck the already weakened gate, one half flying open and left hanging awkwardly, while the other shattered into many pieces. The exhausted men jumped clear at ten yards to allow the men at arms access for their rush to the courtyard.

Dog had anticipated that this next charge would possibly break through the gate, but what the enemy did not know was that a strong rope net had been erected behind the gate entrance. As the enemy rushed through the shattered gate, they were met with a volley of arrows, followed by the thrusting spears through the massive net. The enemy fell in numbers as they tried to slash their way through the net, their bodies piling in heaps, and yet they came on, clambering over their comrades to meet a similar fate. Dog shouted to encourage to his men. He could see the giant Greg prodding away with his spear. One man he impaled was lifted off his feet, as if the giant was using a toasting fork, tossing its cargo on the heap of dead and dying men. Their screams, turning to moans, were soon lost by the dead weight of their comrades. Those still pressing behind, seeing the carnage taking place before their eyes, turned and ran back to main force, dodging the arrows, convinced it was easier to attack the walls than walk into the fury of the defenders with the giant net.

Rogden, informed of the failure at the gate, screamed at his Commanders to stop the running men, and ordered an all out attack on the walls, in spite of their losses. All would be lost if this all out assault were to fail in the next few hours. Ladder after ladder, attempts were pressed forward, and those that were sent crashing to the ground and were still in reasonable condition were used again and again. They untangled the crushed and broken men from the ladders to race to the walls for another attempt. As missiles became fewer from above, some made the battlements, engaging in furious hand combat, causing the defenders to race to meet this growing crisis.

With the fighting beginning to spread along the wall, Lord Grenden was forced to send up reinforcements from the main courtyard to help, while he directed the archers in the courtyard to seek out enemy targets on the battlements should they attempt to make their way down the platforms to the ground. Lackden's assault on the south-east walls was not so successful, only four ladders made it with their cargo to the battlements, and less than forty men gained a footing, and these were sorely pressed by the defenders. To make it worse, he still could not send up Halden's men, as the wall was now fully alerted, with more fresh men eagerly arriving to take on the attackers; things were not going well for him. He shouted at those men still attempting to erect their ladders to keep going, tempting them with promises of great rewards beyond their imagination after victory, but the response was not wholehearted as the defenders threw down the bodies of their comrades at their feet.

Yalden, who had now withdrawn his men from the gate as the charge still seemed doomed to failure yet again, was hit with an arrow, and was lucky to dodge another volley that rained down on him and his men. He had taken the arrow under the left shoulder, which denied him the use of the arm, and he cursed his luck. His place was taken by Redel; it would now be his task to take on the next assault on the gate, and with the knowledge of the rope net awaiting them, they planned on how to beat and destroy it, to take on the defenders on better terms.

Rogden had expected to be in the castle by now, but he could see that his men were not in anything like a commanding position. If he called them off now, he would have to begin again tomorrow. Again, he would have to face losing hundreds of laddermen to reach the walls, and the defenders would have had time to replenish their stock of missiles overnight. With his men still on the walls, Rogden urged his Commanders to use further reserves of men to strengthen their small inroads on the battlements and force the defenders to retreat.

Redel's plan for the next attack on the gate with the ram consisted of using a lighter cart that could burst through the wreckage of the gate by sheer speed and hopefully take the net with it, or a part of it with the impact. Fuel was to be added in the way of pitch and brushwood which would be ignited as it neared the gate. A volunteer would stay to the last few seconds to create an instant inferno, destroying the net in the process; he felt it could work. He urged on his men as they cut the tinder dry thin wood that would burn quickly, and volunteers had been sent under cover from the archers to scoop up the pitch lying at the base of the walls. This was completed successfully. Enough was brought back to be heated up and poured over the whole cart, adding to the fuel. Soon the ram was ready to be wheeled to a position about sixty yards from the gate, and in direct line. There would be protection for the racing crew for most of the way by those with shields, relying totally on speed and fresh men to guide it. It should not present a problem as the men jumped clear, to allow Redel and his men at arms to charge through the burning net, but they were aware they would have to face the footmen and the archers in the courtyard.

On the battlements, the fighting was spreading over a wider area, the enemy now in groups, with fewer one to one engagements. This was making it difficult for the archers to select their targets, for fear of hitting their own. Some of the enemy, who had managed to overcome their immediate opponents on the walls and ambitiously jumped down into the courtyard, were quickly disposed of by the footmen. Many of these defenders had not been sent to the battlements owing to the lack of width there. Due to their chances of using their weapons with effect, only a few could be sent at a time when needed, or when defenders were seen to fall. A full scale battle would soon be developing if the enemy could not be contained on the walls. Horn learned that an attack of the south-east walls had, after a hard fight, allowed the enemy to gain a foothold. The defenders were hard pressed to hold them; some action was urgently needed to force a major counter attack, which would switch the advantage gained by Lackden's men to that of the defenders.

As the enemy Commander roared at his men to press harder, sensing he was nearing a victory, he could see the ram party racing toward the gate. He heard the crash as it bounced off the splintered wood and buckled iron, careering into the net. The glow of the ignited fuel became a roaring inferno in seconds. The cart entangled in the net was exactly what Redel had hoped for; he saw the net literally explode into a mass of fire and begin to collapse from its hooks, amid dense smoke which forced the defenders back. For a moment it halted the attackers; the intense heat generated affected all in the gate area; they could do nothing but wait.

Dog had been taken completely by surprise by this latest charge with the ram, and he knew that as soon as the smoke began to clear, the enemy troops would pour through the gate. He now marshalled his men into a wide circle to await the inevitable assault. Soon the smoke cleared. The net had been reduced to a smouldering pile of glowing ash; the way was now clear for a serious attempt by the enemy to enter the courtyard proper. Dog called for the archers to deal with the first charge, and instructed the spearmen to kneel in front to engage those that survived the first volley of arrows. The footmen at the rear with the giant Greg, would take on any of the enemy who found a gap and gained the yard. Horn's main force in the courtyard was also on alert to strengthen the men at the gate, should there be a serious incursion into the main courtyard by the enemy. Horn wanted to keep his men fresh, as he had other plans should the gate area be held successfully by Dog; the next few minutes would tell him what plan to put into action.

Redel watched closely the result of the burning cart, as he needed to judge his attack without being obstructed by the ram. It was still intact, although now buried into the net engulfed in flames, and fortunately had not skewed across their path. The cart, blazing fiercely, had turned on its side, which gave a clear passage for his men to charge through once the dense smoke had cleared; the acrid fumes had forced his men back to the area outside the gate. Redel gave the order, and his men charged through the gate still wreathed in smoke. Leading the men, he peeled off and took up a position on the right hand side of gate, from where he could command and assess the result of their attack. He pressed his body hard against the wall to escape the archers and defenders above. The first men through fell victim to the eager defenders as they went down one after the other, but the second wave was more successful, as a few actually reached the lines of spearmen and engaged in combat, most suffering a painful death.

The giant Greg, waiting impatiently with his spearmen, could now smell the enemy. Taking on two at a time, he speared one through the chest and felled another with a powerful blow, with the shaft shattering his skull. He then turned his attention to another who foolishly ran at him, only to be brought to a sudden halt as the giant's spear penetrated his lower body, his dying gasp heard above the shouts and din of battle. Many of the enemy did their best not to confront this huge man and tried to skirt round him, taking on other opponents. Greg, in spite of his great size, was extraordinarily quick on his feet, and coupled with his amazing stride and reach, he could engage the enemy within paces of his immense frame. As the successive waves of Redel's men began to show a pattern of most reaching the lines of the defending spearmen, he turned and called for the reserve of Lackden's force to move in for a general attack. At that moment he took an arrow in his shoulder which rendered his sword arm useless. Although in pain from the wound, he broke off the shaft, and with his good arm, waved his men on through the gate, where the fighting was now spreading out into the main courtyard. This had the effect of stifling the archers who shouldered their bows and resorted to the sword.

Horn still expected Dog to contain the fighting in the immediate gate area of the courtyard and its confines, and he had received from Lord Grenden a report from the battlements, which assured him that they were holding their own, in spite of the number of men Rogden was committing to this major assault. Lord Grenden himself had mounted the walls and was taking a terrible toll of the enemy, the defenders being mightily encouraged to see their Lord in action. His athletic movements were tigerish; he moved like quicksilver, and the lightning speed of his sword arm was difficult to follow. Men fell before him or melted away rather than face such a warrior who fought like ten men and seemed indestructible against overwhelming odds.

Rogden, in the meantime, was still urging his men on to the walls. He could see that although they were gaining footholds and parts of the battlements, his losses were beginning to tell. The bodies of those slain in attempting to reach the walls, and met their end from the boiling pitch and crushing rocks, were lying in grotesque heaps, their faces contorted with the horror of their agonising deaths. This was beginning to have a demoralising effect on the fresh men arriving; some taking in the grisly scene lost heart and ran. To have to climb over your own dead before possibly meeting the same fate is not for the faint hearted, and every army had its share of those who would take part in the spoils, but would also save their own skins at the expense of their comrades, to risk the punishment of death for desertion or cowardice.

At the south-east wall Lackden having committed his reserves to Redel at the gate, and now assuming that all was going well, with fighting now taking place in the courtyard, gave Halden and his men the order to mount the weakened part of the wall. He timed it right; no one spotted their group's entry over the wall and make their way down to the yard, the defenders there having rushed to contain an assault twenty yards away. Once in the yard they looked for where they could do the most damage quickly and make their escape, if unable to join Redel's men in the courtyard, bearing in mind that they were heavily outnumbered by the men at arms in the courtyard.

The inevitable happened as Horn had sent a strong detachment to strengthen the guard at the hall and the keep, as the fighting had spread in the yard. They arrived at the precise moment as Halden's men left the cover of the wall to be spotted immediately. As the King's men rushed to take them on, half of them escaped and scrambled back up the wall, but Halden caught out and it proved difficult to overcome. Fighting ferociously, he perished with the trapped men fighting for their lives, his assault ending in failure. Lackden, told of the loss of Halden, reported it to Rogden on his main attack on the remainder of the wall, which was not good news to the Commander. He had to face the fact that the courtyard, although engaged in hard fighting, was still holding out against Redel's men, making no further progress, and would eventually be lost there. He had to make a decision!

He again considered a withdrawal. Three thousand men had been lost since the beginning of the assault on the castle; he could not afford to maintain a continuous attack on the walls, when he may yet lose many more; he would have to regroup his forces for the next day. A messenger was sent to Lackden to inform him there was to be a general withdrawal to the woods as soon as he received this message. With the light fading, that would mean a modicum of cover from the archers, also there would be no pursuit by the defenders, who would still be engaging those left behind. Lackden, having lost many of his best men, felt a sense of relief at the order from Rogden. Breaking away, he was forced to leave those still fighting on the walls. They would be in a short time without support and overcome by the defenders.

And so it was, some tried to break off the fighting, but the only escape for some, with the ladders already shattered, was to jump, and possibly meet their end on the rocks. Redel also received the order and shouted to his men within earshot to retreat at once, except those fighting for their lives. Many made it to the gate and into open ground, only to face volleys of arrows from the archers as they emerged from the gate. They raced away and out of range.

A strange end to the day, the defenders were mopping up the few still showing fight. With no sign of reinforcements from Rogden at the walls or gate, Horn now could see that the enemy's main attack had been called off. The defenders on the walls and those in the courtyard became aware of the retreat and were spurred on to greater effort to finish the remainder of the attackers. Finally, a quietness descended on the castle; the din of battle and the screams of the wounded and dying were now replaced with an occasional moan or a last despairing cough. Men stood wearily, slightly dazed and certainly exhausted, some slumped against the walls, and some lay on their backs breathing hard; it had gone well for them. They had counted the enemy dead as over four hundred in the courtyard when suddenly, and led by the giant Greg at the realisation of the day's victory, the defenders gave a great cheer, which rang throughout the castle and must have been heard by the enemy licking its wounds in the woods.

The two Kings, alarmed and worried at the turn of events, cursed Rogden for his failure to take the castle when things seemed to be going their way, and particularly when they had been receiving good reports. They had been highly optimistic of riding into the castle as conquerors by nightfall, now that was not to be.

Rogden and Lackden met to discuss a new plan of attack on the castle in the morning. Their losses had been substantial, but they still had a slight advantage in numbers. He considered the King's men had taken losses during the day and most of Rogden's latest recruits had been blooded, although the wounded who had made it back to the woods could not be counted. In all, their army could be assessed at six thousand. Another failure, however, and their own lives would be in jeopardy from the angry Kings, who were beginning to see their dreams of vast treasures fast disappearing along with their agreed division of the kingdom of Westerland. Their plan for tomorrow must be one that ensured success. The two leaders talked long into the night at means and ways of entering the castle, rejecting one idea after another as impractical or unworkable. Leaving once again the only alternative of repeating the assault on the walls and gate, using the entire army as one force. The gate could cost them three or four hundred men, but they stood a chance to come to terms in the main courtyard, where Rogden was convinced would be the final battle, and the castle as the prize falling into his eager hands.

For some, the thought of once again attacking the castle proved too much to endure again; they were determined to slip away during the night, when the sentries would be at their lowest ebb of concentration. The Commanders had told them of the treasures that awaited the victors just for the taking, if their will and their sword arm were strong enough. Although the stories of vast wealth had been much exaggerated, these men knew in their hearts that you have to live to collect, and that was rapidly becoming a dream.

Horn was pleased with the victory of the day; he knew that the enemy would now be licking their wounds and planning yet another attack, most likely at dawn, and possibly with the same tactics, plus a few minor additions. More importantly, Horn had not felt it necessary to commit his own picked force during the day due to Dog and his men at the gate area containing the charges made by the enemy's battering rams, and the incursion by their men of foot through the smouldering net. He also worked out with Lord Grenden that the enemy had lost more than a third of the original strength, while his men on the walls who fell numbered one hundred and fifty. The losses at the gate had been light, twenty killed with some fifty wounded, of which a few could still use a weapon if needed. On the face of it, the enemy could not be counted as being three to one, or even two to one; it could be they were at last on equal terms. The bodies of the enemy killed at the gate were taken outside and thrown onto the piles of dead lying at the foot of the walls and the near surrounds. A few still on the battlements were thrown over to land on those below, resulting in a dense black cloud of angry blow-flies noisily rising in mass, annoyed at being rudely interrupted during their attention to what was rightfully theirs.

The boys were sent out to collect sound arrows after making sure that the enemy archers were no longer at their barricade. Weapons in good condition were collected, some having to be pried from dead fingers. The boys moved quickly among the corpses, their keen eyes spotting anything of value which would then be arrayed in the courtyard for the Commanders to inspect. Men were sent out in small parties to recover the large rocks thrown from the battlements; they were rolled or lifted with effort onto carts, ready to be hoisted back up on the walls. Fires were relit under the cauldrons to prepare boiling yet more pitch, still one of the most successful deterrents for the attackers below trying to mount their ladders; all this was completed within three hours under cover of darkness. Vigilance was now the order to all, and the sentries were visited personally by a Commander at regular intervals to remind them of a possible night attack by small raiding parties.

A meeting was called by Horn, Lord Grenden, Lord Sancto, Dog, the Knights of the Unicorn and all Commanders. They met to discuss plans that would be put into operation based on the experience of Rogden's assault methods. The hurling of huge rocks and the pouring of boiling pitch from the battlements could be more devastating if they were to be fully coordinated, which would require more operators. There would have to be a more rapid response to fill the gaps on the walls caused by the loss of men. To that end, extra men at arms, who could respond in seconds, would be stood ready in support of the archers, polemen, and spearmen.

Dog set his men on making temporary repairs to the gate, mainly on one side, which was still hanging on its damaged hinges, and erecting barriers some thirty feet back. He had hoisted another net into place, which had taken the women many hours to make, since the original had been set alight. It had proved the downfall of Yerden, the first attacker with the ram, then Redel, in their attempts to smash through into the yard, in spite of their cleverly worked out plan of firing the cart and setting the net alight. All was now set for the first signs of movement from the enemy camps towards the castle, expected at dawn.

Fires could be seen and scouts Malvin and Fenner reported the comings and goings of men between camps, and the positions of their sentries along the perimeter of the woods area. It would seem that Rogden's camp was guarded well, while Lackden's seemed to be thinly placed and were not really in close touch with each other; his shelter was patrolled at intervals by only two men.

Malvin sent back this information to Lord Grenden, who responded by waking Horn.

"Sire, the Preyden commander is encamped on the fringe of the woods and is not heavily guarded; the scouts have asked if they should take him and bring him to the castle before dawn."

Horn, amused about the possibility, replied, "My Lord, the loss of Lackden would cause Rogden and his allies a great problem. Let them take him if they can, without causing a general alarm; I want no loss of our scouts to ensue from it."

Word was passed to Malvin, who sent Boarset and Latten to deal with the two sentries. Working their way silently to the edge of the woods, within earshot of the camp, they came upon two men engaged in conversation. Waiting until they split up to continue their patrol, and as one paused to relieve himself by a tree, Boarset took him from behind. The pressure on the man's throat stifled any cry as his knife struck deep into his neck. With barely a sigh, he sank to his knees, his lifeblood leaving him in uncontrolled frenzy. Latten had it slightly easier; he crept behind his man, who died with a surprised gasp as the knife thrust through the shoulder, penetrating the heart in one swift movement, never to know who sent him from this world.

Having quietly disposed of the bodies of the two main sentries, the scouts made their way nearer to the camp, dropping on their stomachs as they worked forward in the direction of the tent shelter which housed Lackden. He could be seen lying on a bed of bracken and leaves, his head turned towards them. Both approached the sleeping Commander, with Latten at one side, clamping his hand firmly over the mouth, while Boarset dealt him a sharp blow to the head. Only a feeble twitch of an arm betrayed he had experienced any shock; he lay perfectly still. Gagged and bound, they carried the inert Commander safely out of the woods and using cover, made quick progress to be joined by Malvin. Two scouts were left to watch for any reaction from Lackden's camp; the silence signalled all to be well. The scouts with their captive entered the gate. Lackden, slowly coming round, desperately tried to gain his senses, found he was securely bound and powerless against these determined men. Horn received them in the grand hall, commending their successful mission. He turned to the Preyden commander who now had his gag removed. "My Lord Lackden, seems as though you will not be in command of your force in today's battle after all. We will, of course, detain you in the castle until we decide your fate, but if the Gods are not with us and this day goes badly, you, my Lord, will be put to death."

Lackden replied only with a scowl, and Horn ordered him to be taken to the dungeon and guarded well. The scouts, their special mission completed, returned to their lookout positions in the field, feeling pleased with themselves, and while one catnapped, the others watched for the tell tale signs of the enemy to begin assembling their men on the perimeter of the woods. At first light the enemy could now be seen moving between camps, collecting food and weapons, and gathering into groups into some form of regular order by their Commanders; their shouts could be clearly heard by the scouts.

The early morning was greeted yet again with soft swirling white mist which would later turn to brilliant sunshine, after losing its battle with the penetrating June sun. At the castle the squeaky challenge of a bantam cock woke those of the garrison from their few hours of restless sleep. On the battlements, the sentries could only see the enemy emerging from the woods in a few fleeting moments through the heavy mist rising from the ground. The return of the scouts confirmed that Rogden's army was assembling in force, and that an attack would be launched against the castle within an hour or two. Malvin and his scouts then attached themselves to Dog's command at the gate area behind the ranks of the spearmen, their role for the moment finished; they now would become part of the castle defence.

The disappearance of the Preyden commander had now been discovered with great alarm; search parties in the immediate area had proved that he was no longer within the main part of the woods. Discovering two dead sentries confirmed their worst fears that he had been taken in the night by stealth, and more likely, if still alive, would be a prisoner in the castle. This was, as Horn expected, a major setback to Rogden. His fury on being told was all but uncontrollable. Had the two sentries been more alert, they could have prevented this abduction, instead of losing their lives. Now he had to appoint a new commander. He was tempted to give the command to one of his own men, but on reflection decided it would be in the interest of harmony and cooperation to appoint a Preyden to succeed a Preyden. The chosen man was Hagan, who had caught his eye earlier. He gave him Lackden's command, and to the other Commanders, he gave new orders for the coming assault on the castle. He told them, raising his voice, "The gate has probably been hastily repaired overnight, but should present no problem to the new battering ram. We will deal with other obstacles such as the likelihood of another net confronting them. This means we will double the men." He then added, "All this will not be possible without success on the walls; fully engage those on the battlements and take the attention of those in the courtyard."

Raising his voice again to all to hear and understand, he said, "This time you will attack the walls at two points with every fit man available. We shall put into practice a new method with the ladders, which will defeat the efforts of the polemen to push them away, and will ensure more men reaching the top." He continued, "A rope will be well tied to the top of the ladder. This will be carried by the second man on the ladder, so while the first man is engaging the defenders, he will throw the rope over the wall to act as an anchor. Before the rope can be gathered or cut or the ladder pushed away, five or six men should gain the battlements. All this will require determination by you, the Commanders, to instill courage and spirit in your men."

Redel, in spite of his wound, was again appointed as leader of the ram party to assault the gate. They would use two newly cut trees, with the last two unused carts being strengthened. The surviving men from the previous attempt were joined by fresh men picked for their strength. This assault was to be backed with three hundred men at arms. No order to charge would be given until the laddermen could be seen to be gaining a foothold on the battlements.

The general order to begin the attack was given by Rogden; his archers had already taken up their positions behind the barricades under the cover of the ground mist. These would be moved slowly closer as the laddermen advanced to the wall. The duel with the archers on the battlements would continue, with the opportunity to pick off defenders who were forced to expose themselves while attempting to push away the ladders.

The war horn sounded its warning throughout the castle, propelling those not yet in their positions into action on the walls or their allotted defence point.

All was ready to receive the enemy from wherever those chose to attack, and the south-east wall had been strengthened and was now well manned. The archers loosed their volleys at their counterparts behind their barricades, and they in turn sent their volleys against the defenders with some success. Rogden's army had formed up in four lines at five hundred yards, plus twenty ladder groups of two hundred men supported with reserves; this was to be the spearhead of the attack.

Hagan, like Lackden, was to assault the south-east walls using the same ladder plan, although he was unaware of the heavy strengthening of that section overnight. Lord Grenden, watching from the walls, wondered why Rogden had arrayed his men in four lines; although the mist still hung over the higher ground, it now exposed him. Should he advance in mass formation, the method of battle normally adopted in the open field, and attack a castle, he would take his men into the range of the archers and spearmen. The mist also hid the cart with the ram, and Redel was careful not to give away his position until he began his charge to the gate.

The mist made it difficult for the defenders to make an accurate estimate of the enemy's total strength, nor could the laddermen be seen except in the middle of the front line. A count at this stage could not be accurate, which meant that the enemy would be attacking the walls before that was possible, and the scouts were now part of the gate defence. Sending them out would be too much of a risk, with the enemy so close. However, the defences were in good order; more men had been allocated to back up the missile crews and extra cauldrons had been prepared with boiling water to pour down of the heads and shoulders of the enemy. Although not so horrendous as pitch, which stuck to the skin, inflicting greater pain, it was enough for the victim to forget his assault on the wall.

Horn, in the courtyard, had given orders to his Knights to employ the same stand-off position during the early assault as before, unless the gate defence under the command of Dog should be overrun. The object of this being: should the enemy's attack on the gate fail yet again, and the assault on the walls begin to weaken, with Rogden having to order his men to withdraw, then Horn would order the army of some two thousand men to attack Rogden as he tried to reach the woods. He had no doubt that if Rogden were to fail again, he might well abandon everything and run for the border, escaping the wrath of the two Kings, who would have to run themselves, their plan of conquest in tatters.

Lord Grenden had assumed after the losses the enemy had suffered in the attack the previous day that their numbers would probably be more of a match, heavy losses this time by Rogden would give the King's army an advantage. This would allow them to implement Horn's plan to lead his men from the castle into open ground, where their training would prove to be decisive in field combat. Horn would love to hear the clash of men in the field, and where he would be able to see his enemy. He wanted to attack the weaker lines, charge in mass with his knights amid the din and clatter and the shouts of men and protesting horses, and to end with ultimate victory. He looked across the courtyard to Dog; his men were ready and waiting to counter any attack on the gate, not sure whether there would be another charge by the ram, or a concentrated rush by men at arms to try to enter the courtyard in sheer numbers, regardless of losses. Dog appeared confident and at ease, engaging in talk with the giant Greg, who towered above the others, his massive shoulders shaking with laughter at something Dog had said. *They will acquit themselves well*, thought Horn. *These two warriors would give the men under their command great courage, and bring out that extra strength needed to take on anything sent against them.*

The defenders on the walls were the first to see the enemy's controlled advance, line behind line; the reason soon became obvious when the enemy archers behind their screens loosed volley after volley at the defenders as the lines of men moved forward. An unexpected ploy among the lines of laddermen was that they gave each line their own group of archers. They, in turn, loosed their arrows at the defenders on the walls. The men on the walls were now subjected to twice the amount of fire power, as more laddermen gained the foot of the castle walls. At least twenty ladders were mounted against the two sections of the walls, the first two failing as the polemen pushed them away before the weighted rope could be thrown over the parapet. Their good positioning with the protective shields had allowed more men from the lines to reach the walls, and at one stage men were beginning to queue to mount the ladders, in spite of the missiles raining down on their heads and the victims groaning in agony on the ground. The enemy appeared to be getting more men onto the battlements, fighting again spread along most of the wall. Reports from Hagan suggested that his attack on the other walls was having limited success; one section had been overrun by his men, and this allowed over a hundred to gain access to the battlements, engaging the defenders there.

Redel, sensing the time was right for his entry into the battle and determined the pain of his arrow wound was not going to slow him down, gave the order for the charge of the ram, which again had been primed with fuel. He also detailed two men to attack the net, one on each side as the cart hit the centre. Again the cart gathered speed, and at a hundred yards set its path for the gates. As it hit, the repaired gates splintered with wood flying in all directions as it crashed into the centre of the net, creating a great bulge, which as it burst into flames, also tore the net from the retaining hooks on which the great weight had been hung. The cart and net soon became a raging inferno; the whole area again filled with a choking black smoke. The ram men who had thrown themselves on the ground before the impact were trampled by the rush of the men at arms, who had covered their faces with cloth and surged forward

The first of the enemy to emerge through the smoke were hit by the archers or by the spearmen, but with many more pressing forward, it soon became the scene of bitter fighting. Dog and Greg could be seen taking on and disposing men at will. Dog swung his axe with sickening results, and Greg's clothing and spear were drenched in the blood of his victims who unwisely stood against him. This caused a large part of the attacking force to give ground. Gradually, they were forced back, some actually left the fray and escaped through the gate to the field, pushing past other men trying still to enter the gate to join in the battle. Redel, seeing this turn of events, shouted and cursed at the men in an attempt to convince them they had only to get to the courtyard to be sure of victory, but he began to realise more men were coming out than he could now see going in. The defence was proving too strong and too good for his men, and once again his assault was going to fail. His losses were obvious, and it was only a matter of time before even a retreat would be impossible; also, he had seen through the smoke to the impressive massed ranks of the King's men waiting calmly and unmoved in the main courtyard. Unless Rogden's men could take control of the battlements now and enter the courtyard, the whole attack would never have a chance of succeeding, let alone face this large force of fresh men. Redel, deciding that it was all over for him and his men, gave orders to those that could hear him to make for the gate and the open fields. He turned to join the fleeing men and took an arrow between his shoulders, bringing him down just yards from the gate.

Those still fighting lasted only minutes with no support; Redel had lost two hundred men as well as his own life. A few reached the gate, and most of those never reached safety, the archers picking them off with ease. One of the messengers brought the news to Rogden of the collapse of the attack at the gate and the death of Redel; he cursed he had not given him more men. They still had men in reserve, these being called forward under the command of Ansel to lead the last force of nearly a thousand men to storm the gate, which would still be vulnerable to attack. They both knew that it would be critical if this last attack were to fail; although having success on the walls, it was the taking of the courtyard which would give them victory. To realise this, the men fighting on the walls would have to overcome the defenders and link up with this reserve force coming through the gate. These men were fresh and had not yet been in action, and other small parties from the woods were ordered to join them, swelling the numbers to about fifteen hundred. The plan being to attack the gate in force and overcome the defenders, and a new net would not have been erected. They also decided the defenders would not be expecting another attack on the gate after so many failures and the heavy losses of men.

Lord Grenden's attention from the battlements was diverted to the scouts at the gate who had witnessed the flight of Redel's men from the last attempt. They now reported the latest movement of the enemy, with their obvious intention of attacking the gate area in force using fresh men; their strength could be in the region of nearly two thousand. On hearing this Horn decided that it was now time to act, as he had not expected Rogden's men to descend to the courtyard in sufficient strength to cause a problem. He called Dog to join him with his gate defenders as the warning came that this new force was moving towards them and heading in the direction of the gate area.

Horn gave the order to his army Commanders to move out in force and array their men in the field, confronting the enemy before they could begin their intended charge to the gate. The King's archers were able to pick out their targets as the enemy moved forward into range, and men could be seen to fall. Horn gave the order to advance, and the front rank bristled with spearmen. Soon they were locked in deadly thrust and death dealing blows, with the giant Greg towering above his men and adding to his awesome tally on his advancing and luckless opponents. The clash of steel against steel, mostly through bone, evoked cries of pain as the men at arms came to grips amid the screams of the men who had fallen and now were being trampled underfoot by sweating and struggling combatants, their eyes turned upwards in terror.

Horn, in the midst of the enemy, carved a space round himself wherever he wielded his sword, the explosive energy, The angle of the delivered blow, coupled with the speed of the thrust, drove his men to greater strength and determination. Dog, in full flow, was causing havoc on Horn's right flank, the glint of his axe appeared like a brilliant flash as he swung his favourite weapon. It was soon to be dulled with the blood and human debris as it rose and fell among his victims with devastating results. Greg's spear finally broke into two pieces with the sheer strength of his mighty thrusts. Quickly, he took to using his sword, cutting huge swathes in the enemy ranks with telling blows; one would wonder how on Earth was this man captured in the first place by King Alymer and put into service.

Rogden was aware of the complete reversal of his plans. This last line to attack the gate was showing signs that did not smell of victory for his Commander Ansel. He withdrew men from the assault on the walls to go to the battle taking place in the gate area. Rogden sent a message to Hagan at the south-east wall to release half of his men to join the attackers, who were now seemingly hard pressed and giving ground to the King's men. As noon approached the will of Ansel's men began to falter; it could be seen that some of those at the rear were, in fact, deserting, making for the woods. When the men from the walls arrived they could see the rapidly deteriorating situation, and many joined the flight to the woods and possible safety. It became more difficult for Horn and his men to stand and engage the enemy as their numbers dwindled with alarming speed, and it resorted to pursuit and slaughter.

At the castle walls Rogden watched in disbelief and horror as he saw his reserve force in full flight. For a moment he panicked, then took in the situation on the battlements; he had men on there, and they were fighting well in spite of losses. The defenders were holding them, and the thought of victory began to diminish with this latest setback. Rogden regretted sending some of the wall assault men to join the battle at the gate. He could not expect to take the courtyard now with the King's army in strength outside the gate, and the attack on the south-east walls had proved no better; he had to act quickly before the King's men returned. Rogden had no more cards to play; he must have lost more than two thirds of his combined force and could no longer achieve his object. Giving a last order to the men to look to themselves as best they could, he made his departure northwards with a handful of picked men. Hagan, hearing of the rout of the reserve force, gave orders to break away from the fighting and take to their heels, as to stay longer was to seal their fate.

The defeat of the reserve force and the crumbling spirit of the men, coupled with the deserters returning to the woods in greater numbers, confirmed the two Kings worst fears. Both cursed that they had been influenced by Rogden to take the kingdom. Their thoughts were now on escape to the safety of their own borders. Many of the fleeing enemy were beginning to split into small groups, skirting the woods with the intention of reaching their own lands; it was now becoming a hide and seek problem over a wide area. This was not to Horn's liking, and he ordered the major part of his army back to the castle. At the same time, a small party was assembled to set out on horseback and hunt down the kings and their defeated Commander, Rogden.

Horn had received the news from Lord Grenden that the fighting on the walls of the castle was all but over, with those of the enemy that had remained now being disposed of; the losses to his defenders were less than three hundred on the battlements and gate, although there had been as many wounded.

The fleeing enemy Commander could not have had more than twenty minutes start on the pursuers, and even on horseback, it would take two hours of hard riding to reach the only place where he might escape. It would have to be the open sea; no border would now be his haven, and if the Kings made good of their escape to their kingdoms, there would be a price on his head. Horn assumed that he would have taken some picked men to flee with him, this meant that they should they catch up with him; it would not be a hard fight, but he was wily enough to leave them to fight while he continued his flight.

Dog was sent off with twenty men towards the coastline known as the Black Bay, which would take him about two hours, with orders not to tangle with any stragglers seen on the way. They would be mopped up later, but to take on only Rogden and his bodyguard in a fight. Horn struck out farther to the west towards the village of Geltham with the same compliment of men, which included his six Knights and the giant Greg, although problems finding him a strong enough horse cost them precious minutes. After hard riding to arrive at the village, Horn was told that a party of men had ridden fast through the village, and one was identified by a villager, who had seen him when he and his men raided the village for food and loot. This spurred Horn on to ride even harder, and soon they could make out a group of riders making for the coast. On seeing Horn's men, they split into pairs, taking slightly different routes. At that distance, it was difficult to see which pair involved Rogden. Horn divided his men into groups of five, and the chase was on. Horn took the trail of the pair that had ridden straight ahead; after all, it could be Rogden taking the shorter route to the coast. With his men, which included three of his Knights, Horn closed the gap, but not before they reached the coast itself.

A boat would have to be found by Rogden that was seaworthy and that cost him time. He checked at least two boats: one without oars, the other waterlogged. The search for others in the inlets was not possible as Horn and his men could be heard thundering towards them; there was no option now but to fight. It was the Knight Rogden! He and his companions were prepared to fight for their lives. He recognised Horn and charged towards him; it was three against two.

Horn shouted, "Rogden's mine! Stand back; attend the other!"

The knights made for the other, whose name was Ligard. Horn, sword and dagger drawn, faced his enemy. A tall figure and powerfully built, Rogden felt confident he could take this young man. King or not, he was the son of the man who had banished him from the kingdom. They met as Rogden lunged toward him. Horn easily parried the blow, and with a lightning downward stroke laid open his enemy's left arm to the bone. He gave a cry of astonished pain coupled with a string of curses. For a few seconds he drove Horn back with a ferocious attack with the power of his good arm. Losing a lot of blood, he began to weaken. They thrust and parried time and time again until Horn struck the Knight under the right arm as he raised his sword. It penetrated deep into his chest, bringing him to his knees. He rolled forward as Horn withdrew his sword, and with a final defiant curse, died in the dust, his blood flowing in a thin stream which momentarily interrupted a column of marching ants.

Horn looked down at body of his enemy then across to the other Knights to find that they had been watching his duel with Rogden, their quarry had been disposed off within minutes by the Knight Foxley. The evidence lay a few yards away; Ligard had died quickly and lay in a grotesque heap, the head almost severed from the body. They did not comment on the duel they had witnessed, but their eyes told all; this would be for telling out of his hearing, their young warrior King, to have seen combat such as this, was an inspiration to the Knights.

Horn and his men rode on, hoping to link up with Dog's group, who had run into one pair of Rogden's men and easily removed them, not aware that Horn had caught and killed Rogden on the coast and had carried on to the village of Geltham. Riding hard they arrived in time to find Dog outnumbered in action against a group of the enemy, among them King Aeden of Collona.

Joining the fight, Horn called to Dog, "Dog! Spare the King!" Horn, within earshot of the King, called out across the fighting men, "I am Horn of Westerland! King Aeden of Collona, I call upon you to cease fighting and lay down your arms; accept quarter and be spared!"

King Aeden, no longer a young man, but still brave, answered, "Horn, I knew your father. He would not have spared me. He would have staked me out on a thorn bush for the crows to pick over, so you must take me and my life by force!"

The fighting continued until Dog and Horn isolated the King from his men, his sword knocked out of his hand, and so the King surrendered. Horn then informed him that he would be taken back to the castle at Westerland where his fate would be decided.

So his people could know the fate of captive King, one man was allowed his life to return to the kingdom of Collona to inform his people that he was alive and in the hands of the King of Westerland.

Dog was sent on ahead with the news of the death of the Knight Rogden, the capture of the King of Collona, and disappointingly, no news of the Preyden King Stadd. He could have escaped over his border as it lay but six miles from the woods, but there would be a day of reckoning for this invader. Dog also gave instructions to prepare for a great feast; musicians and dancers were to be engaged; great quantities of game and fowl wer e to be ready; bread was to be prepared, all in readiness for the King's triumphant return to the castle and his people.

Lackden, the captive Commander in his dungeon, could hear the bustle of renewed activity and called the guard to ask what was happening; he was aware that fighting had ceased around the castle for many hours now.

"You better be ready, Lackden, for the King will be returning soon after the pursuit and destruction of your army; Rogden is dead. Hagan, Yerdel and Redel are all dead. The King Aeden is our captive; so, my good Lord, your days will be short, so count the hours." The guard informed him with a hint of pleasure.

Malvin the scout also returning with his men, reported that Horn was but a few miles from the castle and would be in sight within the hour. All rushed to the best vantage points to catch a glimpse of the King arriving at the gate, and to give their victorious King a royal welcome. Streamers were found to tie to all posts, and at the sound of the small force entering the gate, the war horn sounded and great cheers went up from a thousand throats. The cheers rose to a crescendo at the sight of Horn and his Knights with the captive King Aeden. Amid this, Horn and his party dismounted and made their way to the grand hall with difficulty, such was the eagerness of his people to be near their King, and the constant sound of his name in salute rang in his ears. In the grand hall his mother, Queen Aethena, welcomed her son with warm embrace.

"Horn, truly you are your father's son! Your success I never doubted; it was written when you were born that greatness would be your mantle, and I shall live to see it."

The Queen turned and greeted King Aeden, with due respect to his rank. "Aeden, you will be treated according to your station; we will no doubt know of the King's intentions, of which I would not be privy to; your quarters will be made comfortable."

King Aeden, feeling less nervous, bowed. "Gracious Queen, on the way here I was assured that I would be treated kindly; I can ask no more. My army is lost; I am in his hands and at his mercy."

Horn then gave instructions to Lord Grenden to provide a trusted guard comprising of two Knights and two men at arms day and night for his personal protection, rather than his possible attempt to escape from the castle.

As he was taken away to a chamber prepared for him, Horn called Dog to his side, and as he approached, he knelt in homage. The King drew his sword.

"Dog, again you have excelled in battle and in the field. If any man in this kingdom is worthy of a King's praise and honour this day, it is you, my companion in arms. As you kneel, I dub thee Knight of the Unicorn! Arise and take your place with your brother Knights."

Dog's features broke into a smile, that to some would have been quite menacing.

"Sire, you honour me. I am your servant and Knight, always to be at your side."

With that, Dog joined the company of Alban, Bakley and others who were only too pleased to welcome this tried and tested warrior to their ranks. Other men were also honoured in various ways: Malvin, the scout leader; Lord Grenden, who received the King's purse of gold for his defence of the castle walls, which had played such a major part in their victory over Rogden. The giant Greg was called forward. He was promoted to take Dog's command of the footmen and given a purse of silver, coupled with the instructions to the cloth makers to fit the giant with a fine suit of apparel to display his new rank.

The festivities began with the sound of the horn to summon all to the feast; the torches had been refuelled on the walls of the grand hall; they flickered and lit up even the darkest corners. At the main table sat the Queen and Horn, with King Aeden seated on the right of the Queen, a single guard standing behind him. On Horn's left sat Lord Grenden, with the knights of the Unicorn, now including Dog, Chancellor Ancour, Secretary Winloch, and other members of the royal family, with the household officers filling in the remaining seats. The tables groaned under the weight of food constantly being added to with extra delights, apart from the newly prepared food. A great mountain had been stored for a possible siege during the battle with Rogden's army, and it was being consumed in huge quantities with relish. Huge barrels of ale were brought in from the cellars, tapped and set up on their stands for the servants to attend to a constant demand on the tables. Flagons were emptied as soon as they were filled, and should they fail to catch up with demand, they were subjected to a vociferous clamour for more. Dancers twirled between the tables; tumblers performed extraordinary feats of agility of near physical impossibility never before seen. Even the funny men who made contortions of their faces were funnier that ever remembered, raising much laughter.

The celebration went on for many of the men long after midnight; some carried on until they fell asleep at the table, and were either shaken by their wives or servants and steered to their quarters. The Queen and Horn had retired; the captive King Aeden was escorted by his guard to his chamber; all were aware that tomorrow would be a busy day. The Commanders were discussing the battle and future plans, which included the fate of the King of Collona and the Preyden commander, Lackden.

At first light the carpenters and the iron smiths were repairing the gate, adding extra newly designed devices to give even greater strength, and men were digging a wide and deep trench twenty yards back from the gate into the courtyard. This was to deny any attacking force, even after breaching the gate, from making a straight fast run into the main courtyard of the castle. Another feature of this was the erection of a wooden bridge which could be raised or lowered and controlled by the gate guards. Lord Grenden also gave the order to the iron smiths to construct an iron mesh that could be lowered and operated at the gate which would replace the rope net and could not be set alight.

The dead of the enemy, which still lay in heaps, were collected on carts and taken to a series of long pits that had been prepared for burial, as the corpses were attracting swarms of flies. Some of the dead had been in the field for three days, and the heat of the sun made the task more unpleasant. All the missiles that were scattered at the foot of the walls were carried or rolled back into the castle. Boys scuttled excitedly about in the field, collecting arrows that were still in good condition, and if the shaft was broken or damaged then the arrowhead was saved. Small weapons or anything that had been overlooked by the men the previous day and was not saturated with blood or pitch was put onto the cart; the enthusiasm of the boys seemed like a treasure hunt. There were no qualms about sightless eyes staring into the sun, limbless bodies, or heads rolling in the dust for them. These boys stripping the enemy had seen this before. Occasionally, a shout betrayed a real find worthy of the hunt.

Horn and his commanders discussed at lengths the means of dealing with the captive King and the Preyden Commander. Some argued for the execution of both that day, and some raised the alternative of a large ransom for the King and death for Lackden. The grounds for ransom was that the captive King, due to the destruction of his army, could not have the means to raise an army for many years, if ever again. The Queen and Lord Grenden were in favour of the ransom, the Chancellor Ancour voiced his support, and Horn listened to both arguments. Lord Wagnor and Secretary Winloch, who had lost a son in defending the walls in the first attack, were in favour of death for both. Finally, by a majority which included Horn himself, ransom was to be the course taken, and to that end, it was decided to send a small party to the kingdom of Collona to present their terms.

The scouts Malvin and Fenner went on ahead to Bird Valley to look for any signs of possible ambush that could be set by the men of Collona who had fled the battle. Another possibility was that there could be a search party out looking for their King. Alban the Knight caught up with the scouts who reported the valley safe to enter, but they had seen a small party on patrol in the distance. The plan was to arrive at the border under a truce and present their demands to the King's young brother, Prince Aelman. Malvin and Fenner, meeting up with this group, explained their presence. They indicated that the main body of Westerlanders would stand off until Collona agreed to Horn's request.

The Collonians sent off a messenger to the palace with this demand. He soon returned, asking them to present themselves to the Prince. After a discussion which included the Queen, she gave permission for the main party under Alban to cross the border and enter the palace. Prince Aelman was pleased to hear that his father was well and in the safe hands of the royal family. He gave orders for Alban's men to be fed and rested while further discussions took place in arranging their King's release. The Prince really had no option but to agree to the full terms laid down by Horn. Twenty thousand gold crowns would be waiting at the border and handed over on the captive King's safe arrival to his own land. That being agreed, Alban set off Fenner at once to the castle to make sure that the news of the agreement and the arrangements for the exchange were known to Lord Grenden so the King could be on his way without any delay. With this arrangement now in place, Alban crossed the border back into Westerland; he found the journey back to the castle quiet with no sign of hostile enemy deserters, most having been rounded up by hunting parties the previous day.

The castle turned out to greet Alban, and he was quickly ushered into the presence of Horn, where he recounted his talks with the Prince and his mother, and confirmed the plan was agreed to. King Aeden was brought to Horn, and he was pleased to hear of the exchange that was to take place after the mission of Alban, and that his family and people had been told of his safety and well being in the castle.

Chapter 5

The Rescue

A strong force of two hundred hand-picked men were assembled to accompany Horn and the captive King to the border at Collona, while another two hundred would accompany them through Bird valley and to the border under the Knight Dog to look for any signs of treachery from the enemy. The journey began at daybreak, as it had been arranged that the two forces would be leaving together for the major part of the route; they would part company with Dog and his men after leaving Bird Valley. As they arrived at the valley, Horn gave final instructions to Dog to send part of his men to the border to keep watch, although no reports had been sent by Malvin or Fenner of any activity by the enemy. A small band of men had been seen between the valley and the border who had shown no signs of aggression; the scouts had felt sure that they were aware of their mission, and the agreed return of their King.

Horn arrived at the border accompanied by Dog, who had left two thirds of his force at the valley under the command of Foxley the knight, who would be ready to move swiftly to the border if it turned out to be hostile. They were met by a small group of dignitaries sent to escort them to the castle, and after a form of greeting to Horn and their King, who they could see was in good health and unharmed, they led the party from the border and into the kingdom of Collona. After travelling nearly a mile into the country, they were met by a group of armed men under the banner of King Aeden, being the armed guard to the ransom. The ransom itself was contained in leather bags on two horses, which was then under the authority of their Prince, who handed them over to Horn. News spread fast of the return of the King ,and as he passed through the small villagers on the way, the crowds grew in size. Fortunately, no great hostility was shown to Horn and his men. There were only the occasional abuse shouted from a distance, more likely to be the agony of a widow or mother, as surely there must have been many standing in those swelling crowds.

Reaching the steps of the castle, Aeden's Queen, Helda, and her two daughters could be seen waiting anxiously. The party dismounted and the King walked slowly towards them to be greeted first by Prince Aelman, then the Queen. Horn and his Knights were invited into the great hall while the main party remained in the courtyard, giving them time to recover from the journey and enjoy the food and ale which appeared very quickly. Ollten the Chancellor then assured the Prince that the ransom had been paid, saying, "My Prince, the agreed ransom has been paid in two bags and is in the custody of the King of Westerland's men. Your father has now returned, and is unharmed, as you see."

King Aeden replied, "Chancellor, it is so, and I would like to convey my thanks for my deliverance, the kindness shown me in captivity, and on the journey here to Collona."

Horn rose to his feet and addressed the King and the assembled courtiers. "Brother Aeden, I am happy to restore you to your family and kingdom. Let us not cross our borders except in the spirit of friendship and in mutual benefit to our people."

With that they embraced each other in the presence of all the family and court, a sign that the enmity of the past would no longer exist. King Aeden and the Prince wished Horn and his men to stay longer, but Horn was anxious to return to his castle; so taking his leave, he gave the order to the men to prepare for the return journey to Westerland.

As he left the hall, Horn was aware that the eldest daughter of the King Eaden was holding his gaze; he noticed her beauty for the first time; she had waist-long hair, was fair of colour, and her skin had the blush of peach. He stared back, and still she held her look of interest, her clear blue eyes meeting his. Then she dropped her eyes, fearful that Horn would deem her impertinent. Horn was sure that it was more than just a look; he had little experience of females, being for most of his young life totally absorbed in learning the arts of war.

The year sped by, the castle enjoying a relaxed and calm period. The court occasionally dealt with the odd miscreant, which attracted the attention of certain citizens that were always ready to dish out punishment or to condemn their fellow creatures. Hunting for game in the well stocked forests kept the Knights in good form, with Dog excelling, showing his remarkable skill with the spear, and he always took the centre stage when congratulations were handed out. He had become, in a very short while, not only a very competent Knight, but he now carried himself with an air of confidence, almost bordering on dignity. The ladies now engaged his company, whereas before they would run from his presence, or at least turn their eyes away rather than look directly at him, and he had the ear of the King. His propensity to boast of his past exploits to all who would listen became a thing of the past. He had finally learned that it was sweeter to listen to praise from others of his prowess on the field of battle; his skill as a warrior was there for all to see. Dog was pleased with himself, but he did not allow himself to forget that Colver, of the early days in the battle with the Irish invaders, gave him his chance. Now Colver was the King; he would die for him!. Tournaments were often arranged in which Horn entered as a competitor with relish, and his skill on foot with the sword was appreciated by the large crowds who attended. Likewise, his prowess on horseback stunned the audience, who responded with cries of admiration at his feats with the spear and axe.

So the year passed and Horn, who not forgotten the vision of the beautiful Princess of Collna, was sorely tempted to cross the border to see once again if the image constantly in his mind was as beautiful as he remembered. It had occupied his thoughts whenever he retired to his chamber to rest. He reminded himself that it was not a simple task to travel that distance without a strong escort, and to place men at risk just to satisfy his own desires was not the action of a King. One day he promised himself, *if fate wills it, I shall see her*.

And so the months sped on with little or no interruption to castle life. Regular training and a supply of new weapons now forged a strong army that could challenge an enemy twice its size in the field. A new war device had been invented for use in the field; it was a mechanised spear for dealing with charging enemy horsemen and a catapult system which could be set up quickly in the ground. This would be loaded with a heavy spear, which could be released at twenty yards, with sufficient power to bring down horse and rider before they could engage the men at arms. This weapon easy to make; with a light frame it could be carried by two men and set up in a minute. If caught out unprepared, the shaft could be staked in the ground at an angle towards the enemy while the men would still be free to use sword or axe. Other weapons were introduced for use on the battlements, including a gantry from which large stones could be shot outwards to a distance of fifty yards at approaching ladder parties. The smith had cast new and larger iron cauldrons to contain more boiling pitch; he also thought of the addition of two lips, causing the pitch to spray out in two directions at the same time.

Never had the castle boasted such defence. Come a host of armies, they would encounter an aggressive and highly trained force, one that would give no quarter in battle. Regular meetings were called between Horn and his Commanders to discuss reports that filtered in from the scouts, and with Malvin and his men carrying out their duties of patrolling the borders of the kingdom, nothing escaped their attention. Stragglers were rounded up and identified. If proved hostile, they were handed over to small groups of the King's men that operated nearby and taken back to the castle. Thus any contingency that arose would be dealt with efficiency and quickly, but there would be no lifting or relaxing on a guard's part. Those caught doing so would exact swift punishment from the Commanders, justice being dealt with on the spot according to the severity of the lapse of duty.

One fine morning under blue skies, the courtyard bathed in warm sunshine, the courtiers strolled, talking of pleasant times ahead, when they were interrupted by shouting at the gate area. This startled them, and they turned to see a messenger and Malvin the scout in a distressed state. They were running towards the great hall. They asked for an audience with the King and Lord Grenden, which was arranged at once. Malvin spoke quickly.

"Sire, I have seen many people crossing the border from Collona into our kingdom: old men, women and children, all in great distress. They are being held between their border and Bird Valley by our men, who were told by these poor people that eastern Collona has been invaded by a horde. They are most likely Viking or Saracen, aided by the men from the kingdom of Kishland to the east."

News had spread of King Aeden's defeat in Westerland and of the huge loss of men he had suffered in the unsuccessful alliance with the Knight Rogden. Collona now looked like an easy conquest.

Lord Grenden asked the messenger if could estimate the size of the invading army.

"No, my Lord, but they say it is large, and that King Aeden and Prince Aelman have little hope of holding them with what remains of their army."

Lord Grenden turned to Horn and asked if he could call a general council meeting at once to consider this turn of events, as they had established a pact with Collona when their King was returned to his kingdom. Horn addressed the assembly who had answered the call in minutes.

"My Lords, having heard the news of the invasion of Collona, I wish to ask you all for support to aid King Aeden and his people to drive out the invaders;

are we in agreement?"

All were in favour. At once the mobilisation of a force was carried out by Lord Grenden; the Commanders were busy in the courtyard preparing for the march to the border. Carts were being ordered to follow the force with food for the refugees from Collona, as most of them had not eaten for some days. The army streamed out of the castle, Horn leading the Knights of the Unicorn, with Lord Grenden and his Commanders following. Giant Greg could be seen striding ahead of his footmen; a massive sword could be seen swinging in time with his gait, and he was already shouting at the men to keep up with the horsemen.

The army was in a good mood, such a long time had passed since any real action. It would be true to say that they were looking forward to testing their new weapons. For the newcomers, this was a chance to experience their baptism in the field. So, moral was high, and the expectancy of facing an enemy hung in the air. Horn hoped to reach the border before the worst could happen with the Collonians being overwhelmed, or perhaps besieged at the castle, as he was eager to meet the invader in the field. The size of the refugee camp surprised Horn, possibly two thousand, when he was expecting only hundreds. Their eyes showed fear as the army passed, but given the news that within a matter of minutes carts with food would be arriving for them, a few managed weak smiles.

Reaching the border they were not challenged by anyone, and making their way inland, they met up with Fenner the scout, who informed them that a major battle was taking place at the Ulba Heights. The army of Collona was already fighting a rearguard action; they were severely outnumbered by four to one. King Aeden had been forced to leave the field by Prince Aelman for his own safety. He made his way back to the castle to prepare for a siege. Although many good men would fall in the field, some would be able to break away and join the king.

Before Horn reached the Heights, he encountered men fleeing from the battle, who stopped at the sight of the Westerlanders and joined Greg's force of footmen, their courage now returned. After hurried information given by these men on the tactics employed by the enemy and their approximate strength, Horn wasted no time increasing the pace of their march to the Heights. Lord Grenden gave orders for half the footmen to remain at a distance and unseen by the enemy, to give them the impression of a smaller force arriving. This might tempt him into the open ground; the footmen behind would then be able to conduct a pincer movement, while the enemy force was committed to frontal attack in strength.

Horn's army broke cover from the woodland and advanced quickly, joining the men of Collona under Prince Aelman, who was about to withdraw farther, having lost so much ground and many of his best men to the enemy. The impact of seeing the Westerland army now arriving in support, well armed and fresh, gave them extra strength, and a full throated roar from the near exhausted men greeted Horn and his men as he rode up to Prince Aelman. Bloodied from furious clashes with his opponents, Aelman raised his sword in salute.

"Brother, I thank the Gods you are here; our force is near spent; many have left the field for the castle. Welcome, brother Westerland."

Above the din of battle Horn told the Prince of his plan to entrap the enemy on both fronts, but first he gave an order to his men to fight in a retreat formation to the woods, at which time the enemy, more than likely sensing victory, would follow, charging down from the heights, and onto the open plain. At the same time the reserve footmen under the command of Dog would move swiftly through the scrubland to engage their rear and flanks, while Horn's army would move in fast once fighting was assured on open ground. This movement would throw them into confusion, and they would probably not be able to organise a counter attack, giving them no option except to fight for their lives against a highly trained army.

The men of Collona, with the knowledge of the arrival of Horn and his army, fought now with renewed vigour and purpose, and were in fact beginning to hold their own, which was heart warming, but not what was now planned. The order to begin a fighting retreat was given by the Prince. It began slowly, so as not to arouse suspicion, then gathering pace, arrived at the woodland to turn and face the enemy, giving the impression of a last desperate stand. It succeeded! The Kishlanders poured down in mass from the rough ground on the heights onto the open ground, fully confident that any opposition would be overcome easily and quickly by a full frontal attack at the woodland. The giant Greg's men, in two sections, set light to the tinder dry scrub on either side as they raced forward on the left and right at the rear of the enemy. The enemy now were also engaged in furious battle with the newly arrived Horn's army, and the shouts above the din could be heard.

"Horn! Horn for Westerland!"

From two thousand throats it sounded like a death knell to the Kishland men. Dog had taken his place with Horn as they surged forward, eager to get to close quarters with this enemy, the sword and axe coming into their own. They were swinging, slashing, chopping and cutting through their foes. Many fell before them, never knowing which one of the awesome two had despatched them with lightning speed. Their main object was to close on the Kishland Lord and his Knights. The battle intensified; men fought in such close combat that those who received a felling blow never regained their feet, but perished underfoot, owing to the pressure of men literally face to face and shoulder to shoulder, their cries unheard.

A great shout went up from the giant and his men as they arrived unseen and engaged the enemy's rear; his massive sword could be seen flashing twenty yards away, taking a formidable toll of the surprised enemy. When his sword arm was engaged in parrying, the other arm wielded an axe, which with sickening force and sound parted head from torso, or virtually split his victim in two. Both sections of footmen were making good their inroads into the rear ranks and flanks of the enemy to the point of almost sealing them off from any chance of retreat or escape. At the same time Horn and his men were decimating the ranks of the Kishlanders, herding them towards the centre, leaving their dead in heaps behind them.

Now evidence of panic was seen, and such was their destiny; it was becoming difficult for them to use their weapons to the best effect, and Horn's men found the best method was to stab at their opponents at close quarters. The attack by Horn proved successful; the enemy now realised that they no longer engaged the Collonian men, but a trained army, which had not been expected. Their hopes of victory had now vanished as they were now completely enclosed by the Westerlanders. Horn and Dog finally made their way to the centre of struggling men to reach their leader and his remaining Knights. Desperately, they tried to escape their ultimate fate, but the ferocious attack by Horn and Dog spelt their doom; a plea for mercy did nothing to delay their end. Horn, with his telling sword, and Dog's savage and clinical use of the axe were to give no quarter to those who still made any form of defence, or those left with no other option but to fight to the end.

One large group of the enemy managed to escape to the east, and would not stop until they reached their border; some would not make it as the triumphant. Westerlanders spotted this move and gave chase. The fighting gradually died down to almost nothing; all signs of aggression from the Kishlanders had now disappeared, the weapons being cast to the ground by the few survivors. After counting their dead, Horn and Prince Aelman gave orders to gather weapons from the dead from both sides. Horn calculated that the Prince had lost nearly two thousand men, while the losses of his army was in the region of two hundred footmen. The Prince lost most of those men before Horn's arrival in two short battles with the enemy. Trenches were dug to accommodate over three thousand of the enemy, and the Collonians were put into a separate trench; no words were said, no salute given. The few prisoners were never seen again, and no one asked about them.

After the burials, the army made ready to move towards the castle at Collona; there was much banter between the men of both kingdoms, and an occasional burst of song was well received with calls for more, particularly from a small man of Greg's force who possessed a fine strong voice. The scouts had been sent to King Aedan and to the castle at Westerland with news of the victory, and as they made their way to the Collonian castle, people from the villages cheered them as they passed through. At the castle the crowds turned out in force; almost the whole population awaited the arrival of their Prince and Horn's army; many of the boys unable to contain their excitement ran to meet them before they were at the gates. As they entered the gates, the cry went up.

"Horn! Horn! King of Kings!"

As they dismounted, King Aedan and Queen Helda, with their daughters, stepped up to greet them. King Aedan kissed Horn's hand.

"My brother Horn, we owe you so much. Your exploits as a true warrior will become a legend in our land. My kingdom, my family, can never hope to repay your service this day in driving out the accursed Kishland army and their allies, and for the safe return of our Prince Aelman."

This short welcoming speech was drowned by the ever increasing cheers and noise of celebration. Horn held up his hand to speak.

"My brother Aedan, let us this day remember the reason why our two kingdoms fought together at the Ulbar Heights as brothers in arms. For, indeed, we are from this day forward. I shall leave one of my most able Commanders as my ambassador, and we will accept whoever you shall appoint to serve at the Westerland court."

As was expected, a feast was arranged for that night by the King and

Queen. It was gigantic in array, with mountains of food, barrels of wine, musicians and dancers who filled the air with the sound of merriment. Horn, sitting on the left of the Queen, was suddenly aware of the Princess Cleona studying him closely with a half smile on her exquisitely shaped lips. He also caught the look in her eyes which could not be mistaken, sending a message that he could not resist. He rose to his feet; his pulse was racing, but he boldly addressed the King.

"My brother Aedan, sister Helda, since my last visit here, I have seen and much admired your beautiful daughter, Cleona. Should it please you both, and the Princess, I would be so bold to ask for her hand in marriage, and bring about an alliance that will last between our kingdoms for many generations."

King Aedan, surprised by Horn's intentions, but finding it hard to disguise his obvious delight, spoke to his daughter. "Cleona, daughter, you have heard the words of Horn, and he has spoken of his desire, how say you to this? We know you have spoken of him since his last visit here."

Cleona, replying to her father, also turned towards Horn. "Sire, father, I have much admired and thought of Horn of Westerland, and I say that I would become his wife, if you so bless such a union."

With her beautiful face now flushed, she sat down beside her sister as the King rose to his feet. "That is also the dearest wish of myself and Queen Helda. Let us look upon this alliance of our kingdoms as a new age, which promises to be one of strength and prosperity for all."

King Aedan then bade his daughter to stand and come to him. Taking her hand, he escorted her to Horn, gently placing her hand into the hand of the warrior King.

"Brother Horn, I give you my fair daughter Cleona in marriage with our blessing, and let any children of this union uphold the qualities and hopes we all share for the future."

Horn then sat with Cleona, her near presence stirring emotions he had never experienced before. As he looked at her, she seemed more beautiful than ever before. Her golden hair cascaded down on her shoulders like spun silk. Never had he seen such a vision; his heart leapt every time she looked directly at him. His throat seemed to close; he swallowed hard.

"My fair Cleona, my heart is filled with love for you. We must not wait too long for our marriage. Let it be in three months, here in Collona, among your family; shall we agree?"

Cleona looked at Horn, her wide clear blue eyes slightly misted. Her face was flushed with excitement. "Horn, my love, you have taken my heart; you have always filled my daily thoughts of late, which I now know were the seeds of love. Today it has grown and flowered. You and I agree we shall marry in the time you say, in Collona."

The evening strayed into early morning as the feasting ceased and tiredness overcame most. People draped themselves over tables and benches, resembling untidy bundles rather than the once celebrating and victorious warriors of the battle at Ulba.

Later that morning saw Lord Grenden marshalling the men into order for their return to Westerland and the castle. He was pleased to see the giant Greg had already roused his footmen and managed to get them into some form of reasonable order. Horn awoke in time to speak to King Aedan and the Queen about the agreed wedding plans, and took a short while to say his rather moving farewell to Cleona.

"My love, it is time for us to return to Westerland. I leave a part of myself behind. The days and nights will seem an eternity until I return to take you as my bride."

Cleona, looking tenderly at Horn with eyes that seemed to swallow him, said, "Horn, my dear heart, I too will find the days long until we can become one. Take care, my love, for my heart would break should ought befall you."

The sounds of men shouting orders cruelly broke into their world. Horn entered the courtyard, giving his men the general order to move out through the castle gates to join the main army under the command of Lord Grenden. He turned to wave to the watching royal family, but in particular the Princess Cleona.

Both Lord Grenden and Dog made known their happy reactions to the news of the intended marriage as they rode ahead of the force towards the kingdom. Lord Grenden was particularly pleased as he weighed up the potential of the alliance by the two kingdoms in the future years, and his mind danced with the possibility of a son and heir from this union.

As they neared the castle, banners could be seen flying from the battlements in salute, and as they finally entered the gates, the war horn gave out its triumphant sound, causing the crowds to surge forward to greet them. Queen Aethena hurried across the courtyard to her son, while wives, parents, and sweethearts looked for their partners, their shouts of glee rising above the noise of welcome as they found them safe and well. The unlucky ones remained in silence or in sobbing groups, mourning their lost men. Everywhere was the scene of activity and reunion. Dog and the Knights made for the great hall, being joined by Horn and Lord Grenden, with their respective Commanders to review their part in the battle and the conclusive victory.

Horn congratulated them all for their leadership and conduct during the battle, paying particular praise to the Knights, especially Dog, who once again fought alongside him with his usual tenacity. To him he awarded the honour of the Star of the Order; this he accepted with surprising dignity, for in recent months he had become something of a courtier. Lord Grenden was given land in the south of the kingdom, with a purse of gold for his role as Commander-in-Chief of the army. The giant Greg, outstanding in the battle, and for his part in the successful pincer movement at Ulba, received a purse and was promoted in full to the Commander of the footmen with a grant of land in the north-west near the Preyden border, which included the village of Lockney. Other awards for service were made to the Commanders, mainly purses of gold or silver. To some, a sword with the hilt furnished with precious stones was given, while others received a dagger equally decorated. The widows of section leaders who did not survive the battle received recognition by way of grants; also, the families of all common men recorded as lost were to be visited by Lord Grenden with a token purse. He would enquire into the well being of children and the home. This was a task that would be spread over several days, owing the distance to travel to many of the villages and the need to be accompanied by an armed escort to some of the homesteads on the western borders.

The life in the kingdom of Westerland was once again in a relative state of peace, and the threat of any further invasion by hostile kings was no longer feared or expected. Everyday activities could return in full to the castle and its inhabitants. Laughter could now be heard from the children as they played, and tradesmen plied their wares; even the livestock seemed to enjoy the situation as their feed and water was now plentiful. The sounds of the smithy rang out with his powerful blows on the anvil while forging weapons or tools for the land. Carpenters and stonemen busied with the erection of yet stronger staging for the battlements on the south walls, where there had been a weakness exposed by the Preyden Commander in his unsuccessful assaults on that section.

Lord Grenden still maintained, even in peaceful times, a strict training programme, making sure the army was always at a constant state of readiness.

New weapons were devised for defence, and stronger outposts were installed near the borders. These linked up with smaller units between them and the castle, thus creating a better warning system throughout the kingdom. The villages between these posts were visited by Lord Grenden during his distribution of purses, where he assessed their strength and also laid down a form of basic training. He arranged for weapons to be issued and stockades and huts to be strengthened against a surprise attack.

With everything working smoothly in the kingdom, Horn's thoughts turned to his forthcoming visit to Collona, and his marriage to the Princess Cleona. Chancellor Ancour, being told to prepare arrangements with the royal family there for his arrival in the next few weeks, gave instructions to his office to act at once.

As the day approached for his departure, he was informed by Lord Grenden that the prisoner Lackden had been killed trying to escape from the dungeon. The guard had no option, as he had been attacked with great ferocity by the prisoner, who would have killed him had he not been armed. This news did not dampen the occasion as Horn had decided much earlier that Lackden could not be released, and his ultimate fate would have been the axe at some time in the not too distant future. Horn had wisely decided on that course mainly because if they released the prisoner and he returned to his own land, he would forever be looking for the opportunity to join another invasion force. As in the old days, it always resulted with old enemies of long standing turning up on the field.

Horn now had to arrange the party of notables to accompany him to Collona: his mother, Bishop Stelid, Chancellor Ancour, the seven Knights of the Unicorn, and two hundred men-at-arms under the command of the giant Greg, resplendent in his new clothes denoting his rank. Dog had been given the task of commander of the treasure wagon, which contained the gifts for the family of King Aeden and also Horn's State robes and crown, with six picked men as escort. The scouts Malvin and Fenner went on ahead of the party, although there was not a great risk of an attack by any isolated group still in the vicinity of the Collona border.

The journey was pleasant, the weather kind and warm. As they passed through the villages on the route, crowds turned out to greet their warrior King and his mother until they were out of sight. Some of the children ran after them, only to tire and make their way back to their village.

At the castle in Collona, news had reached them that the royal party was on its way; last minute preparations were made for the marriage ceremony, nothing being spared to create a welcome. Beautiful garlands of flowers hung everywhere; the citizens were in high spirits. Royal weddings were a rarity between kingdoms, and this one was to be the most important for over half a century, since King Alymer married his Queen Aethena from the eastern kingdom of Menda. The scouts arrived at the castle to inform them that Horn was a fifteen minute ride away. The guard of honour was quickly assembled in the courtyard, joined by King Aeden's personal guard at the gate.

Everybody who could run, walk, hop or crawl made their way to the main courtyard; no one was going to miss Horn and Queen Aethena enter the gate to greet their King and Queen. A battery of horns sounded in salute as the Westerland army rode in and dismounted. The royal party and Knights made their way to the grand hall to be invited to enter and be officially welcomed by the royal family of Collona.

With the reception over, servants escorted Queen Aethena and Horn to the quarters prepared for them to refresh themselves and rest. As the Princess Cleona had not appeared with family, Horn was a little disappointed not to catch a glimpse of his future bride, but he could wait, for there was to be great feast that night. He was still curious. Was she really as beautiful as his eyes had told him? She was truly the most beautiful creature on Earth. Many times his mind had played him tricks; sometimes he heard her voice and sensed her presence and fragrance. How he had longed to hold her exquisite hands.

The feast was indeed welcomed that night, with much talk between the Chancellors of both kingdoms. Horn, King Aeden and the Queen were in deep conversation with each other. Sadly, there was still no sign of the Princess who had decided to stay in her apartments with her ladies. Although, unbeknown to Horn, she had asked one of her ladies to go and peep at her future husband and tell her how he looked.

The lady returned swiftly and said, "My Lady, his Majesty looks like a God; his strong features would weaken any heart. I think he looks for you, for surely as I entered the hall, he looked across at once towards me. I am sure there was a look of disappointment on his face when he failed to recognise you."

Cleona smiled to herself; she was sorely tempted to rush to the hall to see Horn and embrace him, but tomorrow was their day to meet and join in marriage. With those thoughts she retired to her chamber and easily fell into a dream filled sleep.

Horn did not sleep well that night; his mind was constantly filled with images. He found himself one minute in a tortuous situation under a darkened sky, tormented by a terrible storm, and in the next, in brilliant blinding light. All of this was accompanied by strange high voices forever calling him by name, and when he answered, they did not hear. He woke with a start, for a moment wondering where he was, his dreams still haunting him.

The voice of his manservant broke the spell to return him to full awareness of the daybreak. This was the day of his marriage to Cleona. Was she also awake? Had she been dreaming impossible things also? Horn bathed and dressed; he donned his fine clothes in ruby red made specially for this day. The clothes were decorated with precious stones and pearls. He buckled on his belt of finely spun gold thread from which hung an exquisitely designed silver dagger. He asked his man, "How do I look, Flota?"

"Sire, you are indeed the King of Kings! You carry that colour well. Your bride, Sire, will catch her breath at the sight of her husband to be."

This was interrupted by the Knight Foxley calling Flota to inform Horn to make an appearance in the grand hall where the ceremony was to take place, conducted by an anxious Bishop Stelid. As Horn made his way to the hall, all bowed to him, a youthful handsome figure enhanced even more in such rich clothes. His presence commanded attention; his noble features were dominated by a wide smile as he greeted familiar faces and other guests of the Collonian royal family. Bishop Stelid had already taken his position beside King Aeden and his Queen, and on the other side was Queen Aethena, who greeted her son as he approached the raised dais. He then received the formal greeting from Cleona's family and a special greeting from Prince Aelman, who already regarded Horn as the supreme warrior and was delighted that he would soon be marrying into the family. Chancellor Ancour, standing near the group, offered Horn his crown. Taking it, Horn asked for the crown he had ordered to be made for his bride to be brought forward and placed on a large silk cushion for her.

Servants busied themselves, hurrying among the guests with large flagons of ale or wine to quench the thirst of those who could not wait until the wedding feast. An air of expectancy filled the air; the Princess would make her entry at any time now, although it was her privilege to choose her moment to present herself to the waiting Horn and the assembled guests now filling the hall.

The sudden hush and general hubbub gave way to silence as the Princess appeared and began to descend the steps to the hall. Gasps of admiration from a hundred throats were clearly heard as the vision approached. Her gown seemed to project a brilliance not seen before, her golden hair covered with a silken veil. A silver aura seemingly swirled about her as she slowly descended with her ladies in attendance. Horn was so moved by this vision of sheer beauty that his voice practically froze, strangled in his throat. He tried to pass a comment to his mother, but nothing came; he could only watch in awe as she came towards him and stood by the Bishop. Stelid then bade her to stand with Horn, and as she came close, her very presence seemed to engulf him with a feeling he had never experienced in his life before. Her fragrance, her beauty, was even more than he had ever remembered; he was lost. He had to steady himself as he looked into her eyes through the fine veil, wide with so much feeling. They shone with an intense light. He was, he thought, the luckiest man in the world.

Chapter 6

The Marriage

Horn, with Cleona at his side, kneeling on gold tasselled cushions embroidered with pale blue horns, took their oath before Bishop Stelid, to love and respect each other, and called on all in the kingdom to witness these vows. The Bishop turned to Horn who then gave his vow.

"I, Horn of Westerland, take thee Cleona, the daughter of King Aeden and Queen Helda of Collona, to be my wife and future Queen of my kingdom." Then taking her hand, he placed a gold ring on her finger saying, "My ring you shall wear, my throne you shall share through our life's path, together till death."

The Bishop and all those assembled looked at Cleona who replied, "I, Cleona, Princess of the House of Collona, do take thee, Horn of Westerland, as my husband, and I shall bring honour to thy name and kingdom."

Bishop Stelid then removed her head-dress and replaced it with the crown, solemnly saying, "This is the symbol of the Kingdom of Westerland that honours you today, and whose subjects welcome and accept you as their future Queen. I am, from this day, in your service."

Horn offered his hand to Cleona and she rose to her feet. With a smile, she kissed him and whispered words only heard by her husband.

"My husband Horn, how long have I loved thee; my heart is filled with happiness this day."

Horn, his mouth dry, found it difficult to reply, overcome with nervousness and excitement. "My love, I share your happiness; if I live a hundred years, this day will forever remain in my heart."

A great shout then echoed throughout the castle as the Collonian royal family gave their blessing to the couple, followed by the principal guests from both kingdoms, many laying gifts by the Chancellor's table. The Chancellor listed their names as they paid homage to the bridal pair. Speeches followed, the first was by King Aeden.

"People of Westerland and Collona, this is a happy and significant milestone in our kingdoms. Never before have our people been so united and strong. We will go forward in prosperity and peace, are hearts are glad to have lived to witness this historic day; long may they live!"

Horn, now having recovered from his dry throat, addressed the King, "Kind brother and sister, I also welcome with all my heart this true alliance of our people and kingdom through this marriage to your beautiful daughter Cleona, now my wife. The future years will be proven as you say, and we shall honour all agreements and work together for prosperity. Let no one cross our borders uninvited or harbour ambitions to usurp our crowns, for to do so, their white bones bleached by our sun will be their only reward, which their kin will not dare to collect!"

Cheers rang throughout the hall from the Collonians as the young warrior finished his speech; this was what they wanted to hear. Why had they been so foolish to throw their lot in with the traitor, Knight Rogden?

A feast of feasts was arranged at the castle, everywhere the castle echoed with the sounds of celebration, music, and banter between men, who not so long ago were in mortal combat. Barrels of ale would be consumed in mutual friendship by these men in the courtyard. Chancellor Ancour called for the chest from the wagon to be brought the hall, and Dog returned to the courtyard and ordered the guard to unload the chest and follow him to the hall. Horn had personal gifts for all the members of the royal family, which he found pleasure in presenting himself, and Cleona, looking radiant at his side, marvelled at the variety of beautiful gifts Horn had chosen for them. Thus the day ended, and they left the chamber, escorted by tradition with the family and close friends to the door of their bridal chamber. Then, with the door closed to all, they were left to enjoy their own company at last, to talk of things as lovers, words made only for each others ears.

Everyone rose early the next morning determined not to miss the departure of the party to Westerland with their Princess Cleona. Everywhere there was noise, dogs barking, children shouting, and mothers scolding them for running off on their own. The men of Westerland were ready to move out and were in their respective sections for the journey back when the horns sounded as the royal party appeared on the steps of the grand hall. Servants led the horses, suitably decorated with colourful ribbons, the saddles richly adorned with gold silk cloth, to await Horn and his bride. The Knights of the Unicorn, with their banner flying, were again to act as personal escorts to the couple, and as the royal pair mounted their horses, so the Knights took up their close formation, the procession making their way to the gates. The King and Queen of Collona with their people said goodbye to the couple, calling out their good wishes for the years ahead and to return soon. As they reached the gates, a score of white doves were released that soared into the blue sky as a sign of peace and goodwill. Within a few minutes they had left the castle and were into the open country, soon becoming faint figures on the skyline.

The watching people returned to their homes, but this time with a sense of purpose and in the knowledge they had the most powerful ally among all kingdoms, never again would they have to stand alone against an invader. Prince Aelman had ridden out for a mile with the party, and after embracing Cleona and Horn, he wished them a safe journey and promised to visit them in the next few months at the castle.

Lord Grenden and an escort rode out to meet Horn and his bride as soon as the scouts reported that they were within a mile of the gates, and meeting up with them, he gave his loyal greeting. He, of course, was not only Horn's Commander-in-Chief, but since the death of King Alymer, had taken upon himself the role of father, not that Horn suspected, but the Lord had trained and schooled young Horn and recognised his extraordinary talent, which now, at the age of seventeen, had proved him a warrior. He told himself that the future years were indeed looking promising, and the thought of royal children filled him with great joy as he had shared these hopes with Queen Aethena since her husband, the King, had died. The continuance of the House of Horn was paramount.

The party reached the gates to a tremendous welcome; the horn blasts saluted the royal bridal pair as they came into sight. Gates were thrown wide open and filled with footmen, who were told not to push forward, but to create a path for the royal party to proceed to the courtyard and the grand hall. The sight of the young King and his bride brought a lump to the throats of even the old men as the couple dismounted. Horn assisted his bride, while Lord Grenden escorted Queen Athena to the Hall. There was already great excitement within the hall, courtiers all anxious to glimpse their future Queen. The ladies of the court caught their breath at the sheer beauty of Cleona, still looking radiant after the journey, her golden hair half hidden under her cap, her blue eyes filled with expectancy. The couple were directed to the throne by the Chancellor, where they received the congratulations from the court and the many guests who had been invited to attend the castle on Horn's return. This reception took more than an hour, with the Chancellor beginning to tire in presenting those that had been called, until, at last, the queue was no longer there. The great assembly in the hall bowed in homage as the royal couple left to retire to their chambers to rest and to prepare for the evening's feast in the hall.

The celebrations began almost a soon as the reception was over, and the feast to come was to exceed even that of the great feast at Collona. Huge oxen turned on the giant spit by two sweating men in the kitchen, wafting the smell throughout the castle passages. The servants bustled about their allotted tasks were kept on their toes by the eager headmen of each trade; no one dared to be the cause of a hold up or a disaster on the most important day for many years in the history of Westerland. Secretary Winloch and Chancellor Ancour raced from one part of the castle to the other to make sure that all was going well with the preparations, meeting later in the grand hall to confirm that indeed nothing could go wrong. Feeling satisfied, they both set about arranging the most important and difficult task of seating. Who was to share the long table of the royal family? With so many distinguished guests, it was not going to be easy to please all who felt they should be included. Horn had given the Chancellor the positions of the family, Lord Grenden and Dog, but the rest was up to them, and whatever they did would be a talking point for weeks to come. While all this frantic activity went on, so the couple rested, as this had the hallmark of a long celebration until the early hours.

Extra fresh smelling straw was spread over the floor of the hall to take the impact of spillage of ale and wine and the inevitable discarding of food that would find its way to the ground. Even the eager dogs could not devour all that fell from this overeating, and the more wine consumed, the more was spilled by those who called the loudest. Musicians had been brought in to add to those of the court; a group of acrobats and tumblers arrived from the village of Sabden, famed for their impossible high leaps and tortuous body twisting turns. Dancers from Lowton in colourful dress would perform with non-stop energy. Other entertainers in this galaxy of talent included sword swallowing, jugglers, and deceivers of the eye who could mystify you with remarkable tricks too quickly acted to see how it was accomplished, but intended to fill you with amazement. Wrestling and other combatant sports would give the guests the chance to take sides and lay a wager on their favourite; this then was the programme set before the royal couple and their guests in celebration of their marriage.

The loud blast of the horn sounded above the animated chatter of the guests now assembled in the grand hall, heralding the entry of the royal couple. Horn and Cleona, hand in hand, Lord Grenden, and the Queen were escorted to the long table. Taking their seats, they motioned to the Chancellor to invite the honoured guests to join them. Among those chosen of the army to sit at the long table were the Knights of the Unicorn, headed by Dog; the Commanders, which included the giant Greg; and the court officials such as Ancour, Winloch, Bishop Stelid and the Physician Grindel, also any accompanying ladies of those mentioned. There were gasps of delight and surprise at the sight of the huge platters of food and their exotic arrangement, garland with tiny flowers and fragrant herbs. They were carried to the table by a seemingly never ending procession of servants. Drinking vessels were emptied and quickly filled from the large flagons, which were abundant on the table. All this warmed the hearts of most present, creating a happy and friendly atmosphere in the hall.

The entertainment began with the musicians and dancers leading followed by the others artistes This was greatly appreciated by the guests who were thrilled to see so many varied acts competently performed for their pleasure. The wrestlers drew the most wagers from the guests as they fought with each other for mastery, the cheering crowds backed one or the other as they swayed, arms locked about their bodies looking for a sign of weakness to play on. Horn complimented his officials for the splendid arrangements, not only on the feast, but also the high quality of the entertainment, that had excelled anything seen at the castle before.

As the evening passed into early morning, many on the tables were slumped on their benches, their heads on the table betraying their utter fatigue caused by excess. Loud noises erupted from some, caused by the extreme amount of food and wine consumed, their tired bodies complaining of their overloaded stomachs in the only way it knows to protest to its host. The royal party had discreetly made their way from the hall to their chambers with a certain modicum of dignity, and Lord Grenden, before retiring, gave orders to the posting of the sentries. The hall below was quiet and continued to resound with the occasional discomforts of its sleeping occupants.

The dawn brought a new beginning to Horn and the kingdom of Westerland, for now they had a Queen, young and exceedingly beautiful. The following days were spent together, both totally absorbed in the newness of marriage, which meant that matters of State were temporarily put aside. Chancellor Ancour, anxious to pursue the alliance with Collona, was finally granted an audience with Horn to discuss the exchange of Consuls between the kingdoms. It was agreed to appoint Lord Sancto, who had distinguished himself in the recent battles and had the respect of King Aeden and Prince Aelman. Sancto accepted the position with thanks and arrangements were made for him to leave the next day, accompanied by his wife and servants. A small bodyguard would be detailed to escort them through the villages and across the border. Meanwhile, the King of Collona had chosen as the first Consul to Westerland the son of Prince Aelman and nephew of the King. He would leave on the morrow, a dashing young man who, no doubt, would turn a few ladies heads at court. This pleased Cleona, as this man was also her cousin, and that meant there would always be a link with her family. Letters would be carried daily by messengers between the kingdoms and would arrive safely to the person intended. In this way, court gossip could flow back and forth in confidence.

Military plans for the alliance were organised by Lord Grenden and approved by Horn. Although, as Westerland's chain defences were already in key areas, the chance of a surprise raid was almost remote. Extra defence outposts were constructed inside the border of Collona. Trade had already begun to flow, with the merchants seeing the opportunity to extend their markets. For years the open ground around the castle at Westerland had produced high quality grain This was now exchanged for the bountiful fruit of the extensive orchards of Collona. Along with other mutually beneficial goods, the court settled down to its normal daily activity. Horn called his Commanders to review the state of readiness of the army and their weapons in the various sections under their command, although there was little prospect of an invasion in the near future; nothing would interfere with the training programmes laid down by Lord Grenden.

This had always been the key to their successful actions in the field time after time. They now had a military force in the kingdom that was spoken of with great respect and regarded as the strongest throughout the all known kingdoms; albeit, it certainly was not the largest that could be raised, but it was the most proficient and totally dedicated to the art of war. The fame of Horn as a warrior King was now being coupled with others who had entered the records of other kingdoms, such as Lord Grenden as a tactician without equal,

Dog's fearsome reputation as a warrior without mercy, with axe play impossible to counter, and a giant named Greg, who was head and shoulders above any man, who could use a great sword or huge spear to cut through a whole section of men and toss them aside like paper dolls. So this warning became common knowledge of the seemingly invincible army, spreading to every corner of every kingdom and to the islands beyond. Small boys recounting tales of these warriors in their huts imagined themselves in the role of a Westerlander hero.

So entered a time of peace and happy pursuits of better things. The giant Greg, often admired by few women because most found his size intimidating, discovered romance in the shape of a dancer from Lowton. He had noticed her swirling around the tables at the feast, her flashing smile dazzled and bewitched him. Later, he caught up with this beauty to find a mutual attraction existed. He asked her to become his wife; she agreed and sweeping off her feet, he almost carried her to his village of Lockney. Many other marriages took place, markets flourished and the people prospered.

Dog continued his lifestyle, often to be seen in the company of beautiful women. He was prominent in the occasional royal hunt, excelling in the chase alongside Horn, bringing down the game with his spear or arrow. Tournaments were arranged to keep the Knights on their toes, and Horn was pleased to see the young ones like Kaldon developing into a serious contender for the champions belt, awarded each year to the most promising Knight. This was highly prized by anyone, for it carried not only the title, but a gold purse given by the King.

Thus, this was the story of Westerland and Horn, the young King that came of age. His exploits were spoken of, and his commanders were respected by all. What would the stars foretell of the future of this warrior King? One must not attempt to guess, but that he has a destiny is not in doubt.

Chapter 7

The Expedition

Life continued to improve in the kingdom of Westerland; no troubles of any consequence had been reported in the villages by the headsmen, and it could now boast that they had the finest herds of cattle in memory. The foresters told of the continued increase in quality game, especially the deer and wild boar. With the millers more than happy with the excellent good grade corn, the families were able to eat and work well with a determination to continue this time of prosperity.

It was now a year since Horn took the Princess Cleona as his wife, and much of this feeling of well being throughout the kingdom could be attributed to the happiness of the royal couple, which was evident to all on their visits to the villages. The people were always reluctant to say goodbye and followed them out of the village for quite a distance before returning to their homes. This first tour lasted almost a month before a decision was made to return to the castle, as arrangements were being made for a great feast to celebrate the first year of the marriage. Nothing would be spared to show the royal couple the great esteem they were held in by the whole population. Chancellor Ancour kept everyone on their toes; nothing escaped his critical eye, and the unfortunate member of the household who was found not giving of their best received the full fury of his sharp tongue. Lord Grenden's overall supervision of the all pageantry, mostly involving Knights of the Unicorn and the castle garrison, ensured they rehearsed until he was satisfied that indeed it was perfection. The giant Greg was given the task of arranging his men of foot into orderly ranks; he did not have to repeat his orders. The respect his men had for him was sufficient, for to be the cause of a reprimand was not to be contemplated by the youngest or even the veterans under his command.

Dog had finally won the love and the hand of the lovely daughter of the huntsman in the last few months. This lovely creature was Althreda. Her father and brothers arranged to hold the marriage before the departure of the royal couple's tour of the villagers. It was at the castle, to which the royal family and almost the entire court and household attended. The service, conducted by Bishop Stelid, was followed by the traditional feast. Before the musicians and performers took over, Horn rose to his feet with the Chancellor, banging the table for silence. He honoured the happy couple, in particular extolling the exploits of Dog in his speech, referring to him as 'my companion in arms' and 'my honourable Knight.' Lord Grenden also paid a handsome tribute to Dog, recalling that first occasion on the field against the Irish Kings. He told of the sight of Dog in the thick of the fighting, giving no quarter in spite of his obvious youth. He could see then that there was indeed a warrior in the making, and he had since proved just that. Dog was, for once, overcome by the occasion, as he almost mumbled his response to Horn and the Lord, but expressed his great and humble thanks for the honour of recognition by Horn and the people of Westerland over the last two years. To the once anxious father and brothers of Elthreda, this marriage was indeed welcomed, as she had recently given birth to a son and named him Redweld, on account of his fiery red hair, which was surprisingly long at birth. This was something that Dog had never dreamed of, considering his unfortunate start in life. He had been unwanted, unloved, and committed petty misdemeanours, which one day would have led to the gallows outside the castle walls.

The arrival of the chief scout Malvin at the gates ahead of the royal party galvanised the waiting organisers of the planned reception into action, and as the vanguard entered the gates to report to Lord Grenden, he gave the order to the Commanders to take up their allotted positions in the courtyard. In minutes the procedures which had been so carefully rehearsed were put into action. The chorus of two horns from the battlements heralded the first sight of Horn and Cleona, now riding at the head of their escort, and that was the signal for the entire inhabitants who could make it to vie for the best positions in which to see their King and Queen arrive.

This caused much work for Greg and his footmen, keeping them back from filling the entire courtyard, but at last he managed to exercise control over the excited crowds, giving a clear passage to the grand hall. Queen Aethena, with Lord Grenden, Chancellor, and the Secretary, made their way to meet them as they dismounted, the crowds making much noise. Everywhere one looked, there was genuine joy written on the faces of the people.

Having acknowledged the salute of the Dog and the Knights of the Unicorn, who had greeted them as the guard of honour, Horn turned to his mother, embracing her warmly. Aethena then kissed Cleona and took her hand in hers, leading her to the hall. Banners flew from every vantage point, displaying the emblem of the Unicorn, the national symbol of the kingdom of Westerland. As if in salute, the fresh breeze filled the silk so that they fluttered proudly, uncurled for all to see. Horn, Cleona, and the royal party entered the grand hall to be greeted by the courtiers in their finery, and after the exchange of formal greetings, the royal couple made their way back to the main doors.

Standing on the steps, he spoke to the waiting and still cheering crowds. "Good people of Westerland, the Queen and I thank you for this great welcome on our homecoming. It is sufficient to say that our visit to the villages in the kingdom were a source of joy. We were shown a strong unity and loyalty to the crown, and the reception here today proves that we are indeed a nation committed to the welfare of each family. Other kingdoms are aware of our strength, and only the foolish would now think of invading our land. Under our Commanders we have the finest fighting force ever to be seen for many generations. Again, I thank you for your loyalty to me and the Queen, and our wish is that we shall see peace for many years to come."

Then Horn and Cleona turned and entered the hall with the cries of the enthusiastic crowds ringing throughout the castle. "Horn! Horn of Westerland!"

The whole court took up the cry as they entered. The royal party then retired to their chambers to rest from their journey, the couple alone for a brief moment before bathing and changing travelling clothes for the splendour and finery of the court. The royal servants of the chamber made the final adjustments to their royal regalia and crowns for the feast to come later.

The horn sounded the arrival of the couple to the grand hall and they descended the staircase to yet another welcome as they took their place at the long table. The feast began at dusk; the flickering rushes in their iron holders burning in the hall cast friendly shadows over the people at the tables as the hurrying servants began their everlasting chain of food and wine to the expectant guests. The huge wooden platters were laden with roast hog, venison, swan, geese, and a great assortment of small fowl, surrounded by choice fruit. The great barrels of ale, which had been previously rolled in and set up in their frames at the end of each table, kept the servants busy with the constant replenishing of the drinking vessels, as their thirsty owners banged loudly on the table to attract attention. As the evening wore on, the tiring servants were still kept busy with demands for more ale or wine, the shouting becoming louder. With forty people to a table, there would be little respite until the guests began to slump on their seats, as they inevitably would in time honoured custom.

The royal party bade the guests farewell as they made their way from the hall to their chambers, and with Dog and his Althreda also leaving the hall for their apartments, the feast drew to a close. Gradually, all that remained of the great assembly in the hall were the few who could not be roused or carried away; they would awake there with stiffening joints from unnatural slumbering positions, a head that seemed to be at the mercy of a heavy hammer, and, for a few, the scolding of a wife who had to make her own way home.

The castle, now recovering from the celebrations, slowly resumed its normal activities. Tradesmen were at their benches and smiths were in their iron works. Women washed in the stream, and the court sat to review local matters. The training in military tactics was always a permanent feature, with the younger men anxious to join their fathers or brothers. Particular attention was paid to those who showed a talent for either the sword or spear. When a special gift was discovered, such as that of a natural marksman with the bow, then the young man was taken in hand by the senior archers. The more fortunate boys were given the chance to qualify for the elite household guard, which would allow them a few extra privileges. They could possibly, one day, catch the King's eye.

Thoughts were now turned to other issues. The new relationship through the Treaty with Collona seem to be working smoothly, and many visits by merchants from both kingdoms resulted in a steady flow of goods in mutual demand, which benefited all. The women of Collona had devised a hand loom which was capable of producing exceedingly fine woven cloth, and this was in great demand by the women of Westerland, who, themselves, were experts in dying this cloth with a variety of beautiful colours using vegetable dyes with age old skills.

Ambassadors between Westerland and Collona now proved beneficial to both kingdoms. Lord Sancto, who had been originally appointed as the consul to Collona, was now replaced with the young Knight Alfud, who had been selected for his pleasing manner, coupled with his knowledge, through his merchant father, of trading outside the kingdom. He was also on good terms with Prince Aelman's son Eapden, who had held the office since the exchange of consuls and the treaty between Horn and King Aeden.

The kingdom of Collona had not suffered any further attacks by the Kishlanders since their defeat by Horn's army, and in view of the treaty now existing between them, this ex-enemy was fully aware of the consequences should they be tempted to invade again. The neighbouring kingdom of Preyden to the north had shown no further inclination to cross the border since their great loss of men in the ill fated alliance against Horn. The Preyden lookouts had seen the build up of the strong outposts near their borders which were manned. The scout Malvin and his team visited these posts as part of their role and kept the lookouts on their toes, introducing a weapon check which he carried out on these visits. Although there was a period of quiet peace, there was to be no easing or relaxing of the state of readiness, which Lord Grenden would expect from all sections of the army. Anyone who was charged with the responsibility of a section would, in the event of an invasion or an assault, be severely punished should they be taken unawares by an enemy.

This then was the standard of efficiency which the military had now attained under Lord Grenden and Horn. Such a force could match any aggressor, whether it be within the kingdom or a foreign invader. Thus, the word was spread of the men of Westerland and their particular fighting qualities: their experienced Commanders; Knights who gave no quarter; men on foot with bow and spear, led by a fearsome red bearded giant, who towered above all, wielding a giant sword that took a terrible toll; their King, a warrior; and his companion of most strange countenance that fought with animal ferocity and a magic axe. Many songs were written and put into verse to sing at their feasts by their women, while these men banged their drinking vessels on the table.

The men of Westerland led by Horn,
warriors from hell, of the devil born,
beware their steel or spear or bow,
or lose your head and blood will flow.

No place to run, no place to hide,
It is written why men have died,
They crossed the path of Westerland
And met their fate at Horn's hand.

It was just this reputation spreading throughout the kingdoms over recent years that ensured the people of Westerland the opportunity to enjoy their lives. Threats of invasion were now removed in the border villages. Most had been overwhelmed many times and were always the first to suffer; life could not be better.

Another year passed and a fine day with blue skies heralded another peaceful day ahead at the castle. A hunt had been arranged in Wavelon Forest. Horn, Dog, and the Knights were in good spirits, looking forward to a good chase. Boar and deer were the main quarry. Servants scurried about, leading horses to the riders. Dogs were barking or whining in excitement at the prospect of a good run with the hunt, and all was ready to move off when the gates opened in readiness of the first rush of dogs and riders.

The sound of the horn stopped the hunt at the gates. The guards rushed forward to intercept a group of riders heading for the castle and to ask the nature of their mission. After a few minutes, the captain of the guard walked quickly to Horn, still astride his horse.

"Sire, there is a party of riders from the kingdom of Laswindel, which is over the sea to the west. They had been given permission to cross our land by our scouts at the outposts; they are bearing urgent messages for you alone, Sire."

Horn dismounted, dismissed the hunt, and returned to the grand hall, ordering the visitors to be divested of their weapons for the period of their stay. After the guard carried this order, the strangers were escorted to the hall where Horn had summoned Lord Grenden, and Dog to attend him while he received the men from Laswindel and discovered their business deemed to be so urgent.

Their spokesman was Prince Attaga, the eldest son of King Plachan. His small escort party were Knights of his father's household bodyguard. After formal greetings, the Prince handed Horn a personal petition from his father. Opening the scroll, Horn beckoned Lord Grenden to also read the message it contained.

"Sire, this petition of my father, the King, in which he begs for your help. You are our last hope; even now it may be too late. The Irish have invaded our land with a large army in the north of our kingdom. They are led by the war leader called Brinian, who most thought had not escaped your army when his force was wiped out here in Westerland."

Horn studied the face of the young Prince, whom he guessed was his own age. Anxiety was stamped on his features, genuine desperation was only too evident, and he obviously wanted to return to his own land as soon as possible. Horn spoke to Lord Grenden; there were nodding of heads in agreement.

Horn addressed the Prince. "The invasion of your island and the savaging of your women and children by the Irishman Brinian is regrettable. The evil invader is one with whom we have a longstanding score to settle. My Prince, you will get our support. We can muster an army in a day. The main drawback, which may cause undue delay, is the question of ships. We do not have many of the west coast ourselves, not enough to carry an army. We would have to able to land in force if the Irish have occupied the north coast."

"Sire, that would not be a problem. My father, knowing your reputation and common hatred of the Irish, had already ordered his fleet to stand off from your coast near Lockney, and this can be available to you as soon as you require it."

Horn told his Lord to call the Commanders at once so that they would be able to leave as an army by first light. As the dawn came, the sound of men could be heard checking their weapons. Commanders took stock of their men mustered in the courtyard. A force of three thousand men were assembled, and Horn expected that they would be joined by another thousand as they passed through the villages. It would rest on Malvin, who went ahead the previous evening with a call to arms, and the rest would be up the village leader to have their men ready.

Horn and Lord Grenden decided that the army would divide into three divisions when they arrived on the shores of Laswindel. Horn himself would take the first division, with Dog as his second in command, the giant Greg, a company of footmen, twenty archers and the engineer Torvic. Lord Grenden would take the second division with the Knight Elvil as second in command, a choice of men of foot, and twelve selected archers. Lord Sancto was given the third division with the Knight Briscal as second in command, and a company of men and archers. There had been some slight dissention among the men who thought the third division, being the last chosen, would not be as strong as the other two. Lord Sancto stepped in to remind them that each man would do his best, and that reputations could be made in the forthcoming expedition which would serve them well. It was also decided to leave the Knights of the Unicorn at the castle in charge of the main defence and to guard the royal family.

The order came for the army to leave, and all divisions being ready, they left and streamed through the gate on their way to the west coast and Lockney.

It was clear Malvin had done his job well; men left their homes to join the army as it passed through their village, some calling out to familiar faces with much light-hearted banter on spotting old comrades of previous battles. As they approached Lockney, the scouts were sent on to the coast to confirm that the fleet was indeed to be seen lying offshore, and the men were ordered to eat and rest before boarding for the sea journey, estimated to be about two hours with a favourable breeze, or over three hours with oars.

The scouts returned to confirm that the ships were of good size and were now moving towards the shore to take on board the army; all was as Prince Attaga had stated at the castle. The men moved out and within a short time reached the coast and began to board. As each ship reached its quota of men, it moved out to sea and anchored, to wait for the whole operation to be complete before sailing. Some men had to be left behind, but they were told to stand by for the return of the ships, which would take five hours. The main army on the shores of Laswindel would await them before moving into the kingdom.

As the crossing was indeed choppy, those men overcome with sickness were placed at the rear of the ship, as on arrival they would not be fit to fight on landing, if that proved necessary. They would have time to recover their feet before the last of the men arrived. Horn had hoped that their landing on the east coast of the island would be unchallenged, as they had heard that the Irish had invaded the north-west coast, being the shortest sea route for them. This would give Horn time to assemble the army in its three divisions, without having to engage the enemy in battle on landing.

Prince Attaga had chosen the landing area well; it was near perfect with the men able to wade ashore and onto a firm beach, enabling the non-swimmers to gain land comfortably and join their division. No horses had been shipped in the interest of space, and all would march on foot. Any Commander could take a horse, provided it was given, not stolen or acquired by force. Although, Prince Attaga had assured Lord Grenden that his people would be happy to give horses to drive away the Irishmen.

Lord Grenden awaited the arrival of the last men on the second ships before giving his final orders, then allotted them to their divisions. He lost no time in getting them in to marching order. Horn's division was to go straight to the castle, hopefully not yet under siege. Lord Grenden was to take his division to the right and north, with Lord Sancto and his force would make towards the left and north, the idea being, if the enemy was still in the north-west, it would be faced by the Lords Grenden and Sancto in a pincer movement. The scouts were sent ahead in the three designated directions. Malvin went towards the castle, and Fenner went ahead of Lord Grenden's force, while Boarset took the route ahead of Lord Sancto's march to the left and north. Each scout would take two others to act as runners to the divisions, to report the first sighting of the enemy. They all had to avoid contact with the Laswindel people.

Horn and Dog started their march towards the centre of the island and the castle, where it was expected King Plachan would be, according to his son, the Prince. He also confirmed that the defences had been strengthened to withstand a siege of a few days. The army stood at five hundred trained men. The castle would be the natural target of the Irish if they defeated the Laswindel army, which was reported to be in the region of three thousand strong. Prince Attaga believed from earlier sightings the army were already engaging the enemy a few miles inland, in the northern province. The Prince chose to stay with Horn's division with the hope they would reach the castle before the Irish, and support his father in what would be a major assault should his army fail to hold or defeat Brinian in the field.

The first scout to make a sighting was Boarset, who had seen a group of the Irish attacking a village near the coast. They were estimated to be two miles from their main force who were locked in battle with the Laswindel army. Acting on this information, Lord Sancto gave orders to step up the pace of their march to meet the enemy at this village and deal with them before they could rejoin their comrades at the battle. As they neared the village, the sounds of a desperate encounter could be heard, the screams of women as their men were being hacked down rose above the noise of this unequal battle. Lord Sancto split his men into three sections to surround and attack the Irish, allowing none to escape to give warning that the Westerland army had joined forces with Laswindel.

At a given signal, when the three sections were in position, they closed all escape routes and moved in to encircle the enemy. Every hut was entered as the Irish were taken by surprise; those that were in the lanes or spilled out of the huts were quickly eliminated; none survived, and within minutes it was over. Lord Sancto ordered the bodies of the enemy to be hidden in the nearby copse, and the survivors in the village were told to disperse into the countryside until the enemy army was far enough away from their homes or was defeated. Only three men were wounded in the attack, and then not seriously, mainly cuts which were treated on the spot. Then the Lord rested his men before moving on towards the main enemy force that Boarset had reported were two miles to the north-west.

The scout then sent on one of his men to report to Horn of the skirmish at the village, and Lord Sancto would await the sight of Lord Grenden division before taking any further action. Horn, now nearing the castle and not meeting any of the enemy, sent on Prince Attaga and his party to join his father and inform him of the supporting Westerlanders now in the kingdom.

Two divisions would be joining his army in the battle now reported in the north, and he should halt their advance to the castle. Malvin, now in contact with Horn and Dog, informed them that the Irish had advanced a few miles, and the Laswindel army were suffering heavy losses; many dead could be seen strewn over quite a distance. This meant that soon they would be in a serious position, and on the point of retreat towards the castle. In the meantime, Lord Grenden had arrived from the east and his scouts linked up with Lord Sancto, enabling both divisions to now move in to engage the enemy.

On arrival at the battlefield, it was seen at once that the Irish were in control on this uneven conflict, which was obviously beginning to develop into a running battle, with men leaving the field when able. Lord Sancto decided to attack at once while Lord Grenden would make his assault further down the field. The Irish, seeing a new force approaching them, would turn to face the new threat, enabling his men to engage them from the rear. The attack by Lord Sancto was directed to the Irish right wing, most of which had been held in reserve and were relatively fresh. Sancto's men, sweeping over a small hill which had given them excellent cover, were at the surprised Irish before they realised that this was not part of the Laswindel army. His archers, first loosing their volleys over the heads of their comrades, struck the enemy unawares.

The toll was inevitable, the sun glinting on sword blades being used with devastating effect as they bit into the unorganised ranks of the startled enemy, causing them to be isolated into small groups. This attack of such speed had taken away their natural ability to stand and counter a normal charge. Within fifteen minutes after that first volley of arrows, the Irish reserve force was practically eliminated or running back to join their main army. Regrouping was not an option as their commander had been one of the first casualties. Lord Sancto's men surrounded the last few still showing fight, and it was only a matter of time before they succumbed, leaving him the chance now to advance towards the main army, leaving six hundred of the Irish dead on the field.

Earlier, Brinian, pleased with his ongoing success in the battle, had sent a thousand men to the area of the castle to await his arrival as soon as the Laswindel army was beaten on the field or enough of them had deserted, leaving himself in command of some three thousand, which he considered enough to finish the remainder of the Laswindel men. The Irish sent from the field by their leader did not encounter Lord Grenden's division, who moving up fast, fell upon the rear ranks of the enemy, while Lord Sancto had suddenly appeared at their front to join the still fighting Laswindels.

Brinian realised he had made a mistake in sending off a thousand men, as he now faced a major attack on two fronts; he could see that the new attacking force wore the brown jackets of the Westerland army. He noted, with alarm, the speed with which his men were being pushed back with heavy losses. From what had been an almost concluding victory for him, it had now turned into a battle with a foe of considerable strength, and well trained men who had fought him before. The Irish, elated by their earlier success, were thrown into confusion, their Commanders shouting and cursing them into action; the sight of the well armed Westerlanders bearing down on them was too much for some of enemy. Their leaders, trying to regroup into formation to counter the attack, could not rally the men into anything likely to stop the advance of Lord Sancto. Elvil the Knight was ordered to take on the men of foot. Lord Grenden, in command of his Knights and archers, decided to attack the section directly under the command of Brinian himself.

A hard fight was soon in progress, although the archers had created panic and caused many casualties. The main force of Lord Grenden were now heavily engaged in hand to hand combat with the enemy; spear, sword and axe clashed with oaths and cries of the stricken were heard as the battle increased in its intensity. The Irish somehow began to settle themselves after the initial surprise, and fought hard to get on equal terms with a superior force bent on destroying them. For a while they held their own, until it was seen that a small section had broken off from the battle in the thick of the fighting.

Intent on fleeing the field, a large party headed by Brinian moved at a fast pace towards the dense woodland to the east. Lord Grenden, told of this development, realised the Irish leader had assessed his position as dangerous, and to remain with his army might result in his capture and death; his only chance was to join the thousand men he had sent to the castle area. His army might be able to fight their way out of trouble; he could not take that chance. Grenden sent off two hundred men to follow and delay, if possible, their progress to join up with their men. Lord Sancto's division was now facing a wilting enemy, with many trying to escape in all directions, chased by eager men who showed no mercy. The battle was now drawing to a close; the enemy had suffered huge losses, throwing down their weapons, though many were still put to the sword by men high with the lust for blood. The Irish army in the field had ceased to be a viable opposition. The fleeing men signalled the end of the battle.

The two Westerland divisions had taken a massive toll in their encounters with the enemy, well over a thousand had fallen in the last battle. Added to their loss of the reserve force by Lord Sancto's men, and their attack on the Irish in the village much earlier, this left them with fast dwindling numbers. Lord Grenden, conferring with Lord Sancto, came to the conclusion that the enemy's losses were over two and a half thousand men to the present. This meant that apart from a few hundred deserters, the remainder of the Irish, possibly now in the castle area, would still pose a threat if those deserters managed to join up with them. He was confident, however, that with Horn's division at the castle unbeknown to the enemy, their combined strength would be too much for him. He would be outnumbered in total and was confident that Horn's division, with the garrison of five hundred, could hold them off if attacked before their two divisions arrived.

A rest was ordered for the men and food was distributed as they rejoined their divisions. The wounded were attended to by Ruckle and his magical dressings. Later, they would be escorted to the nearest village to be placed under the protection of the headman; the fifty Westerland men lost in the battle were buried nearby.

It was planned to march at dawn. Fenner was sent on ahead to locate the enemy near the castle, which was the thousand sent by Brinian earlier. These men had been seen resting in a woodland, awaiting their leader's arrival before their assault on the castle. Lord Grenden estimated that Brinian, on the run, would not make contact with these men until much later in the evening, possibly after dark. Therefore, he would arrange his plans to attack the castle at the earliest the next morning, but not until he had as many of the fleeing men that were attempting to reach his force as possible. The Irish Commander had to then organise his men into an army capable of conducting an assault on the castle.

He, of course, was unaware that his army had been virtually destroyed, and had hoped if even they had been defeated, there would be enough men retreating from the combat to be able to muster at the woodland within a matter of hours. Lord Grenden hoped to be in a striking position of Brinian's men by midday with the superior divisions which the Irish could not match. The training and discipline of his army would prove to be final death knell of the Irish invaders. Dog was given the command of the surviving Laswindel men, their numbers a few hundred. They had seen Dog in action on the field and were prepared to follow him anywhere. To them he was one of their godlike heroes and a legend, even in their kingdom.

Horn, at the castle, had been informed of the result of the battle by Malvin, and that an Irish force was encamped in the woodland within one mile from the castle, being joined at odd intervals by deserters from the main battle. All this did not alarm him, as Fenner had also arrived to report the final demise of the Irish main army. The relatively small losses by the Lords Grenden and Sancto meant that they still had a superior advantage of men to deal with Brinian and could possibly destroy him before he attacked the castle. The defences had been inspected for weaknesses, and the result was good enough to withstand a major assault by a much larger force than the Irishman could raise.

The two divisions were now making their way east towards the castle. They had the option of either locating Brinian and attacking him at his position in the woodland, or making straight for the castle. Or, they could combine their total strength for a final battle with the Irish war leader at the castle itself, or better still, on the open field. The scouts, now near the woodland, reported that there was no sign of activity in the woods, which would have indicated the preparation of the building of siege machines by their engineers, but the fact that they were near the forest meant that they had access to the necessary timber.

In spite of this, Horn made sure the castle was defendable; no effort had been spared to maximize defensive strength. The right men were at the right places; boys were trained to collect sound arrows and missiles while under attack, and to keep the supply of water at a state of readiness. As a last resort, these boys were also given a short course in weapons and combat in order to join the defenders if the enemy gained a foothold in the castle.

Now there was an air of confidence that spread through the garrison from the Commanders to the footmen, and the people of Laswindel praised the name of Horn and the fighting men of Westerland, who had answered their desperate call for help without delay. Their own army had fought so bravely in the north of the kingdom and had delayed the Irishmen in their march to the castle until the timely arrival of the two divisions led by the Lords. King Plachan and Prince Attaga now felt that with Horn in command of all the forces outside and inside the castle, their worst fears were hopefully not to be realised. It was a few days ago that they had faced the prospect of their army being totally defeated, and Brinian storming the castle with the horrifying results that would follow: savage slaughter, mutilation, rape, wholesale looting, and the loss of the kingdom to the Irish Kings.

Horn sent out Malvin to contact Lord Grenden, to warn him of the position of Brinian, and to urge him not to engage in any fight unless it was absolutely necessary, but to return to the castle with all speed. He was convinced that it was better to wait until they had the strength of all three divisions with which to defend the castle or attack the enemy before they could launch a serious assault against them.

It was unknown to Horn that Brinian and his army were about to be followed by a second invasion force, already sailing to the north-east of the island, that would be landing soon. This army would march to the woodland to the appointed meeting place, as had been arranged by Brinian.

To offset this, Brinian himself did not know of Horn's occupation of the castle or the strength of the Westerland army; he only was aware of the force that had attacked his men in the north. This was the reason he was in no hurry to attack the castle; it did not offer much of a threat; he could await for the second force. It would be easier to take the castle with his superior number of men whenever he wished.

The scouts, returning to the castle, reported increasing activity in the woodland by the enemy, who seemed to be in good spirits. There were now the sounds of trees being felled, not doubt for battering rams, and machines for hurling stones. This news did not disturb Horn, as he had assumed that the enemy would use all means at their disposal to take the castle, but they first had to overcome his best men, who were eager and ready to deal with Brinian and his men. Boarset the scout had been sent to the north-east of the island by Lord Sancto to make sure there were no stragglers left in that area after the battle with Brinian's reserve force, which had been eliminated earlier. As he neared the coastline, he spotted three of the enemy waiting there, looking intently seaward. Settling down to watch without drawing attention to himself, he became aware that the men had leapt to their feet and danced about with each other in great excitement at something they had seen out at sea. He did not have long to wait to see the cause of their celebration, for there on the skyline and quite visible was a fleet of ships making for the shore. Boarset, counting as he looked, estimated that it totalled over forty, and were crowded with the figures of men. The three men rushed down to the shoreline and began waving their arms furiously towards the ships to guide them to the landing point.

The scout realized that this was an invasion fleet, and carrying possibly as many as two thousand men. Maybe, there could other ships carrying men and horses not yet in view. He made the decision to catch up with Lord Sancto's division already on its way to the castle. Lord Grenden had received the message from Horn not to engage the enemy at the forest on his way to the castle. Speeding up his march gave the woodland a wide berth, and at the same time, it kept all noise at a minimum.

Boarset caught up with Lord Sancto and gave him the news of the invasion force making for the coast. Listening to his scout, he was tempted to march north again and attack the Irish as they landed, but discretion prevailed, and he continued his speedy journey eastwards to the castle. Boarset returned to the coast to watch the arrival of the enemy. Lord Grenden arrived at the castle ahead of Sancto's division, who were some three hours behind, reporting at once to Horn, who made arrangements for a general meeting on Santco's arrival.

The news of the Irish force from Lord Sancto came as a surprise to Horn, but he was still convinced his three divisions would be more than match for Brinian and his new reinforcements. Horn agreed at the meeting with his Lords and Commanders that they should allow the new Irish force to proceed unhindered to the woodland. Whether they met them on the field, or in their advance on the castle, was not an overriding problem. Allowing them to become one army, they could then destroy this common enemy once and for all. On the orders of Lord Grenden, extra lookouts were posted, covering a wide area so that all movement of Brinian's men could be observed, and also the arrival of the new invaders from the coast.

Boarset watched this new force of Irish as they disembarked and waded ashore, forming up under their Commanders. He noted that they seemed confident as though not expecting a hard fight, unaware of the Westerland army in the kingdom. The three Irishmen on the coast had not been involved in the battle, but had been sent to await their ships, so the knowledge of the defeat and destruction of many of their comrades would have dampened their high spirits. He also noted the presence of a conspicuous leader among the first to land. A horse was brought to him; he mounted immediately and turned to face the men, raising his sword he shouted, "Ealcane! For Ealcane!"

This was the name of the Irish King who had been seen to be hit by Fretwin's arrow when he fled the shores of Westerland during their ill fated invasion of King Alymer's kingdom. His men responded to the name with the energetic brandishing of their weapons, giving Boarset the feeling that this was not going to be an easy fight. He could see the men were in the mood for battle; their weapons looked newly forged, and he counted at least three hundred archers. Other men carried spears of the unusual length of ten feet or more, to be used in formation fighting; this was a new development in attack, and particularly effective against horses. This then was a force who had come prepared to fight! The enemy began their march towards the woodland, which would take about two hours at normal pace, making sure to avoid the few villages on the route. Their object was to arrive there without any interruptions or diversions which could result in the loss of men and time. Time to loot later!

The scout had gleaned enough information on the enemy force, so he left when they reached a point some ten miles from the woodland. He made good time passing between his fellow scouts out in the field, warning them of the enemy's route to Brinian's camp. At the castle he was taken at once to Horn and the Commanders, and he gave an account of all he had witnessed, laying emphasis on the condition of the enemy force, which was not raggle-taggle, but well armed and in good heart.

Horn was interested to hear that the name of King Ealcane had been used as a cry of encouragement by their commander, as all were convinced the King had been killed by Fretwin's arrow on board his ship. All this was not good news to the men of Westerland on hearing of the new force of invaders. It was expected that the men on their way to join Brinian would have been of a lower standard than his original force. These were obviously not, and although it was reputed to be less than two thousand, it was going to be a harder fight than first thought by Horn and his Lords. They could not just sally forth and engage

Brinian; new plans would have to be made, and quickly. Horn spoke to his Commanders.

"Well, my Lords, this news means a change of tactics. We had agreed that we would attack Brinian as soon as his new force arrived at the woodland, and before they were in a position to attack the castle. Whilst I think we will be the victors, I also think it would be unwise to risk losing men at this stage."

Lord Grenden and the Lords disagreed. "Sire, we can match the enemy in numbers, and our fighting men have the quality. I believe we would be more than a match for him. Why not let him proceed with his attempt to take the castle? We will, at that point, have lost no men. Many have tried to assault us before in our kingdom; we are well practised in the defence of castles. They, I am sure, will suffer losses so great, they will turn tail and attempt to scurry back to their ships."

Horn answered his Commanders. "You have a point there, my Lords. We are fully prepared to withstand a serious attack; surprise is with us; our enemy knows nothing of our strength. He is sure in the belief he has only have the garrison and the King's bodyguard to attack. And the encounter in the north with his force earlier would leave him to believe he could outnumber us comfortably."

Lord Sancto agreed, but raised the prospect that, by now, Brinian would have guessed that as the survivors of his original force he had left to contain the battle had not arrived back to join him, they must have been heavily beaten. The very few pockets of deserters arriving and making contact with him would confirm this. This meant he would decide to move on to the castle as soon as the new force arrived and were organised into assault groups. So, it was likely to be an attack or siege. At least the defences had been arranged to cause the enemy serious losses of men in any attempt to reach the battlements.

Within the castle all was now in a state of high readiness, Horn felt confident. Wherever he looked, he could see men eager to get to grips with the Irish again, especially those that had made their way with Horn's division and had not yet tasted battle on this expedition. *Time*, he thought, *for the veterans to renew their talents.* As he passed a young fresh face youth of no more than sixteen, his face, in a huge grin, portrayed the mood of his men, and he felt good. He thought of Dog and the giant Greg pawing at the ground, almost champing at the bit like horses about to be given the order to charge into the enemy. They were inspired leaders of the men of Westerland, proven warriors who would rally onto the field, striking fear into those that stood against them.

King Plachan and Prince Attaga shared Horn's confidence, and their men were ready to play their part in defending the castle. First, the King and his bodyguard would protect the royal family within the keep, and Prince Attaga was to be in charge of the Laswindel garrison, positioned in the inner courtyard, but under the overall command of Lord Sancto, who would be in the main courtyard of the castle and acting as a reserve to his men.

Great activity outside the castle brought the garrison to alert, as Malvin the scout arrived at the gates with the news that the Irish force in the woodland area were in celebratory mood, making much noise and laughter. This was the welcome to the newly arrived invaders from the coast, the woodland ringing with the sound of their greeting. The thoughts of these men matched their confidence. Soon they would be carrying off the great store of recently reported treasures as victors, and returning home with as much as they can carry, while their leaders squabbled over the division of the land.

Horn listened to Malvin's report and decided it was time to take action within a few hours. Their earlier plan to attack Brinian and draw him out into the field, rather than wait for him to assault the castle, could work in their favour. Lords Grenden and Sancto were called at once and told of the revised plan of attack. Horn gave the order to assemble all the army in the main courtyard in a state of readiness.

The command of the castle defences was to be under the command of Lord Sancto and his Knight Briscal, with Prince Attaga in the courtyard, and the King and the royal bodyguard in support. This was an adequate force to hold off an assault from a small force that might slip through unnoticed. Horn was to take command of the first division, with Dog as his second in command. They would be with the giant Greg and his company of footmen. They would be strengthened by a company of one hundred archers and a similar section of spearmen, renowned for the attainment of distance. Lord Grenden was to take the second division with his Knight Richel, supported by the two other Knights with a strong force of footmen, plus one hundred archers, almost in like fashion to the original divisions in the early landing on the island.

The familiar and comforting sound of rattling and clinking of steel echoed within the castle walls as men checked their weapons and adjusted the leather straps, looking for any weakness in their equipment. Horn, as always, looked at the faces of the men, and, as always, could see the eagerness and the brisk body movements as they went about their preparations to once more face their despised enemy. The order came for the army to move out of the gate, the scouts being sent on ahead to the area around the woodland to gather the latest information on Brinian's movements, and his intended attack on the castle. Dog, riding alongside Horn, found it hard to conceal his excitement to be in action again.

With his now famous attempt at a grin, he said, "My Liege, my arms do tremble to take the sword against the Irish. I fear my strength has been ebbing away for want of the challenge. The training and tournaments are not designed to raise the blood. I need this campaign to affirm my standing as your Knight."

Horn smiled and looked at Dog. "Dog, there is no other that I would share an hour, or even a day, with in the field, in sport or war. I know you well enough that at the sight, sound and smell of action, you become a warrior of such excellence that it is wonderful to behold, and a tonic for the men."

Lord Grenden rode over to Horn saying, "Sire, there is a small ridge two miles ahead that would easily provide adequate concealment for our forces. It is in the direct route that Brinian would take to the castle, and Sire, it would be easy for him to assume that he had no opposition in that area. He would not have his army in anything like battle formation until he was within a mile of the castle. So, striking quickly from the ridge we would throw his army into confusion. He would suffer a great loss of men before he, or his commanders, could gain control over their army."

Horn could see the logic of Lord Grenden's plan. "I agree, my Lord, but when we attack, I want Dog to remain at the ridge with five hundred men. He will, when it seems the enemy might turn tail, move round the ridge and take them from the rear, thereby causing greater confusion and panic."

And so the trap would be set, and they waited for the return of the scouts as the two divisions approached the ridge taking up their positions. Orders were given for restrained silence and no unnecessary talking or movements to attract the attention of any of the enemy scouts. Horn, looking at the blue cloudless sky, realised that when they attacked Brinian's army, the Irishmen would have the sun full in their faces, which would work to his advantage. Men having to squint with half closed eyes could not defend themselves from every angle against the sword, and would be an easy target for the archers, whose volleys would come from out of the sky itself, unseen. The pincer movement of the two division would create an encircling situation around the enemy, who would, in panic, find himself attempting to fight on two sides. He would have no time to put himself into a defensive position from which he could withstand an attack before he was overcome completely. Horn's army lay resting but on alert to form up immediately when the scouts reported Brinian's approach. It became difficult to resist the temptation to swat the curious flies that buzzed over the sweating men for fear of the movement being seen.

Chapter 8

The Ridge

The scouts returned to confirm that the celebrations by the enemy were now over, and there were positive signs that they were preparing to move out of the woodland almost at any time. This meant Brinian could be at the ridge within a hour, albeit not in disciplined order, emerging from the woodland in groups in jocular manner, pushing or tripping each other over in a playful mood, amid much laughter. Horn's plan to trap them at the ridge was based on the possibility that the major part of the Irish army would be on the march, and any small sections following on could soon be dealt with. Good news came from the scouts who told of their discovering, and dealing with, an enemy scout half a mile from the woodland, and he was acting alone.

The sun blazed down on the ridge; some of the men began to feel uncomfortable and needed to look for shade. Some needed a respite from the swarm of annoying flies constantly buzzing, adding to their discomfort, but orders had to be kept. No talking or sudden movements. The Commanders reminded their men that they might be hot, sweaty and bored, but the approaching enemy would be more unguarded. Their senses would be dulled by the heat and not alert, at least not until they passed the ridge and neared the castle, when they would then take up their assault formations. The scouts were correct in their report that the Irish were on the move in mass and were now a quarter of a mile way, without any forward scouts. Brinian was confident that he only had the castle garrison to deal with. Even a well trained and confident army can be taken unawares while its mind is obsessed with its objectives. They only required an unexpected and sudden change by the enemy to throw it into a momentarily state of confusion and panic.

The men waiting at the ridge gripped their weapons, their sweat partially fouling their sword hilts. The archers, who had been ordered to stay at the top of the ridge when the action began, left their bows idle and arrows in their quivers. This was to ensure they were ready when called to be in a state to launch volley after volley of arrows at the enemy with a firm pull and to loose them with strength.

At last the enemy could now be seen approaching; their banter could now be heard, even curses as someone tripped over a gorse root or got caught up in the straggling brambles and had to painfully release themselves from the thorns. At the head of this army rode the leader on a black horse in the midst of what looked like an ambling mass of men in no great hurry but with high expectation. They were noisy and playful; their weapons, sheathed, swung against their legs.

Perfect! thought Horn. It was as he had hoped. As the mass of men passed on either side of the ridge, which stretched nearly half a mile, he gave the order to attack. The Westerlanders swept down, a line of determined men as the archers let loose with a terrifying hail of arrows into the startled enemy.

Taken completely by surprise, the Irish had no time to organise themselves, but they desperately fought for their lives. They were caught out in the open with no protection, the blazing sun in their faces. The slaughter was inevitable and on a horrendous scale; many threw down their weapons to indicate that they no longer wished to fight. Greg's footmen mopped up these unfortunate men, taking on two at time himself. His magnificent new axe, which he named 'Goddess,' swung and flashed among the heads of the enemy. His height ensured that many of his victims were cleanly decapitated if they strayed into its path. Meanwhile, Horn and Grenden, in their divisions, engaged the oncoming Irishmen, pushing forward into the thick of the masses building up. The enemy, taken by surprise, fell back in confusion. Some attempting to retaliate were quickly disposed by the speed and shock of the attack. Some groups of the enemy, however, were not going to be so easily taken, and clearly were holding their ground. The result was not in doubt; although, there would be a terrible price to pay. The ridge resounded with the screams of the stricken above the curses of the combatants, while the faint sobbing and moans of the dying men were lost to the ears in the clash of weapons.

Dog and his force of five hundred now raced out of the ridge to join in the attack on the stragglers, who were spread over a wide area in small groups. It became a chase rather than a fight, fortunately on foot, in which the fresh men in Dog's section had an advantage. Horn, on foot, which he preferred, ruthlessly swung his sword, thrusting and stabbing, on his way through the disorganised ranks of the enemy. Knight Sancto was at his side, and another was a step behind him to cover his back. So far they had not seen any sign of the Irish leader among the struggling masses or the fallen, now lying thick of the ground.

As most of Brinian's Knights and men of rank had been killed, Horn now assumed that the Irish leader had, once again, left the field on foot, as he had done in the battle in the north with his bodyguard. He was probably back in the woodland among the reserve force he had instructed to wait there until the attack on the castle had taken place.

Finding it difficult to control his anger at Brinian's escape, Horn grabbed one unfortunate wounded man by the throat. He was threatened with untold atrocities he would be subjected to if he would not tell them the whereabouts of the Irish leader, and when or where he left the battle field. Fighting for his breath, the man croaked that he did not see Brinian in the field, nor on the march, and thought that he was still at the woodland with the rest of the force. These were to link up with the vanguard before the attack on the castle at dawn. So, it looked like that a rider had been sent to fool anyone into thinking it was the Irish leader himself attending the battle, but that would not explain the disappearance of the horse. The terrified captive told Horn that it had been killed early in the battle by the archers, along with its rider, and dragged to a ditch only a few yards away. This was confirmed by the horse indeed being there in the company of a heap of dead Irish footmen.

It meant that Brinian was still in the woodland area, but at the moment he would not know of the ongoing destruction of the main force at the ridge by the Westerlanders. If the news were to reach him, he might take an alternative route to the castle with his reserves, or decide he was beaten and flee from the scene towards the coast and a ship, with Horn and Lord Grenden's divisions finishing the battle and moving on towards the woodland in force. The unfortunate captive was quickly despatched by Sancto, his usefulness now at an end, but no mercy was ever intended once they had extracted information from him. Horn, whose thoughts were turning to his next plan, knew that would have to wait until the battle on the ridge was his.

Although Lord Grenden had carried out Horn's orders in despatching all the enemy, he could not prevent some of them escaping from the field and scattering into the countryside; they would be hunted down later. Dog also reported the same had happened, and many men had been seen heading north-west from the ridge but could not spare any men, as they were already chasing and killing the enemy they had engaged in combat.

Gradually the enemy force that had stood and made a fight were overcome, with the battle having lasted nearly two hours in bitter hand to hand fighting. Men sorely needed a rest; their arms were weakened by the exhausting clash of steel on steel, and their throats were parched for the lack of spittle, and the strain of oaths spewed forth from clenched jaws. Some men, so completely drained, practically fell asleep within minutes of sitting down, the air reeking of free running earned sweat and warm blood. The wounded lay in any position that would ease their pain. Useless ligatures were applied to gaping wounds too severe to stop the ebbing of their life and prevent the eventual outcome. Most were comforted by their comrades as they reached the last gasping moments to slip quietly away. Ruckle worked overtime to help those with minor wounds. The hordes of flies increased with their incessant buzzing; they could not be kept away despite furious attempts at swatting the most aggressive. That had to be abandoned when the air became almost black with their merciless determination to settle on their chosen corpse.

Water was brought up from the supply carts, and men drank heavily from the bougets carried by the boys. At the same time food was sparingly handed round to each man. Slowly strength returned to arms and legs. Lord Grenden ordered the fittest men to gather the weapons lying on the field that were in good condition, and the loot, now scattered about, that had been taken in the earlier attacks on the northern villages by the enemy. These were put aboard carts along with other discarded articles; their destination, eventually, would be the castle. The extraordinary light casualties of the Westerland army amounted to thirty killed and sixty wounded; the element of surprise had worked for Horn as had been expected. Brinian's men had not been prepared to engage in a battle mentally and physically at the ridge; their minds had been directed to reaching the outskirts of the castle and assembling in their own time.

Horn called his Commanders to review the situation. They had destroyed, if not the vanguard of the enemy force, then certainly a major part of it. Those that had fled the field would, in time, be rounded up, but they had not taken or killed Brinian; he still remained a threat. Dog suggested he take a strong company of men to the woodland area to seek out the Irish leader, and discover what support he still had. Horn agreed to this, and Dog set off with two hundred men at once, to reach the area in an estimated two hours. He made good time and a forward scout reported that there seemed to be little activity in the woodland, and he did not see any semblance of a force. Dog gave the signal to proceed to the woodland, noting the fallen trees which suggested that some machines had been constructed by the enemy, but where were they? To be of use in the attack on the castle, they would easily have been seen, even in a partially assembled state. Machines would also require many men to haul them overland, owing to the extremely rough terrain. No scout had reported the movement of such machines from the forest area before the action at the ridge, only the details of the force that Horn and Lord Grenden had attacked.

Dog split his men into four sections to search the perimeter of the woodland, with the instructions to meet up within an hour. A blast twice on the horn would give warning that the enemy was sighted. Dog then led his men to the extreme northern edge, which was the densest part of wood, and entered on foot into the dark interior.

Still, there was no sign of the enemy, and no signal heard from the other three sections as they pushed even deeper into the woods. The going proved hard until they reached a clearing of some size. Dog gave the order for them to rest before making their way back to join the others. The men thankfully stretched themselves on the soft leafy ground, finding time for idle banter and recalling their part in the battle on the ridge, quite relaxed, and in good spirits.

Dog noted all this with satisfaction. He was striding into the centre of the clearing, intending to talk to some of them, when an arrow struck him with great force, embedding itself in his left shoulder, spinning him round to crash to the ground. For a moment pandemonium broke loose, as more men fell to arrows from an enemy they did not see until too late. Breaking their cover in the woods, the enemy had completely encircled Dog and his men. No more than twenty of his men were now in a position to face the attackers; they seemed to be everywhere. Dog struggled gamely to his feet to join his men, now defending themselves fiercely. It was inevitable that the weight of numbers would eventually prove too much, but Dog, although handicapped by his wound, took an awesome toll with his sword until he became completely hemmed in by the enemy. A heavy glancing blow from a spear shaft high to his forehead sent him once again crashing to the ground, defenceless and only partially conscious; he expected this to be the end.

He came too through a haze to find he was the only survivor; his men lay all around, their bodies in twisted shapes, formed by their manner of dying. Two Irishmen stood threateningly over him, with the shape of another one, taller than the others, who seemed to be in command.

"I am Terroc, Knight of King Aelcane of Ireland. I command one of Lord Brinian's forces. You, I believe, are a Commander of King Plachan. Your wound will be treated. You may live long enough to give us information on the strength of the castle defence. Do you understand me?"

Dog had heard everything the Knight had said and gave no indication that Terroc's assumption that he belonged the castle was entirely wrong, not that he had any intention of correcting him, now or later.

"You heard me! I don't like to repeat myself. Will you give us the details of the castle, or do I hand you over to someone who will make you talk? I can assure you, he is the best, and with your wound, it will go bad for you."

Nausea swept over him and his frame shook with the pain from his wound; part of the arrow was still firmly buried in the bone and would need a knife to free it. His head seem to burst from the after effects of the blow to his skull, and his vision was still blurred. Dog's mind raced with thoughts. *What had happened to the other three groups? Why no horn blasts? Had they been ambushed by the enemy?* Terroc kicked out at him, catching him in the small of the back.

"Speak out or you are lost!"

As Dog still did not answer, he kicked him again and called to his men. "Right, you two, take him to Maxan and watch him closely!"

Maxan, a brute of a man, stripped to the waist, looked hard at Dog. "I think we ought to get acquainted, but first, let's get this arrow out."

He shouted to the two men to hold down the prisoner. Roughly and with a twisting wrench, he cut with his knife, and the arrow was drawn out of the shoulder, accompanied by a piercing cry from Dog. He was unable to hold back as the arrow head twisted out of the bone and through his flesh; never had he felt such blinding pain. This seemed to please Maxan.

"Ah! My young fellow, you can feel pain; you will tell Terrroc what he needs to know."

Strangely enough, with the arrow head now removed from his shoulder, Dog began to feel stronger. He had noticed one of the guards had laid down his sword. They had not, as yet, bound his arms, believing him to be too weak and handicapped to offer serious risk to them. Dog saw his chance as Maxan went to prepare a tree trunk on which he was to be lashed. From a sitting position he lunged forward, taking the nearest man's legs from under him. Rolling over, he grabbed the sword on the first try, while rising to his feet. A lunge by the other man who came at him was countered easily, and with a lightning stroke, he ran him through. The one on the floor got to his feet in an attempt to reach Maxan and took a blow from Dog, which laid him low. Maxan turned to hear the last man's cry as he died, and with a roar, advanced towards Dog, sword and dagger drawn. Dog allowed him to make the running and stood his ground, but as they clashed, the sheer strength of the man was obvious. Dog was almost swept off his feet. Maxan's dagger arm came up as Dog's weapon swung to deflect the sword slash aimed at his head; the huge man's dagger was sent flying as the sword bit deeply into his shoulder. Again, with a great roar, Maxan charged at Dog, who stepped aside slightly at the last second, so close he could smell the foul breath of the man. His quick upward thrust of the sword brought the huge man crashing to the ground. Almost breathless, Dog looked around, prepared to fight for his life, and was amazed that none of the enemy were aware of the events of the last few minutes. He had expected Terroc to come running at the sounds of the fight, or at least to see how Maxan was preparing Dog for questioning.

Dog wasted no time and made for the edge of the woods, moving as quickly as his strength would allow, stopping only for a moment when a small group of the enemy crossed his path. He decided he would make for the ridge rather than expose himself in searching for the other sections; their fate could have been similar to the attack his section had suffered from.

What all this revealed was that there was indeed a strong force of the Irish in the woodland area, and possibly somewhere in the woods was the Commander-in-Chief himself, the elusive Brinian. Dog made it to the ridge in under two hours with no challenge, except from his own scouts. He avoided a small group of the enemy that the scouts were stalking. He continued on his way and arrived to be greeted by Lord Grenden, who noticed the heavily blood stained jacket. With no men, it did not bode good to the Lord. Dog's lone entrance betrayed the fact that he had met a force of some size and that his men had been lost. Although pleased to see that Dog had survived, some good men had perished in the woodland, which now pointed to the existence of a larger army under Brinian that had been estimated earlier. It also seemed likely that they were still intent on attacking the castle, unaware of the destruction of their vanguard, but the mystery remained. where was Brinian? He had not been seen at the ridge, nor in the woodland, and the scouts, anxious to find the Irish leader to earn a promised reward, had not been successful. Another fact was now that surely with Dog's unfortunate encounter with the enemy, they might have guessed that they were facing another force apart from the remnants of the Laswindel army.

Horn and Lord Grenden decided to pull out their divisions from the ridge and take up a position closer to the castle. This new position would be one of strength to defend with ease, and also a place to launch an attack from, should events dictate it. The men of Horn's force were now beginning to recover from the battle on the ridge, and the wounded had been removed to the castle, with the exception of Dog, whose shoulder wound had been treated at the ridge and now was beginning to stiffen up. He refused to leave in spite of Lord Grenden's advice to rest. By the time they arrived at the hill section, the weather began to change, with the arrival of a steady breeze. It was cooler, and a welcome relief after the oppressive heat experienced on the ridge.

Food and water was readily available, as fresh supplies had been sent out from the castle. The spirits of the men rose as they drank and ate the plentiful rations brought to them by the boys. It would make a difference to their fighting abilities, physically and mentally. As Horn watched the men enjoying the food, he felt a new surge of confidence.

A flurry of movement caught Horn's eye, and turning, he could see Dog, his shoulder strapped for support, giving the impression that he could still account for himself in a fight. After all, the arrow wound had been in the left shoulder. He swung, parried, and slashed at an imaginary foe, and apart from swinging across his body on the turn, which tended to cause him pain during a left to right lightning stroke, he felt he could take on the enemy, and he had a score to settle.

Malvin the scout, speedily returning from a reconnaissance, reported to Lord Grenden that he and Fenner had seen two enemy scouts south of the ridge, making their way to the castle area, expecting to link up with the vanguard of their army, now all but destroyed. Fortunately, they caught up with the scouts and killed them after a short fight. Malvin also confirmed that there had been no sighting of the enemy in the castle area north or east of the hillocks, now occupied by Horn. The scouts they had killed had come from the area of the woodland sent out by Brinian or one of his Commanders. It could also mean that the enemy in the woodland area could be the only force, although, as yet, the Irish leader had not been located. Then again, he could be in command of another force not yet identified and assembled in a totally different part of the island.

The possibility of Brinian being strengthened by yet another invading Irish force in the last few days could not be ruled out, so it could be that Horn and Lord Grenden had seriously underestimated the strength and the intentions of their enemy. He called in his Commanders to assess their position. They were now encamped on the series of the small hillocks in anticipation that the enemy would have to make their way through this area to reach the castle.

The plan was to wait for the enemy to appear, by which time the scouts would have been able to assess their numbers, weaponry and their condition, having marched from the woodland or even farther. This might sorely tire the men and slow down their reactions, while the Westerlanders would be fresh and in good spirits. Night fell, and the men lay under a sky filled with a million stars. The sharp rasping bark of a fox broke the silence and some stirred in their sleep for a moment, then lapsed back in their slumbers, with the sentries peering watchfully into the night for any sign of movement by the enemy.

Horn woke early to find a light mist swirling around the camp. This could mean a clear and possibly hot day; that would be good for them. The enemy, having to march in the increasing heat for some miles, would not bring out the best of their fighting potential. Horn was not going to allow them the luxury of resting before he attacked them. Malvin and Fenner had already been sent out before first light to look at the woodland area for any signs of the enemy assembling, or forming into sections, to begin to their march. Through the mist the scouts could make out a group of men standing in a group, and as they watched, many more arrived, something like two hundred or more. This gave the scouts the impression that they were beginning assemble in that area. This was the start, as all along the perimeter of the woodland men began emerging in numbers, forming up under their Commanders, some moving newly constructed machines for stone throwing from their well hidden sites in the woods into the open by their teams.

Malvin noticed that, as yet, he had seen little of archers, mainly footmen with spear and shield, and only a handful of horses could be seen, mostly the type for carrying supplies rather than carrying Knights. With the numbers steadily increasing by the minute, counting them became difficult to assess, as they rapidly teamed up with their sections. The scouts assumed they could be looking at least at fifteen hundred men ,and the possibility of many more in the next hour.

The sun was breaking through as the mist slowly lifted. It was the beginning of a warm day, which meant that by noon the sun would be creating enough heat to make the enemy sweat with the mere effort of marching, pulling or pushing machines. Malvin decided that the enemy was now on the point of moving in mass, as he could see the Commanders giving orders to the men to keep to their own sections when on the move. Their numbers were now doubled, reaching two thousand. As he and Fenner were about to leave, their attention was drawn to a sudden surge of men at the rear of the columns of the assembled army. It was a small party on horseback; an obvious figure of rank rode to the front and turned to face the army. The rank of this rider was clearly established as the whole of the assembled force roared out his name.

"Brinian! Brinian!"

The men raised their weapons and banged their spears against their shields in noisy salute, which he acknowledged by drawing his sword and pointing it towards the direction of the castle, which again drew further excited shouts from his men. At last the scouts could now confirm that Brinian was alive, in command of a large army, and prepared to lead them in the assault on the castle! It confirmed that the Irish leader had travelled up country and had not taken part in the battle on the ridge, but he had gone to meet the new invasion force, believing that his vanguard were resting in the vicinity of the castle. All this had been missed by the scouts, their attention concentrated on the woodland area and its immediate surroundings, thinking that this was the only place that the enemy could be, confirmed by the incident there involving Dog and his men. They had lost two hundred men, indicating that there was, in fact, a large force in occupation. Fenner was sent back to Horn's position with this important news of the rapid assembling of the enemy, and the appearance, at last, of Brinian himself to lead his army to the castle, in what the Irish thought was to be an easy fight, with great rewards for all.

Horn and Grenden were disappointed to hear of the newly arrived force, as it would now mean a harder fight than first thought; this would call for new strategy. Their original plan had been to await the enemy's arrival at the hills and attack them from a position of advantage, assuming they were a thousand strong. Double that number would mean that it could allow some of the enemy to carry out evasive actions during the fighting, instead of being fully occupied in ongoing combat. Horn was still not sure that Brinian was aware of his vanguard's destruction; some of his scouts had been accounted for by Malvin and Fenner. Perhaps he had heard news from the many deserters from the action; one or two may have made it back to the main camp without attracting the attention of any Westerland men. However, the signs of confidence that were observed by the scouts was of an army under Brinian that had not suffered a reverse. Of course, he would, most likely, be passing through the area of the ridge, and it would be very obvious, with the amount of dead that still lay there in that heat; the swarming flies and the carrion overhead would not be missed by him. He would realise that his men had been overcome by a larger force than the Laswindel army could have raised after their losses in the battle in the north. It was a chance Horn would have to take; they could choose another route, although the ridge was the most direct. It was too late now; although, they had buried their own away from the ridge, leaving only the Irishmen to be identified.

The Irish leader gave the order to march and was in high spirits, soon to join his vanguard in the castle area. He was relishing in a short fight with great rewards, relaxed and certainly not expecting any resistance before his assault on the castle itself. The two scouts, Malvin and Fenner, still watching the Irish army, noticed that they were now in two formations. Following them for the first two miles, they were surprised to see them separate; one force swung out to the east, led by Brinian, while the other marched straight to the south towards the castle.

Malvin decided to report this maneuver to Horn and set off at a great pace, covering the first two miles in good time, outpacing even the mounted enemy. He paused only when two enemy scouts ahead of their force appeared and realised that they were on course to encounter the Westerland army in the hills. He made the decision to attack them, and with his silent approach he was able to skirt round to their front, noticing that they were in deep conversation and quite relaxed. It would be his speed of action that would decide the outcome. Fortunately, there was good cover from the thick gorse, and as the first man came into his range, his well aimed dagger struck him in the chest, dropping him like a stone without a sound so that his companion almost fell over him. The other thinking he had been hit by an arrow, drew his sword as Malvin stepped out into his path. He proved that he was no pushover; an experienced swordsman, the enemy scout squared up to Malvin and made the first move, which although he parried, he could sense the strength of the man. Malvin was to fight for his life; he must not fail to get his report to Horn and Grenden before the enemy arrived. So they parried, cut and attempted to slash, the sounds of ringing steel and oaths conveyed this desperate message. It was Malvin that took the first serious blow, his left shoulder laid open by a powerful swing which momentarily threw him off balance. With the strong instinct of survival, he swung his sword and by his efforts drove the Irishman backwards, his sword flashing in the sun as they clashed chest to chest, the man spitting in his face with his exertion. Every ounce of Malvin's energy surged forth as he finally penetrated the man's defence with a fierce thrust to the middle of the body, which made its way through flesh to glancing off bone and emerged through his back. Malvin sank to his knees, almost entirely spent, his chest heaving and sweat pouring down his face and body. Trembling, he staggered to his feet. He wasted no time dragging the two bodies of the enemy scouts into the gorse bushes to conceal them from any approaching Irishmen. Having completed the concealment, he cut some cloth from his enemy's jacket to stem the blood which oozed from his wound, and which was already beginning to congeal on his body with the heat and his own sweat.

It was not easy to start his journey to the hills; it took a while before he could maintain a steady pace; the pain of his wound was now being replaced with a soreness from which he managed to gain some relief by discarding his tunic. This was causing pressure on his shoulder with the rapid movement of his body pushing forward in a shambling gait, the best he could adopt to maintain something like pace. He still had some distance to go to reach the camp. He suffered bouts of nausea but was able to keep going until he was almost at the camp. His breathing became difficult; he sank to the ground, his legs failing to respond; blackness finally overcame him.

At the camp a sentry had already seen Malvin drop to the ground, and seeing no movement, sent out a party to investigate his condition. He was recognised at once and carried into the camp. Many gathered to see what had befallen their chief scout until they were pushed away by Lord Grenden, who cleared a space around him and called for Ruckle, the experienced wound dresser. Many men owed their lives to his methods of treatment. As Ruckle started to uncover the wound, Malvin began to come round and tried to get to his feet, but he was restrained by two of the sentries. This added to his distress; he tried to cry out his message, which was lost. Malvin, now fully aware of his surroundings, shouted above the noise that he had to see the Commanders with important news of the enemy, and if they did not release him now, they would soon be up to the waists in Irishmen looking for blood.

Soon Horn joined Lord Grenden at the scout's side and listened to his report. They congratulated him on his heroic action in disposing of the two enemy scouts who would have seen the Westerland force in the hills. The scouts could have alerted Brinian of their presence, not only in the castle area, but on the island itself, thereby eliminating the element of surprise which had served them well so far. The news of the appearance of Brinian was certainly important; now they knew where he was. He was in command of a force heading southeast, the other force possibly led by the Knight Terroc, heading towards their position.

Plans were made, for delay could be costly. Horn and Lord Grenden would take their force to intercept Brinian, while Lord Sancto, Dog and the giant Greg would hold their force to meet Terrroc at the hills. If he missed them, they would then follow and engage them in the open area at the castle. It would also be the chance for Dog to settle his own account with Terroc the Knight, and he gave orders that when he was identified, he was to be singled out for his ex-captive to deal with. Lord Sancto would hang back with a small force and await developments. Dog would have the easier fight with the enemy and an element of surprise, while Horn would have to seek out Brinian's force and decide on his action when the enemy was in his sights at close quarters.

So, the die was cast, with Dog expecting to be the first into action as Terroc's men were reported to be on a direct route to the castle and would pass through the hills towards them. Fenner the scout came into the camp at the hills, breathing hard from his punishing run and shouted to the sentries to be on watch as he had sighted the enemy force approaching; they could be in the hills in less than an hour. Dog received this news with relish; all was set to welcome them with newly sharpened steel, and soon the sound of the enemy carried to the waiting men. Their banter, the clanking of their weapons against shields, and their mood and noise betrayed the fact that they were not expecting to be challenged, and certainly not by a force. Dog gave orders that no one should make a move or sound until the enemy was at the foot of the second series of hills, so as to entrap them between the first and second points. Then, at a given signal on the horn, they were to descend in mass to attack them before they were fully aware what was happening.

The enemy came on in the direction expected, and as they approached the first hill, they climbed the slope with effort in the heat. Grateful to be at the top, they stumbled down, in nothing like good order, to the other side to be confronted with yet another hill to be climbed. Momentarily they paused to get their wind, which gave the rest of their force time to descend the first hill and join their comrades, puffing and blowing in jocular manner. The shrill blast of the horn rang out, resounding in the hills, which had a startling effect on Terroc's men. Before they could gather their senses, the Westerland force, lying in wait, were given the order to attack, descending the slopes with great speed and falling upon the enemy, putting them into complete panic. Dog's men took a terrible toll, and the giant Greg could be seen hacking his way through the enemy, followed by his footmen at such a pace that they actually reached the bottom of the first hill, cutting off the escape of many of the Irish, forcing them to fight. Terroc, witnessing the slaughter of his men, tried to urge them to stand and fight, rather than attempt to escape the trap and organise their ranks. This was proving difficult and costly, because of the actions of Dog and Greg who had now been joined by Lord Sancto, cutting his way through, leaving a trail of dead and dying Irish. The enemy were stumbling over their own men who had gone down in the packed disorganised ranks, and those not yet dead, groaned, some screamed in agony as heavy feet added to their pain.

Dog at last had sight of Terroc, now dismounted and holding his own. He fought his way to within a few feet of his enemy, and those around him made way for these two to meet. The look of hatred on Dog's face as they came together did nothing to offset his sheer ugliness, and the Knight faced the grim task of taking on this seemingly inhuman caricature of a man, shouting as he recognised him.

"You! Ugly as you surely are, I should have killed you myself in the woodland, but I will leave you broken on the ground for the beasts to devour after my sword has done its work."

Dog scowled, his features distorted, and replied, "Come, Knight! This is your last combat! Your bones will whiten in the sun when the maggots have done with you. Your sword will lie rusting at this place, should not a peasant deem to pick it up."

The clash of steel heralded the struggle of these determined men with one object in mind, the destruction of the other, which also might turn the tide of the battle by example. Terroc, the taller of the two, and in his prime, would have the advantage over Dog, being able to swing his sword to cut a chest and head with his long reach. Dog, stocky, and of great strength and stamina, had met tall men before. He could thrust at the body with one of his favourite moves, coming upwards at such speed that his sword penetrated leather clothing and equipment, to strike and pierce the body with a fatal thrust. For a tall man Terroc moved very quickly to meet Dog's first move, a probing stab at the Knight's chest, his reply to a parry and a cut that swished so close to Dog's head, he could almost feel the blade through his hair. They cut, stabbed and parried on equal terms, but as Terroc stepped up his attack, Dog was forced to retreat a few paces after receiving a slight cut on his right arm. Although it was not serious enough to dampen his aggression, in fact, it spurred him into a ferocious reply. Now driving Terroc back by the sheer weight of renewed energy, he caught the Knight with a glancing blow on the shoulder which exposed a gaping wound, which rapidly began to stain his tunic with flowing blood. This caused Terroc considerable pain and put him at a great disadvantage, knowing he had to finish Dog before he would lose consciousness. Dog, sensing he had his man in trouble, kept up his attack without mercy, and Terroc, exchanging blow for blow without any telling hits, began gradually to feel that this could be his last fight. With one final rush at Dog, he exposed his body as he swung his sword at head height; this was the moment Dog had hoped for! Up came his sword with a lightning thrust to enter the Knight's body and take his life, while his sword still hung motionless in the air. The falling Knight gasped as Dog pulled his sword free from the body, curses screaming on his dying breath. Standing astride the fallen Knight, Dog shouted for all to hear, "Go quickly to your sad maker! Tell him it was I, Dog, that sent you!"

Terroc had gone from his world before he had finished the words.

Elsewhere, the Westerlanders were doing well, and taking a great toll of the enemy now trapped in what was rapidly becoming a valley of death, between the first and second hills. Above the struggling men towered the giant Greg, whose occupation at the bottom of the hill was a foreboding sight for the Irish, as he spurred on his footmen. His huge axe flashed and flayed among the enemy heads, some never aware of what had decapitated them so neatly as they joined the bodies of their comrades, and those still in the last desperate throes of life with thrashing limbs and feeble groans. Within a short time the force had been virtually destroyed by Lord Sancto and Dog's men, only a hundred or more escaping from the battle to scatter in the countryside and into the cover of the gorselands, but they would be hunted at a later hour. The losses were slight in spite of the nature of the battle, some thirty of Dog's men had been lost, and twenty wounded. Greg had lost forty of his footmen with two wounded, and the count of the dead Irishmen reached the total of almost a thousand.

After a short rest period the dead were stripped, the weapons collected, and any small item worth picking up pocketed, their own dead carefully buried in a large pit nearby. Dog ordered the men to be fed and watered, as Lord Sancto rode to the castle to report the outcome of the battle in the hills to King Plachan and Prince Attaga. He told them that Horn was in pursuit of Brinian and his men, who had taken a different route to the castle. He then returned to join Dog and Greg sending off Fenner to locate the other force, who would, by now, be closing in on Brinian, who was expecting to link up with Terroc in the castle area. Lord Sancto and Dog agreed it would be sensible to move out their force north, as they judged the enemy would eventually cross their path. Should Horn's force have caught up and engaged them, and if fate continued to be kind, they would be in a position to entrap the enemy between their two forces, preventing any chance of escape or desertion.

Horn, having travelled some miles since leaving the camp in the hills, awaited his scouts to report the sighting of the Irish army under Brinian's command, which now should be well down country. Horn, not wishing to tire his men in the heat, kept them moving slowly through the gorse, providing cover and part shade, which the men appreciated. Boarset the scout returned to Horn with the report that he had seen an enemy scout, but had not intercepted him; he assumed that this scout was not too far ahead of his force and was still travelling in a southerly direction. This meant that he was moving away from Horn, and they would have to change direction if they had hoped to confront the enemy head on.

Rapid instructions were given to section Commanders to prepare the men in this new maneuver and at the same time to warn them there was to be no undue noise, as they could shortly be in sight and sound of the enemy. The force quickened their pace towards the direction anticipated by the scout of Brinian's route with the hope of arriving at a point that would give them some advantage, either with cover or height, from which to attack. Horn was still hoping that Brinian had not reckoned on, or had confirmation, of the Westerland army's strength on the island. Fortunately, the ground was covered with gorse, in most areas head high, and many a small copse, which proved a relief from the heat as the sun blazed down relentlessly. Maybe the enemy would have more open exposure as they had marched the greater distance from the woodland, burdened with their machines needed for the assault on the castle.

Boarset returned from his mission to warn Horn and Lord Grenden that he had seen the forward section of the enemy, who were struggling with the machines over the rough terrain and heading directly towards them. They had been sent to the front of the force to set the pace so that they would not be left too far behind on arrival at the castle. Horn halted his men at the perimeter of a small but dense wood, as it would be a good place to launch an attack should the enemy cross the open ground directly to their front. Boarset also had confirmed the result of the battle in the hills, and the great success of Lord Sancto and Dog at little cost. This news coming on the eve of a likely battle with Brinian warmed the hearts of the men, and would certainly be a boost to their determination to deal the enemy a further mortal blow.

Another report by a scout confirmed that the Irish army was now spread out for some distance, which meant that Horn could not launch a successful attack on their front or a pincer movement to surround him. Too many would have time to take evasive action and escape to form up as a threat elsewhere. Horn decided that they would attack the Irish when more than half of the enemy had passed their position, then Lord Grenden would attack with half of his men wheeling to the left, which would divide them, and then pursue them from the rear, while Horn and his men attacked the enemy by turning right, with the intention of containing him with a frontal attack. If the planned movements by them were perfectly timed to act as one, it would create instant panic, and they would be forced to fall back on themselves, creating more problems in an attempt to organise themselves into defence.

Fenner had informed them that Lord Sancto and Dog had begun to move their force out from the hills, with the object of intercepting Brinian, and joining in what could well be the final battle. It would be possible for these two to attack from the east of the wood, thereby ensuring that the enemy was trapped between the three wings of Horn's army. They would be easy prey for Sancto and Dog in attacking the vanguard, encumbered with their machines. The problem was the main frontal attack on Brinian's force by Horn. As however disorganised they might be by the unexpected confrontation, it would give large numbers of stragglers in the rear the chance of escape, including Brinian, and it was Brinian Horn wanted above all else. The proven death or capture of this man was paramount to him; after all, that was the main reason why he had come to the aid of King Plachan, in the expectation of ridding their kingdoms of his threat once and for all.

The enemy could now be heard, and a scout ahead of the vanguard was swiftly dealt with by Fenner with his usual skill. Within fifteen minutes the machine men and the first groups were slowly steaming past the woods where the Westerland army was well hidden, only two hundred yards away, and waiting for the signal to attack. The enemy seemed relaxed as they passed, calling out to each other, making much noise, which was a welcome sound to the ears of the waiting men. Reports by the scouts were correct; they were indeed in straggled form as Horn and Lord Grenden watched their progress closely. It took some ten minutes before it was judged that half of the enemy had passed the point, from which the attack was to be launched by the two commanders.

The blast of the horn rent the air as the two attacking forces emerged from the cover of the woods as planned, the enemy being completely startled. Even the war horn had played its part, with the enemy temporarily frozen to a standstill and not really aware of what was happening. Horn drove into the middle of the confused men, and at the same time, Lord Grenden began his incursion into their ranks. Both Commanders then turned to their chosen direction as the enemy tried desperately to get their ranks into some order. Cursing, the Irish Commanders screamed at their men to respond and defend themselves against the rush of the Westerland men, eager to get to grips.

The enemy, now engaged in battle, tried to present a front from which they could counter-attack, but by spreading out, they had unwittingly exposed themselves to Horn's men who had soon outflanked them, and were cutting them down at will. It meant now that the enemy were forced to fight on three sides; one section of the Irish came up from their extreme rear, which was comprised of experienced men, who then enjoyed limited success before being overwhelmed by their eager foe.

Lord Grenden and his force were having a comparatively easier task than Horn, as the enemy he had engaged were not the pick of the Irish, mainly engineers burdened with their machines. Their archers had little chance of being able to loose their arrows, as they were forced to take on the role of foot men, which was not their strong point. It was not long before Lord Grenden realised that his success was rapidly turning the enemy to premature flight.

That was not what they had planned; it would mean turning the action into a running fight or hunt, which, in turn, would force him to split his force into sections to scour the countryside. This would effect his force being unable to join with Horn's men for a combined attack on Brinian's main army, which was the original plan of the two commanders before the battle began. However, Lord Grenden made the decision to send off a party of men, under the command of the Knight Briscal, to skirt round the action, and race to the area beyond the enemy, in order to pick off those that had already fled, and others that were on the point of deserting. Briscal arrived quickly to the area of the main action and began at once to mop up the running enemy, most in panic, looking for the nearest cover. Many were caught in the open and the situation was soon contained.

Horn's force, now fighting hard, began making good inroads into the enemy ranks with Horn constantly searching for the elusive Brinian, who could be anywhere amongst his men. The Irishman knew it was always better to take action on foot rather than on horseback. This then would not identify anyone of rank, and would also encourage the men around them to fight harder, side by side by example. He was not the type of leader to lead at the head of his army in action on the field of battle, but would be in the midst of his men, unseen, directing them by using subordinates, and, of course, he proved in earlier battles he could actually leave the field. This then was the nature of the man, who had long been a threat to the kingdoms that lay to the east of King Aelcane's land, and his raids were always designed to plunder the treasures and grain of other lands.

Now Brinian, the King's most experienced Commander, having invaded the kingdom of King Plachan, had placed his army into an ambush by a stronger defender than he had ever expected to deal with, and his army was being systematically destroyed piece by piece before his eyes. They were driving his men apart, making it almost impossible to form a rallying point, and his losses were staggering, great gaps appearing where men had fallen. This he knew was not just the Laswindel army, but a force of considerable military experience that had come to the aid of King Plachan. Brinian could only guess that it was Horn of Westerland, and as he closed with them, he could again recognise the clothing peculiar to their footmen, which was dyed dark brown and studded with small metal disks. He also knew that there would be no quarter given, and no mercy shown to him or his men who might be overcome by these warriors.

He now contemplated withdrawing from the field when one of his remaining scouts reported that yet another force was approaching them at their rear and would be on them within a matter of minutes. His men would then be trapped between these forces, and there was no way they could fight this new threat, as they were fully committed at their front. Their best men had already been lost, trying to hold the punishing assault by the Westerland men, in their steady advance through their ranks. With the mortal struggle progressing Horn's way, it surely could only be a matter of time before the Irish leader would be forced to make a counter move which would possibly expose his presence. Brinian also realised that his army had been split in two at the outset of the ambush, and with those attacked by Lord Grenden being the most vulnerable, he may well have lost them, along with the machines for his intended attack on the castle. He was right, of course; it was all but over for his vanguard.

Lord Sancto and Dog arrived at the battle, and the scouts reported on the successful maneuvers carried out by Horn and Lord Grenden. All was going well, and they were informed that Briscal and his men were blocking the route to the north and mopping up the escaping Irish. They made the decision to round the battle and attack Brinian at the rear, while Horn was attacking successfully at their front.

Hearing the news of the new force coming up fast to his rear, which could mean the likelihood of his whole army being defeated, Brinian took the decision to leave the field with his bodyguard of six Knights. Virtually unseen in the general melee, he slipped away into the interior of the wooded area, and struck out in a northerly direction. Horn, still pressing forward, his tally mounting of the enemy slain by his own hand, still had no sight of the enemy leader, unaware that he had left the field; he fought fiercely on. His Knights around him created a spear shaped wedge that was now gaining ground towards what was left of the rear, where they hoped to find Brinian.

Dog arrived at the rear only minutes after the Irish leader had entered the interior of the woods, and to the dismay of the enemy, who now realised that they were trapped between two determined forces bent on their total destruction. Many tried to escape to the gorselands on their right, as Dog's men swooped on them with the enthusiasm of hunters with their tails up, looking for trophies. Horn could also see the arrival of Dog ahead of him, and ordered his

Commanders to fan out with their men to stop or hunt the fleeing and scattering enemy, intent now only on survival, their appetite for combat completely exhausted.

As the battle was drawing to a conclusion, it became obvious that the enemy for some time had been leaderless, but there was no time to check out the dead and dying underfoot. Horn had to finish the main action while a few of the enemy still offered resistance. There was a slim chance of Brinian being amongst them. Gradually, all resistance was finally crushed with the exception of the fleeing men being hunted at the rear by Dog's men, and at the front by Briscal. Horn was now sure that Brinian had left the field and his army to its fate, and Horn gave vent to his frustration as he shouted to his men to spare no one; none of the enemy must be allowed to reach the coastline and their ships.

Meeting with Lord Grenden, he praised Lord Sancto and Dog for their part in the successful battle at the hills and here at the woods. He gave Dog the command of a select force made up of the fittest men to reach the coast quickly, to prevent any of the enemy lucky enough to escape the slaughter from reaching their ships. Dog set off after a short rest, expecting to reach the coast within two hours, which should guarantee their arrival before the Irish, who would be going from cover to cover to avoid being seen as they made their way to the north-west part of the island. Lord Grenden, having achieved a great result with his men in destroying the vanguard, reported to Horn his views on the battle, and those of his men under Briscal were having great success in stopping the enemy from entering the gorselands. Denying any safe cover would mean that within a short period of the hunt, very few Irishmen would escape their attention, and those the did would eventually be reported while hunting food by the villagers.

Horn decided to make camp, and gave orders for the wounded to be attended to, and the dead counted. Weapons in good order and undamaged equipment were collected before the disposal of the enemy bodies from the battle. It took two hours to dig the huge pit of some thirty yards long by the tired men. Their own dead were afforded a separate burial as was the custom of the Westerlanders. Always, the fallen were never buried with an enemy. It is said, slain by an enemy in battle did not give him the right to lay beside them. Divided by battle and divided in death, the Gods would not see their struggle; they would be committed to fight until time itself ceased.

Chapter 9

The hunt for Brinian

The evening brought a welcome respite from the heat of the day. Moving away from the burial site and the persistent flies, the exhausted men could relax, their work done. Some fell asleep while others talked of their part in the battle. Horn and Lord Grenden strolled among the men, stopping at one group or another to comment on their efforts in the battle that had come to their notice. Awards would be made, and favours granted to the bravest. A messenger had been sent to the castle with the news of the destruction of the Irish army by Horn. Prince Attaga, King Plachan ,and other members of the family went to the courtyard to announce the good news to the people and were greeted by hundreds of voices raised in cheers. The news had spread in minutes throughout the castle.

Now the kingdom was safe; there would be no threat from the Irish leader Brinian. The order was given by the Prince to the defenders to stand down and resume the normal day to day routine. There was, of course, to be the official celebrations when Horn and his army eventually arrived back at the castle, the people of Laswindel being determined to fete their deliverers with all the best of their resources. Banners and streamers would fly from the highest points of the castle walls and decorated with the unicorns of the royal House of Horn.

Brinian, meanwhile, had made his way through the interior of the woods to the north, and with no one in pursuit, he decided to rest under the cover of the approaching night; tomorrow he would make his way to the coast striking north. He also knew that there would be a strong possibility of being hunted down by his enemy, therefore he would have to be extremely careful of exposing his cover at all times. However, he was confident that they would not attempt to take any action that night, as the woods themselves adopted even a darker threat, being an ideal place to ambush small parties of hunters. The slightest sound would carry some distance in the still woodland, betraying an approach by even the lightest of foot. He and his Knights were comparatively fresh, not having been in the thick of the fighting, but he detailed one of them to keep watch as they prepared to settle down until first light, when they planned to move out to towards the coastal areas.

He believed he and his bodyguard could outstrip their pursuers if they left early enough and resisted the temptation to sacrifice safety for speed. They took the precaution of splitting into two groups. They agreed to stay within sight of each other for protection, should one party be discovered and attacked. Brinian pondered over what his return to the kingdom of his Lord would be. His record was not good; he had hoped to redeem himself on this invasion; his achievements would be nil. The promised plunder of treasures had vanished with his army; many good men had been lost, including some of his Lord's best Knights, against what had been the promised easy task of taking the castle at Laswindel. If he managed to take a ship to the country of his birth, he would have to think of the real possibility of not returning to King Aelcane with the news of another lost cause. Maybe he would make his way to the south and his family in the mountains. The King's vengeance had a long arm; his role as a Commander was finished for he had nothing left to lead, and his bodyguard would look to their own once they reached the safety of the ships and, subsequently, their own land.

Dog reached the coast before the sun went down. He did not stop for a handful of his enemy seen skulking in the gorseland. Although sorely tempted, his prime objective was to reach the coast with all haste. There were sentries on the shore. They had to remove them, scuttle any of the ships close to the shore, and then lie in wait for any Irish to arrive. He easily took care of the few sentries on the three ships still lying there. His men stove in the hulls and bows, watching in satisfaction as they slowly heeled over in the water. Now unusable, they would never sail again with Irishmen aboard. Dog posted his sentries in case there was an attempt by the small bands of the enemy to reach the coast, but none were heard to try during the night. Probably, most had been outpaced by Dog and his men in their forced march during the afternoon. During the night, the enemy would be moving for cover to cover, knowing they would be, in time, relentlessly hunted down by the Westerland men.

There was one obvious and direct lane through the scrub to the ships and that was narrow and gorse covered, which meant that the enemy could reach the quayside before they could be identified and dealt with. A small party was sent down this lane by Dog to a point where there was a bend and a suitable place to trap the unwary. They would lay in wait for the first of the unfortunate arrivals. Brinian, now on the move, and his party, in two groups moving a hundred yards apart, hoped to reach the coast in less than two hours.

At the same time, Horn and his rested and much refreshed force were ordered to carry out a wide sweep towards the north-west, and Lord Sancto had previously taken a small force into the woods to the south-west. He had already accounted for over a hundred Irishmen, leaving small pockets of them scattered in different directions for some distance. Horn took one of the sections in the sweep which would press directly to the north, while Lord Grenden took his men to the north-east; this would then encompass the area most likely to have hidden men from the battle. The enemy would be making an attempt to reach the coast, hopefully into the arms of Dog and his handpicked force.

Scouts were sent ahead; their experience in tracking always proved to be a great benefit, enabling a Commander to know which direction the enemy had taken and their approximate strength. On this sweep of the countryside, they still had all their scouts. Only Malvin, still recovering from his wound, was left at the castle, which, fortunately, he had been able to reach before he succumbed through loss of blood. Horn's men started out a good pace and were now fanned out among the gorse, being careful not to fall into it or brush against the wicked thorns. Most of this species of gorse in Laswindel oozed a toxic secretion, which had been known to be fatal to a person suffering multiple punctures of the skin. It was imperative that the wounds should be cleaned at once, not that it would guarantee complete recovery.

There had been no sighting of any enemy for some time until a great whoop rent the air as two luckless Irishmen were brought down on the run as they broke cover, flushed out by the footmen and finished off by the eager archers in hot pursuit. Fenner the scout came running toward Horn with the news that there was a small party of the enemy, consisting of what looked like a person of rank, making their way north using cover, obviously having emerged from the wooded area that day.

Horn quickly assembled a small group from his force. He carried only a sword, which would allow them to move with maximum speed and be accompanied by Fenner. He had already estimated their route, and together they raced off without delay. It took nearly an hour at fast pace before Fenner brought them to a halt with a cautionary signal, as ahead they could make out three figures, although he had originally seen six, so that meant they had split up to make pursuit difficult. Horn, in this small group, took out six men and decided to skirt round and close on the enemy at speed, to cut off their escape. The three Irishmen, seeing them now emerging from the gorse, shouted as they prepared to defend themselves. This gave warning to the other three not so far away on the right and slightly ahead.

They were experienced Knights and a hard fight ensued that lasted nearly half an hour, until they were finally overpowered, but not without the loss of two of his men. Again, there was no sign of the Irish leader among this group. The sound of clashing steel and oaths could be heard nearby from the main force who had stumbled on a group of the enemy. Desperate fighting was taking place there. It was becoming clear that a lot more of the experienced men had escaped from the battle than was first thought, and Brinian could well be very close to them, using the same route to the coast.

A few more isolated pockets of the enemy were located and dealt with by Lord Grenden's men. Horn, in turn, routed a small group, totalling about sixteen, who offered little resistance, mainly due to half of them having discarded or lost their weapons since the battle. With the two forces meeting up, it was decided to rest for an hour then proceed towards the coast to within two miles. At that point they would be able to operate with smaller parties and fan out across the ground cover, over which the majority of any surviving enemy would have to use to gain access to the coast and the quay. Whether they would appear that evening or first light did not matter. Dog had been fairly successful with his plan, and his tally had risen to sixty caught, some in small groups and others as lone fugitives, and at no cost to his own men.

In the fading light of a warm summers evening, Dog felt pleased with himself; all was going well. Fenner the scout, having left Horn's force, arrived to inform Dog that the combined forces of Horn and Lord Grenden would be making camp two miles west, and in the early morning, they would begin their sweep across the countryside to flush out any of the enemy that were still attempting to reach their ships. He could expect Horn to arrive at the quay by noon, provided all went to plan.

Returning to the main force, Fenner informed Horn of the success of Dog's action on the ships, and the mopping up his men had carried out in the coastal area. Horn smiled to himself. He could not have a better and more able Knight than Dog. He had always excelled himself as a warrior, and now he had emerged as a most capable Commander, one who he could rely on in any action in the future. With his natural talent, he had proved himself worthy of the rank of Knight. Lord Grenden was, of course, of the old school. He had served and fought time and time again with the old King, and had taken it upon himself to teach the young Horn the art of war as soon as the boy could hold a sword. His loyalty was never in question. As Commander-in-Chief of the Westerland army, he led by example. His prowess in the field was quite awesome to behold. It became common practice to give him space as he wielded his sword above his head to cut through the opposition like butter. *I am, indeed, fortunate*, thought Horn, *to have such men to lead my army*. They had become a military force with no equal across the many kingdoms that bordered their land, and their reputation had spread even to those lands beyond the seas.

The combined forces arrived at the point chosen to make camp, and as the evening closed in, sentries were posted with instructions not to raise an alarm, but to observe any movement nearby of straggling Irishmen. They were confident there could be no threat of an attack by the fast dwindling numbers of the enemy still out in the gorselands. Food and water were taken round to the men who were now settling down to rest. Once again they were told to keep talking to a low level. There was no need to attract attention, and with the heat, it was unnecessary to think of fires. Cooked food was out of the question, unless it was cold meat saved from a previous meal, often carried wrapped in a piece of cloth in their jerkins. Some of the veterans, being more experienced, had adopted the method of eating half of their ration, which benefited them later, while most of the young men and boys would eat all or anything put before them given the chance. Most would look on enviously as the older men produced their cloth wraps to reveal extra rations at a time when there was no food forthcoming.

After a well earned rest for most of the men during the night, they awoke at first light, eager and ready to continue the hunt. Once more scouts were sent out northwards to locate any of the enemy on the move. Some returned to report very few sightings, which could mean that some of the Irishmen were closer to the coast than was assumed the previous day. It was decided that each force would be of sixty men, each to cover an area almost half a mile across and to work their way towards the coast.

The great hunt was on, and the groups moved out of the camp to their respective starting points to the west and to the north, their orders being to search the land inch by inch for the Irishmen. An added incentive was announced of a huge reward to be paid to the man who actually caught or killed Brinian, or was instrumental in locating him at close quarters. This was, of course, assuming that he was still alive and on the run. Not a single man would deny that apart from the huge reward itself, the glory alone would enhance the status of the fortunate warrior, and would undoubtedly lead to promotion and numerous favours being bestowed. It was, after all, common knowledge that Horn, and his father before him, were noted for their generosity towards anyone of any rank who distinguished themselves in their service.

Horn chose the middle route to the north with his group. Lord Sancto and his group were on his left, the idea being that the extremes of each group would have sight of each other at all time, so that the slightest movement by the Irish would be seen. It was also possible that the few settlements across the country could have been sought out by the enemy, the occupants taken as captives or forced to supply them with what food they had in their huts. Therefore, it would be necessary to also search these crude dwellings and not to take the word of the locals that no enemy was in hiding there. Gradually, the sweep began to move with purpose and now and again came the shout of triumph as a discovery was made of some unfortunate man, either taken on the run or killed in the cover which was hiding him.

Horn and his group could see a small settlement directly ahead of them, and being surrounded by a small defensive stockade, it was not possible to see over it at a distance, so a scout was sent forward to look at close quarters for any signs of the enemy. He returned soon to report to Horn that there was no apparent sign of the inhabitants or the enemy. To all intents and purposes or for whatever reason, the place had been abandoned. Horn's group, moving carefully into the settlement, confirmed the scouts findings; no occupants were in any of the huts. Items of clothing were scattered about the floors, as if they had been hurriedly sorted. It was also discovered that the dogs had been killed and thrown into a pit near the stockade. No livestock could be found, and it all seemed unnaturally quiet.

There being no point in looking farther at what was obvious in the settlement, Horn ordered his men out and assembled them to continue their sweep to the north. He sent out his scouts to try to locate the missing people as well as the enemy who may be scattered among the thick gorseland, which would slow them down as they tried to make their way through it, risking being torn to shreds by the thorns. One scout returned to report that he has seen a group of people ahead that seemed to be under a form of control, being hurried on when they stumbled on the rough ground or slowed down. He also confirmed that the group contained a number of children. This then was obviously the people from the settlement, being used as hostages by the enemy, who would not hesitate to use them as human shields in a desperate attempt to reach their ships. It was imperative that these people be released as soon as possible, but to attempt to rush them or make a direct attack on them might result in the loss of life of some of their numbers.

The plan to save the captive villagers was to be carried out by a few picked men under the leadership of the Knight Briscal. Without delay they set off to catch up with the group still heading north. Soon the group were within sight, and Briscal decided that he would overtake them, skirt round and watch for any of the enemy that might peel off to the gorse for various reasons. The problem was that the enemy would soon discover that a man was missing. Part of the answer to this was solved when it was realised that the last few people of the group were being pushed along by three of the enemy, and that group were mainly women and old men. Only four of the enemy seemed to be in control of these people at the front.

It was as this group entered a denser part of the gorseland that Briscal saw his opportunity. Noiselessly, six of his men crept close to the rear of the group and the three Irishmen. At a signal they attacked in pairs, swooping on them before they could make a sound; thus, now three of them were disposed. The frightened villagers in the rear were cautioned to be silent as though nothing had happened and to keep in their original order in the group. The six men made their way carefully and slowly through the walking people, bending low, imitating the old men, while Briscal and the rest of the men outflanked those at the head to lie in wait for them. As the four Irishmen in the front of their captives were spaced out, and keeping to the edge of the path, it would have to be like the attack at the rear, in unison, before any of the enemy could warn each other and endanger the lives of the villagers.

The four Irish at the front were unaware of the loss of their comrades, and the subdued light in the dense gorseland was in favour of Briscal. The enemy were confident that these people would provide them with a safe passage to their ships, and they felt good, so good that they were beginning to relax their vigilance; now they were nearing the coastal area. The attack had to be as quick as the first! They moved with great speed to each man already targeted.

As they approached, leaving their cover of the gorse, three of them were despatched before they knew of the presence of the men that killed them. A fourth man, who had been in the act of turning, saw his two attackers. Grabbing a woman captive, he backed off into the gorse with a knife at her throat. Briscal now ordered the group to begin to collect themselves and instructed some of his men to escort them back to their settlement and then rejoin the first hunting group they met. At the same time he gave the order to two men to follow the escaping enemy with the woman hostage and to await the opportunity to overpower him and release the unlucky woman, hopefully unharmed.

Horn was pleased at Briscal's success in rescuing the captives. As it was nearing noon with the heat increasing, he called his force to a halt to take a short rest. The scouts were reporting with good news that some twenty-six of the enemy had been flushed out; they had also observed others ahead, either alone or in pairs and all heading northwards. At this rate the enemy could be eliminated within a day or two, and Horn and his army could return to the castle with the news for King Plachan of the total destruction of the Irish invaders. He would able to assure them that the Irish Kings would never be able to seriously challenge any kingdom for many years to come.

At the coast Dog's men were not idle; the few enemy who managed to reach the coast were easily rounded up. The flow of these men gradually slowed down, which meant that there were less of the Irishmen who had escaped from the battle than first thought. Orders were given for Horn's men to begin the sweep once again, and the Commanders of each section moved out their men quickly, eager to continue the hunt with the thought uppermost in their minds of being the lucky one to collect the reward offered for the Irish leader.

Brinian, moving cautiously on his own through the gorselands, had seen the group of villagers being herded along by some of his men, and laid low with no intention of joining them or any of his force making for the coast. He knew that before long the group would be sighted by their pursuers. Their chance of survival would be considerably reduced, as they were still a few miles from the coast. He recognised one these men as one of his Commanders called Ribatt, who had a reputation for extreme cruelty to his own men, and would take prisoners for the sole purpose of satisfying his sadistic nature to experiment with new methods of torture.

As he watched the group moving ahead, he suddenly became aware of movement behind them, six men not of his army, following close to their rear. Moving swiftly, they had, within seconds, taken the lives of the three men at the tail of the group, and began to move slowly up the column towards the front. He was sorely tempted to call out a warning, but to do so would expose his own presence and turn their attention to him, should they deal effectively with the rest of his men with the group. As he feared, the men at the head of the column were also dealt with in the same manner, with the exception of the man Ribatt, who made his escape with a woman hostage into the gorse, and made directly towards his position. He dived heavily into the thickest of the gorse, which covered a deep hollow, and gasped in pain as the treacherous thorns embedded themselves in his flesh, inflicting many deep gashes and punctures. He crawled painfully back to the edge of the hollow and watched as another party of men came near. Part of Briscal's small force passed him, escorting the villagers who had been captives until their release a few minutes ago. These were followed by another two men, obviously tailing Ribatt and his hostage.

This was, for him, the signal to move on. He merged with difficulty from the gorse, his jacket torn and shredded by their cruel onslaught on his body. He kept to the path to continue his journey towards the coast, his arms and legs causing him great pain. His whole body felt on fire, and he knew he would have to find water quickly to try to bathe his wounds. He decided he would have to rest. He sat down, partly closing his eyes, when he heard a movement which brought him to his feet. Drawing his sword, he turned towards the sound and found himself looking straight at Ribatt with the terrified woman. Lowering his sword, Brinian stood facing his Commander, who had recognised his leader at once. With his knife pointed at his captive, he motioned for her to sit down. This was not what Brinian wanted! This could be a problem in the making; he must remain on his own to have a reasonable chance of eluding the pursuers of what was left of his army. He had also seen and knew that there were two men tailing Ribatt. The two must be close; they may be watching them!

The Irish leader spoke sharply. "Ribatt, get rid of the woman! She will only slow you down. It's the only chance you have of evading the Westerlanders! The life of this woman will not spare you from their vengeance."

Ribatt did not answer. Brinian swore at him to dwell on his words. "You must understand that your only option is to let her go; it could work in your favour. There were two men following you; they will find her and you!"

Ribatt looked with almost contempt at his Commander. "I will take my chance with her, the woman's mine! I will get rid of her when it suits me." He spat the words out.

Ribatt was still convinced the hostage would ensure his survival if he was challenged, but it meant he would have to defy his leader. This was a direct challenge to his authority. Hearing of the two men on his tail, he would have to act quickly and be on his way.

Brinian, sword in hand, took a step towards the man, sensing he was not going to act on his advice. Ribatt, standing his ground, realised he would have to take on his Lord in combat or concede. His mind told him to obey, but his pride told him otherwise. He was now a fugitive, as was Brinian, his destiny was in his own hands.

Stepping back, he drew his sword and lunged forward, hoping to catch Brinian off guard, who was quick to read his intentions by stepping aside and aiming a lightning stroke at head height. The terrified woman, rooted to the spot, watched as the two men she knew were not enemies clashed and circled around each other, looking for an advantage. Although Brinian was clearly the better swordsman, Ribatt possessed great strength, as steel met steel. Many times Brinian's sword was all but knocked from his grasp by the stunning blows of Ribatt. At one stage the men closed chest to chest with swords locked, sweat and spittle exchanged with curses. A sudden surge of brute strength from the commander all but sent Brinian staggering backwards off balance. Recovering at once, he ducked the vicious blow that was meant to finish him. He struck hard under Ribatt's arm, the force of which met flesh and bone, sending the commander cursing with pain down on one knee. The woman, sensing what was to come, turned away her head as the sword descended on the neck of Ribatt, sending him spinning forward, his head all but severed. His life blood quickly spread over the ground in a thick dark stream before its progress slowed to thin rivulets taking up the form of some giant hand.

Brinian turned to the woman, her face a mask of sheer terror in the expectation of her own death from the Irishman. To her surprise he told her to run and keep on running if she wanted to live, as there were more of his men in the area. For a moment she was rooted to the spot with her fear. She collected her senses within seconds and raced off towards the south to almost collide in minutes with the two Westerlanders. Recovering, she told them of the events that taken place since she was taken from the group. Her captor, she said, had been killed by one of his own kind in a terrible fight. They both appeared to be important and knew each other instantly, the victor telling her to run if she wanted to live. One of the men took off in the direction indicated by the woman in the hope of finding the Irishman near there, while the other decided to take the woman back to her village settlement.

Brinian was exhausted from the combat with Ribatt, and as the pain from his encounter with the gorse returned to rack his body with increasing pain, he needed to find a place of rest before he could resume his way to the coast. His hope of reaching it before dawn had now become impossible. In the late afternoon he came upon an isolated dwelling, and waiting for a moment, he moved closer. His first thoughts were for water and food if they were available without having to challenge and betray his presence. The dwelling was surrounded by gorse and shrubs, making it easy to move in very close. Crouching low, almost touching the walls, he heard the sound of voices raised in argument and knew that there were at least two men involved. In spite of his great need for water and food, he realised that in his seriously weakened state he could not take on one fit man, let alone two. Regretfully, he made his exit painfully and slowly headed north. After spending some time outside that dwelling, he had unwittingly allowed his pursuer to close the distance between them. The man, sensing that he must surely find his enemy at any time, stepped up his walking pace to a jog; his mistake would be that he would betray his presence by stepping on dry twigs that might carry the sound down wind.

Brinian although in dire trouble physically, still had his hearing and became aware of the man approaching; he now had to stand and challenge him. He could press on while he could still walk, hoping to outwit him in the cover of the gorse. He decided it was too difficult to elude him for long; he would have to face him eventually. Stopping, he listened again intently. Brinian could now plainly see some movement through the gorse, betraying the man's nearness. Moving himself into a position directly in the man's path, whose heavy breathing could be heard, Brinian closed upon him. The man came upon the Irishman as he rounded a slight bend on the rough path. The shock of suddenly seeing his quarry almost on top of him delayed his action in drawing his weapon. The Irish leader summoned all his remaining strength and made no mistake; his sword cut short the man's gasp of surprise as it cleaved through his jerkin and entered deep into his chest. The unfortunate man crumpled to the ground; his face still wore an expression of bewilderment. Brinian, with great effort dragged the dying man with his fading strength into the thickest of the shrub, collapsing beside his victim. Trying to regain his breath and with the realisation that he was now completely spent, he drifted into a state of heavy sleep.

Some time later he came round; he had lost all sense of where he was. The sight of the body of the man laying near him brought him back to reality. An attempt to rise using his sword as a prop failed; he fell heavily back into the gorse. Once again the thorns tore into his body; he listened to himself scream out in renewed agony.

Horn continued to have success in flushing out more of the enemy during the day, and reports from scouts and section commanders continued to confirm more sightings, and also that little resistance was offered by the enemy when captured. Lord Sancto and his men had joined the hunt in the south-east and had practically cleared up the whole area with ease, apart from one exception. A group that were trying to make their way westwards when caught fought with purpose, costing him three of his men. Regrettable as it was, but when balanced against the total destruction of sixteen of the enemy, it was considered good odds in a hard fight.

In the western part of the island the chance of any odd straggler escaping was practically nil, and if they did reach the coast, very little fishing took place there. Boats were few and far between the scattered villages. Even if they managed to find one, it would be fraught with danger unless they were experienced fisherman in those waters. With the knowledge of the destruction of the main Irish army, Prince Attaga also joined in the hunt in the south with a small force. After a meeting with Lord Sancto, he took the extreme route to the south coast, reaching it within a hour. With no sign of the enemy in spite of all villages being searched and confirmation from the inhabitants that they had not seen the Irish, he returned to the camp of Lord Sancto. The Prince requested that he may stay with them until the main force with Horn and Lord Grenden arrived after clearing the enemy in the north. Rations were sent out from the castle as they settled down. They posted sentries after finishing their food to keep a lookout for any lone fugitive moving through the gorse.

Up at quayside, Dog had accounted for six more on the enemy on the last day, but it was becoming clear that very few of the Irish would now be arriving as Horn and his Commanders were effectively mopping them up before they could reach his position. Had they been successful, they would have found no ships to take them to their homeland, as they had been scuttled.

Fenner the scout had made his way to the north-east and had seen nothing of the enemy in that area, so he turned and took the route directly to the north, along a rough path heavily bordered with tangled gorse. He kept himself away from the cruel thorns by staying as much as possible in the middle. He was making good progress towards the coast, hoping to link up with Dog's men before nightfall, then make his way back to the main force. As he moved quickly down the path, he could see someone coming towards him. His reaction was to wait and ambush the man, but to his relief it was another scout who had been sent out earlier by Dog. He told Fenner that he had seen a lone figure at a distance who was not travelling at any pace. He thought, perhaps, the man was injured, but he had not engaged him, as his orders to report to the main force was his first priority as scout to the commander.

Brinian began to stir, his head buzzing with peculiar noises. His body felt on fire. He struggled to get himself in an upright position. Staggering forward, he crashed back on his knees, his unsteady legs too weak to support him. Also, his sight was beginning to fail him; he peered through half closed eyes. It was an effort, but he tried again to get to his feet and stood swaying, his head swimming, tongue swollen with the heat and lack of water. He could not go far in his weakening state. He was like a child, almost helpless. He thought now that he should have kept a companion. It was too late now. He had shunned the company of his Knights, and they were lost in the belief he could travel faster and safer on his own.

Diving into the gorse and rolling through the gorse into the hollow to take cover was proving to be fatal, as the deep wounds and masses of punctures were throbbing with an intense heat he had never felt before. By removing part of the wrappings on his legs, he could see that most of the wounds were suppurating, and now were septic. He was racked with a fever. He began to hallucinate. Believing he was surrounded by enemies, he swung his sword at imaginary foes. Curses streamed from his parched throat. With the full glare of sun beating down on him, he swayed and crashed to the ground, rolling into the hedge. Brinian, barely conscious, tried to focus his eyes on the sky but could see nothing but a mist. His strength was now completely ebbed, and his breathing became shallow as he finally entered into a dark world.

Fenner kept on his course, taking a more easterly route on the advice of Dog's scout. He had mentioned the lone figure he had seen who might have been an enemy deserter. The heat of the day was now lessening a little, so he could keep up a better pace that was fast, yet comfortable. As scout for Lord

Grenden, he had to move quickly with sightings or messages from one Commander to another. With the chief scout Malvin still injured, he had taken on his role. Observant by nature, he had exceptional eyesight. He could spot a movement a long way ahead. Many an enemy that lay hidden in trees or woodland had been found and reported by him to their ultimate dismay and demise. Fenner had covered nearly a mile to the east and then took a narrow and rough path which gradually turned northwards. Its high sharp gorse gave a warning not to get too close to the hedge.

He was taken by surprise when he came upon the still figure of the Irish leader Brinian. Stopping a yard away, he studied the figure laying there. His clothes and equipment, although muddied and torn, were of high quality, his sword had a decorated hilt of precious gems. This man, therefore, must be a high Commander of the Irish Force who had died of his wounds. Fenner bent down to remove the sword and was startled by a long sigh from the man. He was still alive! Turning the body over, the eyelids flickered in an effort to open; his cracked lips parted as if he wanted to speak but nothing happened.

Here was dilemma for the scout. There was a helpless enemy with the spoils of his equipment, particularly the handsome sword. A quick knife thrust was all that was required to despatch him. He had done this many times, but he sheathed his knife and took his skin flask from his belt, which held water, pressing it the man's lips. The water at first ran off his lips and down his face, but then his lips parted and the lifesaving fluid entered his throat with the magical effect of returning life. Now Fenner was committed; he had an enemy at his mercy, and he had partially revived him. What to do now? He could not walk; he was not to take prisoners, especially these Irishmen. He could leave him to expire on his own and take the sword, although he would have give up equipment of that value to his Commander.

This man was undoubtedly of the highest rank. Fenner, excited by his find, knew this was no ordinary Commander. He could be worth a reward, and, no doubt, they would kill him anyway, but he might be of use in extracting information. Fenner made the decision to report his find. He gave the man his remaining water. From his pouch he fed him slowly cold deer meat. The Irishman was breathing, although faintly, and Fenner was confident that he would last until he could return with others; there was no way he even stand or drag himself off, let alone escape.

Moving fast, the scout reached the main force and made his report to Horn, who listened with great interest as Fenner described the man he had encountered. Horn picked six men. With the scout leading, they left the main force at once to return to the path in the gorseland where he had left the Irishman.

Brinian found he could move his head but not his limbs. Brinian heard the men approaching and painfully squinted at the hazy shapes coming towards him. His sight had improved slightly; he could see the figure of one who seemed to be in command. He thought, *at least I am to be confronted with a Commander*. Horn could see that Fenner had been correct in his assessment of the enemy's rank and importance. Bending low, he asked him whether he could hear.

"Who are you, Irishman?"

The man's hoarse reply carried a hint of arrogance. "Who is it that asks?"

Horn replied, "I am Horn of Westerland, and the Irish army is destroyed!"

Silence greeted Horn for a moment, then the Irishman, with difficulty, opened his mouth. Speaking through cracked lips, he said, "I am known as Brinian. I know I shall not return to my homeland and shall die like a animal here on this cursed island. I salute you, Horn, as a warrior and King."

After he uttered these words, he gasped as if in overwhelming pain. His body jerked in agony. Trying to lift his arms, he finally looked directly at Horn. With a long soft sigh, he died.

This then was the final end for his old enemy. Never again will he lead an army to invade another kingdom, carry off their treasures, bring death and destruction, and take women from their children and families. Horn stood for some minutes looking at the body of his old enemy. Brinian was on his back, his mouth open as if to scream and curse his victors. The eyes still seemed to carry a burning hate. Horn ordered the men to bury the body quickly where it was found, minus the equipment and the beautiful sword, which he presented to the surprised Fenner. He had never owned anything of that value, and now he was to rightfully own it with the King's blessing. He knelt in homage to his King and thanked him. Horn smiled at the still surprised and grateful scout.

"I have long been aware of your good service as a scout, Fenner, and now you have justly earned the reward for the capture of Brinian, the leader of our old enemies. When we return to our shores you will attend me to receive the promised reward."

They turned and left the scene, making their way back to the main force.

Soon the news of the discovery and death of Brinian spread throughout the army, with a great feeling of joy at the end of the Irishman. Of course, for some who had hoped to have been the lucky one to earn the reward, there was disappointment.

Now it would hasten the efforts to finish the hunting down of the few Irish still on the run in the north, and they would soon be returning to Westerland and their families. The main talking point among the men was the lucky scout Fenner, who was not only presented with Brinian's sword and equipment, but on his return home would receive the great reward promised by Horn, who, smiling broadly, related the events that led to the discovery of the Irishman, with due emphasis placed on Fenner's role. Fenner, to his credit, asked that Dog's scout, with his chance remark of seeing a lone man making slow progress to the north, should be recognised. This, and this alone, had led to the discovery of Brinian, who could have lay there forever. Horn confirmed that the scout would, indeed, be given a reward for his part.

The news was carried to Dog at the quayside by the same scout, who carried orders from Horn to remain for one more day before returning to the main force, then proceed to the castle of King Plachan. Dog felt an overwhelming desire to shout and dance, but remembered he needed to show by example some restraint as a Commander. He permitted himself a huge grin, the result of which created the well known scowl, sadly often taken as a sign of anger rather than happiness on those contorted features. Only two on the enemy had been intercepted in the last hours. There could be very few in that part of the island, if any at all were still out in the gorse, attempting to reach the coast. Dog kept his men on their toes with frequent visits to their lookout posts. He had not found it necessary to reprimand a single man; all had taken their task very seriously, and their tally of the enemy bore testimony to their vigilance and skill.

Lord Sancto received the news of the death of Brinian and informed Prince Attaga. He was delighted to hear that his father's kingdom was indeed safe, not only from the scourge of the Irish invaders, but from their leader; never again would he command a force to invade. The Prince left immediately to convey the news the royal family and the people of Laswindel. He arrived in such haste that the garrison at the castle at first thought there had been change of fortune or a disaster , and the Prince found it hard at first to be heard. Surrounded by yelling men, he again shouted at the top of his voice.

"Brinian is dead! Brinian is dead! Hear me, Brinian is dead!"

Suddenly they grasped the meaning of what he was saying. In complete contrast there was a stunned silence for a few seconds, then the whole castle erupted with the sound of cheers as the word spread like wildfire, even beyond the walls. The royal family came down into the courtyard to receive a great welcome from their excited subjects; a tremendous feeling of relief and joy was felt by everybody, who not so long ago were in the fear of their lives from the cruel invader.

On the order of King Plachan, a great feast was to be held on the return of Horn and the Westerland army to the castle. They would be feted as victors over King Ealcane's force. Beasts were to be slaughtered, bread baked, the best ale brought from the cellars, tables scrubbed and clean straw put on the floor of the grand hall. Nothing would be spared in the welcome to their great ally and their saviour. The courtyard was to be decked out, with barrels of ale set up for the men of both armies to drink and celebrate their victorious alliance in the recent battle.

A special royal messenger was sent to Horn from the King, giving him the whole kingdom's gratitude, and that they waited his arrival at the castle with their most humble salutations to a great leader and warrior King. The people of the island could now resume something approaching a normal life with the threat of possibly being ravaged and slaughtered removed, thanks to Horn and his Commanders.

Horn received the message from King Plachan and conveyed its contents to his Commanders. He sent back the messenger to confirm that his army would be leaving their camp later that day, but they would make detours to flush out any of the enemy still in the gorselands. The army was expecting to arrive at the outskirts of the castle by first light. Horn also sent a scout to remind Dog to leave the quayside and join the main force when they left camp, as he wished the whole army to enter the castle together.

As the scout arrived, he could see two of Dog's men bringing in a very frightened Irishman, who had been caught close by and was in a pitiful state. He had been cut and torn by the gorse and, obviously, had not eaten for some days. Dog studied the man's face for a moment, intending to query why his men had not finished him where they had found him, but changed his mind. Here was an opportunity to present a great insult to the Irish King Ealcane. He sent his men to find a small boat, one of the few he had hidden on arrival at Quay from the enemy, before he destroyed their ships. The unfortunate captive, expecting to be killed, was in mortal fear, trembling with the thought of what method would be employed to despatch him. He knew that this was to be his end; the Westerland treatment of an enemy was well known. Dog ordered the man to be brought to an old tree stump and told the men to hold his left arm over the stump. With a lightning stroke, he brought down his sword on the man's forearm. With a scream, the captive slumped forward in a heap, losing consciousness at once. The Irishman's arms were tied off to arrest most of the blood spouting from the stump. When he came round ten minutes later, he was carried to the boat. Dropping him in the middle with one oar, he was told to go to his King and to tell him of the destruction of his army and the death of his leader, Brinian.

The luckless man lay in the bottom of the boat for some time, suffering from the shock of losing an arm, the real pain to come later. Eventually he struggled to a sitting position and tried different ways of propelling the boat one handed and with only one oar. Eventually finding a method that took him forward, he left the shore and headed out to the open sea. If he ever reached his homeland, his fate would be in his King's hand, but most messengers of bad news paid the penalty of their King's wraths for causing grief. Perhaps it might have kinder to have sent him to his ancestors, but the sea might be kind and spare him that fate by swallowing him in its ever voracious appetite for humans souls and boats.

Dog gave the order to assemble at the quayside. They checked their weapons and prepared to start their journey to meet the main force, a good hours march to the camp at a normal pace, with the reminder to be on constant guard for the remote possibility that there may be a fugitive still in the gorselands. The journey was, however, uneventful and Dog's force became part of the main army, with many a cheerful reunion between old friends taking place. Dog gave his report to Horn, who welcomed him warmly as he recounted his time at the quayside and the tally of the enemy caught attempting to reach their ships. Horn informed him that his scout would be rewarded, along with Fenner, for his part in finding the Irish leader Brinian, and they both would be called to receive it on returning to Westerland.

After a short rest, the whole force moved out slowly, with Horn, Lord Grenden and Dog at the head. They were in great spirits! Everything had more or less gone as they had planned, and their losses had been comparatively light in all the actions that had taken place in the last few days, at the ridge, the hills, and the woodland.

Horn felt pleased with himself; his men had proved yet again that their quality and their character could take on any army, mainly due to Lord Grenden and his strict supervision of their training in the arts of war. Sadly, he was also aware that his Commander-in-Chief, who had also served his father with great distinction, was no longer a young man, and would soon have to retire to a much deserved and gentler life in the country. After travelling for over an hour, the main force met up with Lord Sancto and his men, who also were in great spirit, having accounted for many of the enemy with little loss to themselves. They, like all the men, were in the mood to enjoy the reception that would be awaiting them at the castle. Their thoughts of returning home in a few days lifted their hearts. This could also be the last battle for the Westerlanders for some time, so it was a good feeling to have survived this campaign and be able to tell of the events that took place on the expedition to Laswindel.

The arrival of the Westerland army was reported when almost a mile away from the castle. Everything was in a state of readiness. The total garrison, men, women and children, were eager to see the arrival and welcome the victorious King Horn and his army. Some, particularly the young children, wanted to rush out of the gates to be the first to greet them, but the guards had been ordered to close the gates by Prince Attaga until the army were almost at the castle, then they would be opened with a salute of the war horns.

And so it was, the gates opened at the right moment to admit the army with Horn, Lord Grenden, and the Commanders all riding at the head. They were the first to be showered with thousands of flower petals thrown. Eager maidens danced between the lines of men, as the horns again heralded their welcome to the warriors. The happy and excited population roared out their welcome as they swamped the men, so much that Horn and his Commanders had virtually run the gauntlet, to where the royal family stood waiting their arrival, to greet them officially. After the embracing ritual with various members of King Plachan's family, they made their way to the grand hall where the King and Queen addressed Horn and his commanders.

"My brother Horn, our hearts are filled with thanks for your great part in ridding our kingdom of the hated Irish and their leader, Brinian. We will forever, in our future years, recall the heroic deeds performed on our island in our defence, and this shall be written and recorded as an important part of the history of our country. Your brave warriors who fell in the defence of our land are our greatest sadness. I will make amends to the families of those men by awarding a large purse of gold, which will be distributed by my own son, Prince Attaga, who will be returning with you to Westerland for a short period. Again, I thank you all. It is our pleasure and pleasant duty to invite you all to a magnificent feast that will be prepared in this hall. Our armies will be lavishly entertained likewise in the main courtyard."

Horn thanked the King and replied, "My brother Plachan, we are happy to have shared the rigours of battle with your army, and we share the joy of destroying our common enemy, Brinian, and his force. I am grateful to you for the provision for the families of the fallen men, and I welcome Prince Attaga's intention to stay awhile in our country. He will find good hunting in our forests, and will be warmly welcomed by our people. My Queen and I will look forward to his company at the castle. So, brother, my army and I accept your kind invitation to feast. Let us talk no more of war; rather, let's have the talk of continued trade and our friendship in filling the flagons with ale to our health and our people."

Almost at once the servants were dashing from the kitchens with a continuous supply of food and ale to the hall and courtyard, the huge platters of meat eagerly seized upon. It had been some days since they enjoyed such good food. With the accompanying whistle and pipe player keeping up their merry tunes, men danced on their own, or the lucky ones were picked out by the maidens. Everywhere the sound of laughter rang out. Tumblers performed their feats to loud applause, while in the grand hall, the dance of the swords took place. There was a dance where the swordsman's flashing blade cut the air while the dancer spun in and out of his reach, sometimes the closeness of the daring dancers brought gasps from the ladies. The celebration last until most had fallen asleep, some where they had sat, taking huge quantities of ale. The sound of heavy snoring drifted the early morning air, occasionally interrupted with the rumble and grunt of an overfilled stomach protesting its treatment.

Dawn broke to a clear blue sky and the promise of fine day ahead. Orders were given to the army to assemble at noon to begin the journey home, a short sea crossing with the fleet that had left Westerland early that morning. Farewells were made to new found friends among the men; a few romances had begun among the maidens on the island, no doubt that would lead to one or the other adopting a new country.

As usual, Horn rose early, his mind now on his army's return to their own land and his beautiful Queen awaiting his homecoming later that day, but first he asked to see King Plachan before he took his leave at noon. The King received Horn, attended by the whole royal family, and again thanked him for bringing peace to their country. On behalf of his family and the grateful people of Laswindel, he presented Horn with a magnificent torque of twisted gold, and for Queen Cleona, a beautiful necklace of sparkling precious gems, the quality of which was obvious as it flashed with brilliance; it was accepted by Horn. Lord Grenden has assembled the army and waited only for the order to move out through the gates of the castle. The crowds were packed tightly at the point in front of the guardhouses, intent of saying their farewells to the men; it was moving sight that would be long remembered.

As the army moved out, the cheering and shouting gradually quieted. It was almost silent as the last section of engineers and their equipment passed out of sight; the crowds sadly moved away from the courtyard. Scouts had been sent to the small harbour to signal the ships to sail inshore to make ready to take the army on board. The wounded would be on hand carts and would embark first. The more seriously wounded had been left in the care of the men of Laswindel until they were able to return to their own homes. On board all was ready, and the fleet moved out to begin the short crossing back to their own kingdom. Some of the men were in such high spirits that they began singing, while others thought about their reunions with loved ones. A few still thought about the last few days and the battles.

The familiar coastline of Westerland appeared closer, and the men as one cheered, knowing that within an hour they would setting foot on their own land and making their way to their villages and families. The crossing, as predicted, had been good, with a fair wind in their favour. Closer still, a giant fire had been lit on the cliffs; great activity could be seen; figures were streaming down to the harbour near the village of Lockney. Some families had been alerted of the appearance of the fleet nearing the shore and had run or walked to be the first to greet the returning warriors, determined they would join their men on the march back to the village, young girls holding their loved ones hand, and the boys, as was the custom, proudly carrying their father's weapons.

The local men tumbled off the ships and rushed to the waiting families. The remainder formed into their sections under their Commanders and began the march to the castle and the approaching villages. Although it was now early evening, they expected to be there before dark. With heat of day rapidly cooling, the journey was less tiring, with each step taking the men closer to their homes. Some peeled off at their village, with many shouts to old friends as they ran into the arms of their families, the children whooping with delight as they grabbed their fathers around the legs, almost causing them to stumble.

The main army finally were in sight of the castle, and it was obvious the word had reached them of the ships off the shore at Lockney. A great reception had been prepared for their warrior King and his army. Queen Cleona rode out with her bodyguard to meet her husband. As the army drew ever closer, their pace increased with the anticipation of seeing their loved ones. Horn halted and dismounted as Cleona, helped from her horse, moved quickly to embrace her husband, then both remounting, rode side by side the short distance to the gates of the castle. From the very highest points of the keep, Queen Aethena, the mother of Horn, watched the reunion of her son with his Queen with a little difficulty, but with the help of the young eyes of her personal servant, who described the meeting in detail to her, she felt a great joy; a tear dropped onto her cheek; the kingdom was safe with Horn and his Queen. The deafening noise of the excited crowds rang throughout the castle as the army reached the gates and entered the courtyard. Most of the women could be not restrained and literally threw themselves at their men, causing Lord Grenden to give the order to the men to break ranks.

It was useless to try to control the high state of emotion of the people as they surged through the ranks for their men. The atmosphere reached a pitch within half an hour, and it became clear that the courtyard, packed with relatives of the returning men, had become completely chaotic. It took a long blast on the war horn from the battlements to draw the crowds attention to the royal family and the army Commanders gathered at the entrance to the grand hall. Horn addressed his subjects.

"Men of Westerland, my loyal people, this is a proud day for our country. We have returned safely from the expedition to rid our good neighbour Laswindel of the invading force of the Irish. I feel great pride in having led our warriors once again into battle against a cruel enemy. The fighting qualities they displayed will send a message throughout all kingdoms that any ambitious or envious king who thinks to challenge the might of Westerland or our allies had better employ his army in cutting wood, growing grain, or feeding his hogs, and throw away dreams of conquest. I charge you all to comfort the mothers, assist the widows, and help the children of our warriors who did not return with us. So, again, my Commanders and I salute you. Enjoy the night with your families, for tomorrow will be a feast day for all."

The crowd responded at once. "Horn! Horn of Westerland!"

Horn raised his hand, acknowledging their praise. Commanders were called to the hall to be personally thanked by Horn. Lord Grenden, Lord Sancto, Dog, and the young Knight Briscal received special mention and awards. The scout Fenner was sent for from the courtyard. He was given the right to land in south of the kingdom for his discovery of Brinian and a gift of a purse of gold. Then followed the young scout from Dog's men at Quayside, who received a purse of silver for his part in spotting Brinian. The fact that the Irish leader's main cause of death was blood poisoning, leading to a fatal fever because of his seriously weakened physical condition, did not lessen the importance of his discovery by the scout. Other awards were made to individual men whose actions in the three main battles had come to the notice of Horn or his Commanders. This normally would have been a purse or a sword fashioned by the top swordsmith, Blandon, which were highly prized by every man.

So as the evening drew to a close and most retired to be with their families, Horn and Cleona made their way to the royal chamber, where the necklace presented to Horn for his Queen by King Plachan was placed around her neck to her great delight. The brilliance of the gems brought a gasp of delight from her as they flashed, casting fingers of light throughout the chamber as she moved about excitedly. The beauty of his Queen still took his breath away as he watched her. He blessed his good fortune that he gone to the aid of his one time enemy, King Aeden of Collona, for he had taken the pearl of that kingdom as his Queen, and she had fallen in love with the young warrior at first sight when he had returned her father safely to his family and people.

The morning light streamed through the chamber, and Horn and his Queen had slept soundly. Suddenly, the sound of greeting and laughter fell on their ears; the castle was coming to life on this special day. The men were home; life could begin again for most, and today was to be a feast day. Gaily coloured cloth hung from posts and high points, fluttering in the slight breeze. The women had started to bake early, as a mountain of bread was required for the coming feast, while the men lit the great fires to roast the huge ox and many swine over the massive iron spits. This particular roasting had to be just right, somewhere in the region of four to five hours, so timing was of the utmost importance. Ale of the best quality had to drawn from the great barrels, ready for the vast quantities that would be consumed. This was last years, brewed to perfection, and had been saved for just such an occasion. No one would be hungry today, nor would anyone be thirsty.

During the morning, Horn and Lord Grenden, with Prince Attaga of Laswindel, visited the widows and families of the men killed on the expedition in their homes. Those in the villages would receive theirs later, and the Prince gave each a purse containing two gold pieces from his grateful people.

Dog, meanwhile, returned from the hall to his wife, Althreda, the daughter of the huntsman, with their young son, Redwald, to inform her that she would accompany him to the great hall for the feast and sit with his Lord among the Commanders, Knights and their ladies. As the evening approached, the guests made their way to the hall, and the sound of pipe music heralded the start of the celebrations. Outside the entire garrison, warriors, and inhabitants filled the courtyard, jostling for the best tables, eager to begin the feast and enjoy the entertainment, come what may. All the delights to please the eye, to flatter the stomach, and to satisfy the thirst were laid before the men, women and the older children of the castle. It also included those from the nearby villages who had walked since daybreak to be there. Strong men carried or rolled the huge barrels of ale from the castle cellars and set them up in the hall and again in the courtyard. No time was lost in tapping them, as the thirsty men roared their approval as the amber liquid flowed sweetly into their flagons. The feast was to be followed by music and dancing until almost dawn, or when sleep claimed them, whichever came first. The grand hall had been decorated with green branches and entwined with strips of coloured cloth to lend a festive air to its usual stark appearance, and the floor had been cleaned with new earth and fresh smelling straw.

The tables were literally groaning with food for the royal family and their Lords; there were baskets of fruit, mountains of fresh bread, and platters of fish and sweetmeats. As was the custom, the giant hog was carried in by two men and set up beside the royal table to be carved by the servants. The appetizing smell of the roasted animal carried to most of the guests, causing some of the men to take great sniffs in anticipation of the taste yet to come.

Horn and Cleona entered the hall when all were present, being escorted by the Chancellor Ancour, who then proceeded to instruct the assembled guests to their places chosen by the King. All at the royal table waited for the couple to sit before they took their seats, and the feast began with the servants at their elbows to carry out any request or demand. Dog, to his great surprise and pleasure, was given a place of honour with his wife on Horn and Cleona's left, with Lord Grenden on the right with Queen Aethena, and a very special and unusual honour for the scout Fenner to sit with the Lords and Ladies.

Long into the night the feast lasted. There was continuous music for the dancers, while other entertainers performed feats of strength, and magical illusions delighted the royal couple and guests. Funny men brought tears from the guests with helpless laughter as they slapped each other about and performed hilarious cameos which brought deafening applause. Another list of awards for service was read out by the Chancellor. This was the custom of rewarding, which Horn was particularly pleased to do, and the men who received these small gifts would serve better and inspire their comrades to do likewise, either in battle or in their daily lives at the castle.

The next day arrangements were made to strengthen the outposts, even though the chance of an invader to the kingdom was now almost remote. Lord Grenden and Dog began a new form of training in warfare and siege tactics, as they had not yet been afforded the opportunity to take a defended castle in their recent campaigns. At the same time, the giant Greg put his footmen through new routines of defence and attack. The archers, under the command of Fretwin, began to compete with each other in distance and accuracy, eagerly watched by the hopeful young boys who aspired to join their ranks. It was always so in Westerland that there was an inborn ambition of the sons to follow their fathers or elder brothers into battle. Very few wanted to be employed on the land, to become fishermen or woodsmen; although, with a trade, it could provide a better and much safer living. Figures like Lord Grenden, Lord Sancto, and now Dog were held in awe, the subject of hero worship from afar by these young aspirants in the kingdom, their appetites whetted as the seasoned veterans recounted their deeds and the exploits of their Commanders.

A peaceful future was now envisaged in the kingdom, and life in the villages around the castle began to improve with record harvests of grain. The coastal settlements were landing catches of fish that exceeded anything previously caught in their home waters. Horn and his Queen Cleona resumed their duties as monarchs of the kingdom, holding court and listening to the advice of their Chancellor on matters of State, with old Winloch, the secretary, preparing the necessary documents. Life was almost perfect. The strong relationship with the kingdom of Collona continued with increased trade, and the news that Queen Cleona was with child delighted both Horn and his in-laws, King Aeden and Queen Helda. They hoped for a boy, who would carry the blood of both Houses and cement their kingdoms forever.

And so the kingdom waited through the next few months until at last the day dawned, so eagerly counted. At midnight, with a star-filled sky and a full moon, amid great excitement, the birth was announced of a royal Prince of the Kingdom of Westerland. Thus it was destiny fulfilled; the hopes of so many had become reality. Lord Grenden and Queen Aethena embraced each other; now they were confident the kingdom and crown would be safe for many years to come.

What would the future for this child of a warrior King hold? What would be his role in the years to come? Perhaps, he would succeed his father, but then the destiny of Horn himself had not been written, but his fame had spread even farther throughout the kingdoms. To all he was a warrior born, a ready defender of the weak against tyranny and cruelty. He was a champion of Kings, a King's champion, and his purpose would never be done.

THE END